Summoned

Summoned

*Identification and Religious Life in a
Jewish Neighborhood*

IDDO TAVORY

The University of Chicago Press   Chicago and London

IDDO TAVORY is assistant professor of sociology at New York University.

The University of Chicago Press, Chicago 60637
The University of Chicago Press, Ltd., London
© 2016 by The University of Chicago
All rights reserved. Published 2016.
Printed in the United States of America

25 24 23 22 21 20 19 18 17 16   1 2 3 4 5

ISBN-13: 978-0-226-32186-8 (cloth)
ISBN-13: 978-0-226-32205-6 (paper)
ISBN-13: 978-0-226-32219-3 (e-book)
DOI: 10.7208/chicago/9780226322193.001.0001

Library of Congress Cataloging-in-Publication Data
Tavory, Iddo, 1977– author.
  Summoned : identification and religious life in a Jewish neighborhood /
Iddo Tavory.
     pages cm
  Includes bibliographical references and index.
  ISBN 978-0-226-32186-8 (cloth : alk. paper) — ISBN 978-0-226-32205-6
(pbk. : alk. paper) — ISBN 978-0-226-32219-3 (e-book)   1. Orthodox
Judaism—California—Los Angeles. 2. Jews—California—Los Angeles—
Identity. I. Title.
  F869.L89J575 2016
  305.892′4079494—dc23

                                                                2015026511

For Jack Katz

Contents

Acknowledgments

Any project that takes as long as this one has benefited from countless comments, suggestions, readings, and presentations. It is through a community of inquiry that ideas take shape. My intellectual debts seem endless.

First and foremost, I am grateful to the Orthodox men and women who let me into their homes, their synagogues, and their lives. It is hard to be an ethnographer's friend. The line between observation and conversation, a meal and a "field visit" is all too fluid. I thank them for their patience, trust, and generosity. I put on about ten pounds from Sabbath meals while I was living in the neighborhood. Let this be a measure of their friendship. As readers will quickly note, this is not an ethnography that proceeds as a character study. The real protagonists of this tale are situations, the rhythms of interaction. I hope, however, that the human protagonists will recognize the situations, the dilemmas, and the world as their own.

My first intellectual home is still Israel. I am grateful for my friends and teachers there. Foremost, the friends who started our G. H. Mead reading group at Tel Aviv University: Lior Gelernter, Tom Pessah, Inna Leykin, and Tama Halfin. Their warmth and intellectual depth are reminders of the possible fusion of friendship and a community of inquiry. Sasha Weitman, Yehuda Goodman, Yehouda Shenhav, and Avi Cordova mentored me through my early years as a sociologist. I think Sasha, especially, will recognize the marks he has left. The idea of summoning has more than some traces of his notion of "socio-erotics."

I have been extremely lucky to have then found a home at UCLA. Jack Katz got me into this work, into phenomenological sociology, and read my work through the years. My debt to his mode of thinking, seeing, and sensing the social world is obvious and deep. He also lent me a bike (which I lost) and let me stay at his place for over a month, drink his sparkling water, and ruin a big chunk of his house by clogging the toilets. Stefan Timmermans turned quickly into a friend and co-conspirator. Our writing together about methods and pragmatism runs through this book—and as I develop further in the appendix, it is an example of the kind of "abductive analysis" we have been crafting. I am also grateful to Rogers Brubaker for giving me unfailingly incisive comments, and to David Myers for keeping me honest on the Jewish front.

Friends at UCLA, and especially Josh Bloom, Kate Choi, Philippe Duhart, Noah Grand, Jyoti Gulati-Balachandran, Shawn Halbert, Hazem Kandil, Jooyoung Lee, Tara McKay, Kristin Surak, and David Trouille all suffered through drafts and long conversations. Later, at the New School, I was lucky to work with and to enjoy the passion and erudition of Andrew Arato, Richard Bernstein, Jeff Goldfarb, Eiko Ikegami, Elzbieta Matynia, Virag Molnar, Rachel Sherman, Terry Williams, and Vera Zolberg. I think this book bears their mark. As I write this, I have moved to NYU, and the friends I have there already, and those I am getting to know, are exciting.

I developed my thoughts in countless colloquia, talks, and working groups. I thank members of the UCLA ethnography working group, the "Craft of Ethnography" book-writing group at the Institute for Public Knowledge with Colin Jerolmack, Lucia Trimbur, Harel Shapira, Erin O'Connor, and Tyson Smith, as well as the New School junior faculty colloquium, various lecture audiences, and my grad students at the NSSR and at NYU. I thank Fabien Accominotti for his help with thinking and constructing networks, Adam Murphree and Jacob Faber for some help with the figures, and Eman Abdelhadi for help with proofreading. I am also grateful to Doug Mitchell for his insight and his support. Doug understood what I wanted to do with the book immediately and took it on without hesitation, all the while exchanging emails regarding the important question of the proper collective noun that should be given a group of ethnographers (a gaggle? a troop? a misbelief?). Howard Becker and William Helmreich not only provided incredible feedback on the manuscript for the press but were good enough to identify themselves so I could pester them with questions.

Of the endless conversations I had with colleagues and friends, there are also some moments that stick out—the minor turning points of thought. Eviatar Zerubavel invited me to present my work at the "soon-to-be-author-meets-non-critics" session, where I first crystallized some of the ideas in the book, and pushed me to think about the notion of social worlds. Over dinner, Ivan Ermakoff gave me clarity when I was at my most muddled. Robin Wagner-Pacifici recommended Calvino and had a hunch about Thomas Mann that ended up providing wonderful bookends for the narrative. Rob Jansen and (again) Colin Jerolmack read and reread the entire manuscript and made it better, tighter, and simply more interesting. I also thank Nina Eliasoph for her ongoing friendship, insight, and general woppiness, and Ann Swidler for her friendship, intellectual generosity, and enthusiasm.

And then there are people who I just want to thank for their conversations about the book and about sociology more generally: Eli Anderson, Chris Bail, Mathieu Berger, Daniel Cefai, Matt Desmond, Mitch Duneier, Gary Fine, Amin Ghaziani, Andreas Glaeser, Alice Goffman, Neil Gross, John Heritage, Eva Jablonka, Eric Klinenberg, Monika Krause, Michele Lamont, Paul Lichterman, Eeva Luhtakallio, Doug Maynard, Terry McDonnel, Harvey Molotch, Alex Murphy, Mel Pollner, Richard Sennett, Doron Tavory, Ada Ushpiz, Susan Watkins, Jack Whalen, Andreas Wimmer, Dan Winchester, Chris Winship, and Amit Zoref. Thank you all! The book may not be as good as it could have been had I listened to all your ideas and suggestions. But then again, it is much better than if I hadn't at all . . .

Last I would like to thank Nahoko Kameo. Depending on mood, she is my toughest critic and my most avid supporter. She read each page. Some she deleted, others she simply made better. Living with her, and then with our daughter Eliana, is a kind of joy I never knew possible.

ONE

Toward a Sociology of Summoning

I walk through the dark suburban-looking streets of my middle-class Los Angeles neighborhood to a Hasidic evening class. There is one every Tuesday evening. I get a phone call from David, the organizer, on Friday, before the Sabbath kicks in. It is always a variation on the same conversation, "Are you joining us this Tuesday? We have a really great speaker, Rabbi . . ." The name of the rabbi changes almost every week, as David scrambles to get one to come this late in the evening for no pay whatsoever. I get another call on Monday evening, just to make sure that I actually make it. If I can't come David sounds disappointed on our next conversation. It is important to have enough people, he tells me, "it's been going on since the 1980s." He is in real estate for a living but seems to relish the effort he puts into organizing these weekly get-togethers—cajoling people on his phone list each week in order to find a host in the neighborhood, a rabbi to take over the class, men to attend.

Each time we meet in the house of a different Orthodox Jewish family in the neighborhood, and although I tell myself that this is a wonderful way to get to know people better, I am usually too exhausted to be on my best ethnographic behavior. I find the house, only a few blocks away from my rented garden backhouse. It is one of the small, detached, bungalow-style houses of the Beverly–La Brea neighborhood, belonging to someone I have never met before. I see a couple of bearded men walking in and can see, from the window, that the living room features a large bookcase full of religious books, the sine qua non of an Orthodox household. In the living room, beneath the shadow of the bookcase, a large table has a modest spread: soft drinks, nuts, cake, a bottle of vodka that some jokingly call "Hasidic health food." Some men are already seated.

There are usually between eight and twenty men—and only men—at these meetings. Most are what others call "ultra-Orthodox Jewish," sporting long beards, yarmulkes, and hats (although, this being a weekday, some are dressed in working clothes and substitute berets or baseball caps for their signature black hats). A couple of regulars are less obviously Orthodox-affiliated—a retired engineer who puts his yarmulke on for the occasion and tends to make tangential *Star Trek* jokes, another quiet and close-shaven retiree who seems quietly engaged but never asks a question.

The class goes on for about an hour. This time the speaker is a young guy from Brooklyn, in his early twenties, who is doing a service year in the local yeshiva in Los Angeles. He talks about the difference between levels of the presence of godliness in the world. It is mystical and a bit abstract, touching upon Kabbalistic literature and distinctions, what Orthodox Jews call "the Torah's secrets." But for all the mysticism, the people around the table are not listening in rapt attention. They have probably heard most of it before, the speaker is young, and his audience is tired. In fact, a couple of people fall asleep around the table, and I have to gently nudge one of them who snores a little too conspicuously.

On the verge of falling asleep myself, I can hardly blame them. Some of them, myself included, started their day at 5:45 a.m. with forty-five minutes of Talmud reading, then spent between forty-five minutes to an hour in morning prayer. As most of those around the table are not religious functionaries, they then went to work in what some called "non-Jewish" jobs—a couple of them are software engineers, one works in the aerospace industry, a carpenter, someone who owns a moving company, a real estate agent, a lawyer. After work, most of them stopped at home for a short while and then went for evening services in one of the many Orthodox synagogues in the neighborhood. Evening services are somewhat shorter, but many of the men will hang out in the synagogue for a while longer, sometimes to learn, sometimes just to chat a bit and catch up with friends. They then had little time to spend with their families before hurrying to the class. After the class ends, David asks if any of us still haven't prayed the evening prayer. Most did in synagogue, but some didn't, and we spend some twenty minutes praying before we disperse.

We are not alone in this. On any given day in the neighborhood there are dozens of such group meetings, classes, and study sessions. In fact, both I and a couple of others who show up that day were torn between going to this meeting and joining a new class that the rabbi of the synagogue we usually attend has just begun. On Wednesdays I go for an evening class in the local yeshiva, on Thursday evenings I have a one-on-one study session with a good friend whom I met in synagogue, Friday afternoons and Saturdays are completely organized around religious practice, as the Sabbath is spent mostly in praying, eating, and sleeping. And although men's schedules tend to have more of these occasions, there is a plethora of women's classes being organized on any given day.

Living in the Orthodox Jewish neighborhood for three years, I found something thick, almost palpable, in the quality of neighborhood life. Like everybody else I knew in the neighborhood, I found myself constantly fielding calls to participate in classes, asked to donate time and money, sometimes called at 6:35 in the morning by someone in the small synagogue I usually attended. Trying to explain the texture of everyday life to friends outside the neighborhood, I often resorted to metaphors of thickness, of viscosity—living an Orthodox life in the Beverly–La Brea neighborhood was like swimming in honey. And as some of the men around the table that evening probably felt, it was often exhilarating, but sometimes tiring or even overbearing.

This book is about this "thickness" of communal experience and the situations that give it flesh. What does this thickness mean sociologically? How is it sustained? How do the structure and rhythms of different situations that people routinely navigate end up constructing the kinds of predictable relations and the sense of self that emerge therein?

Perhaps, one could say, the neighborhood engulfed the residents, providing a "total" world, an enclave such as the one some imagine parts of Brooklyn, New Jersey, or Israel to be—where Orthodox Judaism reigns supreme, where it seems inevitable for people to participate in Orthodoxy. But this is a mystification of most Orthodox enclaves, and, at any rate, such a notion quickly dissipated if one simply strolled through the neighborhood. The neighborhood was only about 20–30 percent Orthodox Jewish, mostly non-Orthodox white middle class. And far from the centers of Jewish Orthodoxy in New York and New Jersey, Orthodox men and women walked through a space that was recognized more for the aspiring artists and trendy teenagers who lived there or came to shop than for religious life. Large billboards, hanging just above the people walking through the streets, advertised the remake of the sexy soap opera *Melrose Place*, named after one of the main arteries of the neighborhood. The three subtle slogans on the posters read "Tuesday is the new Humpday," "Tuesdays are a bitch," and "Ménage-à-Tues," and featured pictures of the actresses and actors casting suggestive glances at each other and at the passersby. Below, at street level, quite non-Orthodox retail stores thrived between synagogues. Two doors down from one synagogue was a marijuana dispensary, just next to a storefront marked "Tarot and Palm Reader." On the same block as one synagogue there had been, until recently, a gay movie theater.

Orthodox residents walking through the streets seemed not to notice their surroundings. People talked to each other but almost never stopped to look at the stores they passed, as if reality were layered and they somehow inhabited a different street; some seemed to ponder the sidewalk as they walked along in quick strides, rarely lifting their heads, their whole bodily posture set apart from the street life. But this was mere appearance. Among themselves, residents often laughed at the painstaking work it took to ignore these surroundings, the "look at the birdies attitude," as one young Orthodox man called it. When a restaurant that had had a sign depicting a pig wearing sunglasses and wielding a knife and fork closed down, the comments were quick to come. A couple of Orthodox men I had dinner with the following week said it would be interesting if they could have a kosher restaurant there instead, maybe even a synagogue. After all, one of them quipped, there is a well-known prophecy in the Kabbalistic literature that holds that, when the Messiah finally comes, pork will become kosher.

Instead of explaining the density of neighborhood life as the result of the isolation of a religious enclave, then, we must seek other avenues.[1] As a way to begin approaching this question, it is useful to turn to literature. In one of the imaginary cities that Italo Calvino brings into being in his *Invisible Cities*,[2] the inhabitants draw cords of string between their houses. Each kind of relationship between them would be marked by a different-colored string. But finally, as relationships thicken over time, the strings become unmanageable. There are simply too many relationships to allow people to move around in the streets. In Calvino's imaginary world, the city then has to be abandoned, and all its inhabitants must move away, with only the ghosts of relationships past remaining to mark where the city once stood.

The image Calvino conjures is evocative. One can imagine a birds'-eye view of the layered ties in the neighborhood, an image thick with cords of string of different colors. One could see how Orthodox households were joined by a multiplicity of ties, while the houses of the non-Orthodox in the neighborhood (Jews and non-Jews alike) had far fewer local ties to boast of and were quite weakly linked to the Orthodox Jews living next door. This is a useful image, capturing some key aspects of Orthodox Jewish life in the neighborhood. In sociological terms, there were multiple network ties bringing people together within the circumscribed space, coalescing the Orthodox neighborhood, and transforming it from a geographically delineated area into a buzzing hub of activity.

Calvino and network analysts provide important insights that I draw on extensively. But such an analysis takes us only so far. There was something about the *quality* of the relationships that neither Calvino's imaginary city nor the painstaking depictions of network analysts capture. To use the example of the Tuesday evening class: people in the neighborhood didn't go simply because they knew people who asked them to come, although that was certainly a prerequisite. They often went because they enjoyed the learning and the sociability, but they also went because they felt *needed*, because that was part of what it meant to be an Orthodox Jew. As some have observed,[3] what happens in a "tie" cannot be captured solely by drawing colored cords of string. Most of us have very few friends who would dare to call us at 6:35 a.m., and that only if some kind of emergency had occurred. What kind of ties allows these kinds of interactions to happen? What kind of ties brings people to a class at 8:30 p.m. when they have to wake up at 5:30 a.m., when they know they will probably fall asleep in front of their teacher?

This experiential "density" of the Jewish Orthodox neighborhood thus cannot be reduced to its vibrant associational life. This is an important part of the picture, no doubt, but only a part. If we remain with the network image we will be led to imagine social life as if we were talking about nodes being pushed and pulled in social space. But even a short ethnographic vignette such as that presented above makes it clear that it is also about being a specific kind of person, about being constantly reminded that one is an Orthodox Jew.

As they walked the streets of the neighborhood in Orthodox Jewish attire—the beard, the yarmulke, the hat, the black clothes—there were other small acts reminding Orthodox Jews who they were. Orthodox Jews they didn't know nodded to them, inadvertently reminding them that they were also instantly recognized; non-Orthodox Jews in the supermarket assumed they were a religious authority on what is, or isn't, kosher. The streets themselves reminded people in the neighborhood who they were, with nonkosher smells and profane images acting like a moral obstacle course they traversed on a daily basis. Living an Orthodox life is being enmeshed in a system of laws and a moral organization of purity and danger. There are many things that you can and can't do, and so many more things you must be wary of. To use a metaphor other than ties, nodes and networks, Orthodox Jews in the neighborhood were constantly *summoned*, brought into both interaction and existence as inhabiting a specific identification category.

Taking Summoning Seriously

Summoned; a religious metaphor. But what does it mean for someone to be summoned? On one level it is a physical movement. In being summoned we move from one social situation to another. We are summoned to be *with* certain people, summoned into specific activities. But being summoned is more than that—it is about being summoned *into being*. When Orthodox residents realize that they need to navigate the neighborhood streets so as to avoid impure sights, sounds, or smells, when they are approached by strangers in the bus station and asked, "Is it true that Jews believe that . . . ," they aren't directly summoned into associational ties. Indeed, they may be summoned when no other Orthodox Jews are in sight. This, then, is a different matter. It is about the array of situations in which one becomes, or becomes once again, a certain kind of person—something that can happen alone or together, a specific pattern of social situations.

Louis Althusser, a Marxist philosopher and sociologist, had something similar in mind when he positioned "interpellation"—which, not incidentally, is French for "summoning"—as a core concept in his theoretical framework. But in his image, summoning acquires not religious overtones, but juridical ones. His image is that of the police officer shouting, telling you to turn around. As you turn around, you accept that you were summoned into a certain kind of being—"interpellated" as the subject of the state.[4]

Although the juridical and the religious metaphors share some similarities, there are some problems with this juridical image. First, a juridical summoning is too violent an image. Social life has its moments of coercion. But although there was an element of subtle coercion in the Friday phone calls, and although the question of "what would the (Orthodox) neighbors think?" is an aspect of much religious summoning, it would be simplistic to claim that power dynamics always form the core of such moments. What the juridical metaphor misses, and what religious "summoning" better captures, is the sense of fulfillment, responsibility, moral failure and elation that being summoned can sometimes entail. In developing a sociology of summoning, we need to be careful not to reduce participation and identification either to a dour command or simply to a warm and fuzzy feeling of communal attachment.

The juridical metaphor may also give us an overly passive view of summoning. When you are summoned to court, or by a police officer on the street, you must react. At first blush at least, it seems as though the power of the summons cannot be ignored. This, however, would present a skewed picture of the men and women I came to know in the Beverly–La Brea neighborhood as objects of religious ideology, as though the external world were producing and shaping a largely passive object. If a few decades of interactional studies have shown us anything, it is that in order for meaningful interaction to be sustained, people must recognize and participate in a shared project. As sociologists of different stripes show in detail, social situations are sustained in *interac-tion*: meanings in a conversation are negotiated and solidified not only by the person uttering her turn-of-talk but by her listeners. This aspect of meaning and identification is obvious for conversations, but it is no less true in street fights or even armed robberies—videos of stickups and street violence show that victims and perpetrators must orient toward one another for a "successful" interaction to take place.[5]

Summoning, then, has to be thought of as an active interaction be-tween "being summoned" and the act of recognizing and shaping this summons. In order to be summoned, we must learn to be invoked—that is, we must recognize that something happened, and happened to us. But this is not enough. In order to be "correctly" summoned, we must act in a legible manner—a way that both we ourselves and others can read as meaningful. As I quickly learned in the flesh, specific ac-tions were legible for others in ways that were at first illegible for myself. Certain prayers, for example, connoted specific personal occurrences in people's lives that everybody around me knew how to decipher, and that I couldn't see. In a very different register, I literally couldn't un-derstand the first anti-Semitic encounter I experienced—I couldn't be-lieve that the person shouting at me from a passing car was shouting "Jews" while giving me the finger—although it was crystal clear for the Orthodox friend I was with.

This book is an attempt to specify how and when Orthodox Jews are summoned in everyday life, how interaction emerges in the meeting of people's ongoing projects and the summons of others, and the ways in which different moments imply and construct their identifications. Although we are all summoned in our lives (as students, as immigrants, as parents, as academics, etc.), it occurs to different extents and with different stakes. What made the Orthodox Jewish neighborhood of Beverly–La Brea a strategic site to study this aspect of human life is how "thick" these acts of summoning were, in terms of both their frequency and their implications for the way that people thus summoned understood their lives.

But to take this metaphor seriously also means that we must specify some of its assumptions: What exactly is being summoned? And when? Who summons? What kind of work goes into being summoned, or summoning? Does summoning involve simple cognitive recognition, or is it entangled in webs of emotion? And although the answers to these questions must be given in the context of actual lives, they do have certain theoretical contours that need to be spelled out, if only to set up the framework that animates this book.

So what exactly is summoned? Two answers present themselves— answers we can call "minimalist" and "maximalist." A "maximalist" answer is that what is summoned is a particular self or subject. In social psychological parlance we could say that a specific "identity" is being evoked. After all, in every case the summoning produced a similar subject—an Orthodox Jew. Of course, not all acts of summoning are precisely the same. Sometimes people were simply summoned as Jews (as in anti-Semitic remarks), sometimes as *Orthodox* Jews (as when someone asked an Orthodox-looking man in the supermarket what was, or wasn't, kosher), sometimes as people belonging to a specific subaffiliation of Orthodox Judaism, sometimes as an Orthodox man or woman, sometimes as someone with high standing in the Orthodox world, and sometimes as a newcomer occupying the lower rungs of the Orthodox status hierarchy. Thus, as in any social world, there were different positions that people occupied, and these different positions were usually experienced as important for their self-definitions. And yet there was a family resemblance among the different acts of summoning: although a different *kind* of Jew may have been summoned, they all summoned "a Jew."[6]

The problem with the concept of identity is not so much that it is "incorrect" to say that what was summoned, in almost every case, was an Orthodox Jew. Rather, the problem with the maximalist solution is that the notion of identity is often constructed in an overly static manner. The self, as different theorists have argued extensively, is most productively conceptualized as an embodied process.[7] As anthropologist Thomas Csordas puts it: "self is neither substance nor entity, but an indeterminate capacity to engage or become oriented in the world, characterized by effort and reflexivity." The concept of identity tends to make us forget this point, luring us to think about the self as an entity rather than as a process, a thing rather than an achievement.[8]

If "identity" is the maximalist answer, the minimalist answer is that what is summoned is what sociologist Harvey Sacks called a "membership categorization."[9] A membership category can be thought of as an "identification," a specific category of personhood that is being evoked, constructed, and sustained in interaction. When David called to cajole me to come to the Tuesday classes he organized, he was calling me as an "Orthodox Jew," as belonging to a specific membership category. By accepting the call and acknowledging that it made sense for him to call me—giving excuses if I couldn't come, or assuring him that I would—I retrospectively validated his summons and his identification of my selfhood. Rather than a fixed entity, categorization is seen as a situational and interactional accomplishment.

The difference between these interpretations can be understood in terms of a potential and its actualization. In the "maximalist" interpretation, identity is always there, and the act of summoning only actualizes what was hidden from view. The metaphor is one of unveiling—the object was already there, albeit invisible for a while. In the minimalist interpretation, on the other hand, the processes of selfhood are seen as a contingent and situational accomplishment. We completely bracket the question of whether and what exists between summonings—and assume, at least methodologically, that we are re-created anew each time. In the first case, summoning brings forth a preformed self; in the second, the act of summoning and its acceptance co-construct the summoned self within the act.

The approach I take in this book leans toward the more minimalist interpretation. This is for two reasons: first, it is simply more prudent to assume that things happen when we can see them, rather than that they are always-already there. This is especially the case with an object as slippery as the subject. But it is also more true to the actual observations—people were constructed within the act of summoning, sometimes in novel and creative ways that they could not quite expect before the fact.

And yet we should not simply go from one extreme to another, from a static picture to a completely fluid and situational one. The minimalist interpretation of identification has its own limitations. The most important point, which serves as a backbone for the book's theoretical project, is that living in a specific social world entails a *patterned structure of summoning*; indeed, as I will argue in more detail, this is what it means to live within a *social world*.[10] Occupying a particular self means not only having "an indeterminate capacity to engage or become oriented in the world," but also knowing when and what to expect, and from whom. In that sense, the capacity to engage *is* in fact determined—it is determined by learning when we will probably be summoned and how to effortlessly reorient ourselves when summoned. Indeed, it is this pattern of summonings that makes the milieu we live in a unique social world, that gives identification and interaction not only their situational, but also their *inter*situational, texture.[11]

Moreover, this intersituational texture of identification already exists within a single act of summoning. When we are summoned into being, we are not only accepting a tag, a moniker. Being summoned, and accepting the summons, we also construct a plethora of assumptions—expectations regarding the things such a person would care about, assumptions about pasts or futures, things that such a person would see as defining his or her innermost core.

Conceiving of "identification" as a situationally circumscribed achievement neglects the fact that being identified has temporal ramifications that extend beyond the situation. In most situations in which we are being identified as a specific kind of person, the identification includes not only who we are in the present but a host of expectations about actions in the future, as well as some expectations about our past.[12] To take a simple example, coming to synagogue in the morning also meant that people began to expect that I would continue to do so, so that when they were missing a man for a morning prayer, it seemed only natural to call me and ask me whether I would come down. Thus, the critique of "identity" must be careful not to conceptualize the situational properties of the construction of self as happening in a situational present, while neglecting the fact that both pasts and futures already exist in identification, and that the situation always overflows its temporal boundaries through people's histories and expectations.

Related to the extension of identification in time, most expectations of summoning also include what can probably be termed the "depth" of identification. Not all membership categorizations are the same: some define us in a neatly circumscribed set of situations, while we understand others as defining us across situations; some are seen to define a relatively trivial aspect of our self, while others operate as "master statuses" that seem to color the totality of our being. These definitions of self also come with an emotional apparatus: there are things that people "like us" should want to do, and things we shouldn't; there are things that should be important for us and things that aren't—there are some definitions of self we try to resist and others we embrace.[13]

When I was summoned to come to class, my acceptance of the "Orthodox Jew" membership categorization also meant that I should value religious learning. I could worm my way out of coming to class. I could say I fell asleep, twisted my ankle, went to another class, or was out of town—all of which I am ashamed to say I used at one time or another, and, as Orthodox friends confessed, they sometimes did too. I couldn't, however, say I didn't *want* to come. Making this particular move would not be rude, it would be almost nonsensical. It would be much like being invited to an academic conference and answering that I dislike intellectual exchanges. Not only is it something you can't tell the person inviting you, it is something you can't tell yourself. In accepting and coconstructing a summons, we take on a host of expectations about what we should and shouldn't want, what causes us pleasure and what evokes dismay. There are moral and emotional expectations that are played out in such interaction, and part of knowing how to be summoned is to be overcome by the right kind of feeling, or at least to know what kinds of emotions one is supposed to be overcome by.

These aspects of summoning are, as I will argue in the conclusions, important in any social setting. They are all the more central, however, in a social world in which religious practice is a defining axis of self. This is for two reasons. First, as I will show in more detail below, religious identification in the neighborhood was seen as a deeply important identification, which other identifications should be secondary to. In that sense, the kind of self summoned was supposed to be a deeply cared-for morally imbued self.

Second, Orthodox Judaism today—even in its most stringent anti-Hasidic pockets—stresses the role of religious experience and emotion.[14] Although Orthodoxy stresses adherence to the law as a defining feature of the religious self, being moved, and praying with zeal and religious intent (*kavanah*), were a constant topic of conversation and rabbinical admonishments. One of the most interesting insights emerging from social studies of religious experience is just how much work goes into being able to be overcome by experience. Rather than something that simply "happens" to the believer, or that is always the same across history, having a religious experience is something that devotees spend much time and effort cultivating.[15] There are manuals as well as endless conversations about ways to cultivate the right attitude; it is a project that people are actively pursuing and that they define themselves through.

11

Thus, some of the work that always goes into learning to be effectively summoned is more visible in the Orthodox Jewish settings.

Two more questions remain open: who summons, and how? Obviously, the guy who muttered "talking about money, eh?" when I was walking down the street with an Orthodox friend was not summoning me in the same way that I was summoned when a friend from synagogue called me to synagogue (much too) early in the morning, when David called me for his Tuesday class, or when I was invited to a wedding of someone I didn't even know. They all summoned me as a Jew, but in different ways, evoking different reactions and emotions. It would be tempting to say that summoning followed a hierarchy of religious power—that the "higher up" someone was in the religious hierarchy, the more he or she could summon others. This, however, would be too simple. Although rabbis and other "religious virtuosi" had more power to define proscribed and prescribed religious practice, the fact that the summoning was highly moralized played an important role. Religion was a kind of ace in a symbolic card game of summoning—doing it correctly could allow a homeless Jew to scold a respectable middle-class congregant, a guest to tell his hosts what they could (and more importantly, couldn't) do in their own kitchen.

Last, we turn to the processes of summoning—the mundane ways in which summoning was done, understood, and embodied. As much of the book revolves around a description of these processes, suffice it to say at this point that these included multiple forms: from organizations such as schools and synagogues to the ways that Orthodox prayer was organized; from the passing comment on the street to tracts and speeches expounding upon the superiority of Jews. Indeed, rather than confining our analysis to either "institutional closure" or interactional achievements, either boundary mechanisms or solidarity-forming rituals, it is more useful to look at how different forms of summoning coalesce in action, how different social processes sediment over time and articulate each other's meanings to form specific figurations of summoning.

To account for the ways through which people are summoned requires us to pay careful attention to the daily lives of the people we study. People are summoned into being not only "on special occasions" but in very small, mundane ways, ways that they usually don't think about much. What we are looking for are the patterned ways in which such summoning occurs. For unlike the paradigmatic case of religious summoning, the sociological summoning I speak of very rarely entails a burning bush, an exceptional miraculous appearance of the transcendent. Rather, it is the patterned texture of small moments that pervaded Orthodox Jews' lives in the neighborhood, the specific ways in which living as an Orthodox Jew in Beverly–La Brea afforded people with opportunities, or pressured them. To depict the specific patterns of social life, we need to know quite a bit about Orthodox Judaism, but also to understand how the neighborhood came into being, who lived there, and how they lived their lives.

What Lies Ahead

The book, then, is organized around the specific arts and situations of summoning that constituted this aspect of Beverly–La Brea's Orthodox Jews' social world. Each chapter in the book takes one facet, a few processes that share a family-resemblance to each other, and shows how they operated in everyday life.

The next chapter describes the neighborhood as it exists today and outlines some of its history. In part, history serves as a way to avoid the danger of a static ethnographic "present progressive." But excavating the neighborhood's past is also important if we want to understand how summoning occurred. The people I lived with were often summoned through the mediation of religious edicts and ways of life, so that residents of other Orthodox Jewish locales may recognize many of the processes and patterns I describe. But neighborhood residents were also summoned in particular ways because of the specific ways in which the neighborhood emerged. Especially important in this context is the rise of a particular form of Orthodoxy—what counted, and what no longer counted, as "Orthodox" in the neighborhood. No less important is the constantly unfolding organizational history. As I show, the particular history of the neighborhood made both for a proliferation of organizations and for a tight relationship between different subaffiliations of Jewish Orthodoxy, "thickening" neighborhood ties and pooling together subaffiliations that are at each other's throats in other centers of Orthodoxy.

With the historical stage set, chapter 3 deals with organizations and their role in everyday summoning. What does it mean to live in such a dense organizational space, with about twenty-four synagogues in one square mile, multiple schools, adult education organizations, and volunteering associations? I show how multiple ties among people who have specific primary organizational affiliations emerge, so that people who "belong" to one subaffiliation of Orthodoxy still find themselves summoned by a host of other organizations and social circles. I then delineate some ways in which the structure of participation is translated into a thick web of summoning in everyday life. Taking the examples of schools and the unique institution of Orthodox Jewish transnational panhandling based in Israel, I show how organizational rhythms are layered on top of each other. Paraphrasing Lewis Coser's term, I explain how, organizationally, the Beverly–La Brea neighborhood operates as a "greedy neighborhood."[16]

Although chapter 3 already presents a rudimentary picture of organizations in the neighborhood—especially schools and synagogues—this still tells us little about the predictable interactional patterns that emerge within the organizations themselves. Chapter 4 focuses on the way religious proscriptions and prescriptions provide opportunities, openings, and pressures for members to interact. I look at the structure of prayer, of Sabbath gatherings, at the everyday psalm reading, the attempts to garner a quorum of ten adult males on a daily basis in a small synagogue, and the laws of the Sabbath—some of the patterned occasions in which ties between congregants were formed, cemented, and reconstructed. Focusing both on the minutiae of mundane moments occurring in everyday prayer, and on more dramatic episodes of neighborhood life, this chapter not only fleshes out *that* people are summoned in everyday life but also looks at some of the forms and relationships that such summoning routinely takes.

The next two chapters examine what can be thought of as a semiotic picture. While summoning reconstructs a specific membership categorization, it also provides us the contours of what and who we are not. Chapter 5 delineates the internal variation and distinctions within the neighborhood's Orthodox social world. These distinctions were made between those seen as more or less observant (or *frum*), among people belonging to different subaffiliations of Orthodoxy, and between those who were born into Orthodoxy and those who became Orthodox (or, indeed, Jewish) later in their lives. The chapter shows how such internal distinctions worked to further locate Orthodox residents in interaction. Although often summoned as a generic Orthodox Jew, people were also summoned in far more specific ways. Far from simply denoting a totem pole of domination, these forms of identification were often a source of interaction and a way to further locate the self summoned.

Having looked at internal differentiation and distinction, in chapter 6 I describe how people differentiated themselves from the non-Jewish other. With most people working in white-collar "non-Jewish" jobs, this was especially pertinent. The (often explicit) challenge that non-Jews posited was the construction of strong differences against a backdrop of relative similarity. How does one deal with the fact that during the day one works with non-Jews, has non-Jewish friends and professional identifications, yet returns to a social world in which Jews and non-Jews are sharply separated and differentiated?

This focus on difference in the summoning of the self brings us, finally, to the way that the material environment itself—from nonkosher hotdog stands, to the lingerie shops of Melrose, the billboards, and the comments of complete strangers on the streets—acts to summon the Orthodox self. Chapter 7 follows the almost invisible ways in which the Orthodox people I knew religiously mapped the streets they lived in, and how by passing through the streets, and through everyday anonymous interactions in the street, they reconstituted themselves as specific kinds of people.

I conclude the book by making two kinds of comparisons. First, I synthesize and compare the different processes presented in the book. What patterns and mechanisms scaffolded the texture of Orthodox Jewish life in the neighborhood? Moving beyond the case, I then think comparatively about how summoning acts in different social worlds. I examine political affiliations, neighborhood identifications, religious sects, and celebrities, as well as more mundane forms of identification such as occupational and familial identification as a way to construct a comparative spectrum of summoning in social life. Although summoning is an inevitable aspect of any social world and any pattern of identification, it is also a variable feature. The variation in the mechanisms of summoning, its experienced "density," and the moral stakes involved in a particular identification could be used as a way to compare different social worlds.

A Note about Ethnographic Involvement

As in any project based on participant observation, my relation to people around me structured my data collection. Thus, it may be useful to know something about how I came into this project and how others, I believe, saw me. I am Jewish, male, and grew up in Israel. I am also of European origin, from a secular, middle-class family. In Israeli terms, this is the closest you can get to being a WASP. This also means that although I am Jewish, my Judaism was, like being white in the United States, a transparent category I usually didn't place much emphasis on precisely because it was so self-evident. I knew practically nothing beyond the stereotypical about Orthodoxy, although, like all Jewish Israelis, I speak Hebrew as my mother tongue and learned the Old Testament at school.

I started fieldwork almost by accident. Arriving in graduate school, I was hired to conduct some interviews with Orthodox Jews by Jack Katz, as part of a large-scale comparative neighborhood study.[17] In order to get into the neighborhood, we made connections with the local Chabad-Lubavitcher Hasids at UCLA. Any entry into the Orthodox world—granted one has a Jewish mother—is basically made effortless by Chabad. As this Hasidic group sees bringing nonaffiliated Jews into the Orthodox fold as a key part of its mission, I was immediately accepted, even courted.[18] I was told that although I might think that I wanted to come into the neighborhood to conduct research, it was the most inner recesses of my soul driving me to find a connection, the spark of holiness I possessed as a Jew who was yearning to return to Orthodoxy. My vegetarianism was understood in the same way—my Jewish soul's struggle to keep a kosher diet. Research was just an excuse.

One of the relatives of the chief Chabad rabbi on the UCLA campus lived in the neighborhood and volunteered to make introductions in a Chabad synagogue he thought I would enjoy. His choice was inspired—a small synagogue, with a deeply intellectual (and, as I found out later, an extremely funny) rabbi. It catered to newly religious Jews, many of whom were highly educated, including a few with PhD degrees. The rabbi, whom I will call Rabbi Chelev-Chittim,[19] was not overjoyed about the prospect of being the target of ethnographic petit-espionage, but welcomed me nonetheless.

For a Jew, entry into Orthodoxy is entry into a world where one is constantly invited over, attended to, made welcome. This welcome, combined with a misplaced feeling that I had somehow "managed" to enter a world that was entirely foreign—I had never spoken more than a few words with an Orthodox Jew in my entire life—made me decide to conduct my dissertation research in the neighborhood, and I stayed for the following five years, three of which I lived in the neighborhood. Although I entered through Chabad, and spent the first year or so mainly with Chabad friends, and in Chabad synagogues and yeshiva, I branched out. As I will show in more detail in chapter 3, the neighborhood itself intimately connected people from different subaffiliations of Orthodoxy, and people from other subaffiliations—non-Hasidic ("Yeshivish"), Modern Orthodox, Satmar-Hasidic, and others—were soon among my friends and acquaintances. Thus, although the data collection started with Chabad, and although my "regular" synagogue (what people call their *Shabbos shul*) remained Chelev-Chittim's synagogue,

I conducted sufficient interviews and made enough friends in other subaffiliations to be fairly confident that what I say in the book applies to more than this small part of one subaffiliation. However, the structure of the neighborhood also presented its challenges. Although a few of my best friends ended up being women, I was inducted—especially organizationally—into a world of men. The sociology of summoning I present below, although attentive to women wherever it can, is thus primarily that of men.

Living in the neighborhood, I tried to keep the same routines and strictures as did my friends. I mostly kept the laws of Sabbath and ate kosher (which was, indeed, much aided by my vegetarianism). Although I didn't don a yarmulke outside the neighborhood, I did wear one when in the neighborhood. I also did not take observational field notes on the Sabbath, as that would have constituted a religiously proscribed form of work. My field notes suffered as a result, but I believe it would have been unethical to do otherwise. I also, genuinely, became interested in Jewish theology and law, an interest that will probably keep me occupied for many years to come.[20]

Most of the people I knew were highly self-reflexive, and many were extremely widely read. I had to defend ethnography not only in conferences but in conversations with friends in the neighborhood (some comments included "how is your work scientifically valid if you are so obviously affecting the observations?" and "when you take notes, do you write only what we say, or also how we move, like they do with chimps?"). For a long while, however, and although I was explicit about my research, my Orthodox friends assumed I was the model "returned Jew," or *ba'al tshuva*. Some of them had gone through this process themselves, and my learning, my interest, my being, made sense through that lens. When I let a few friends read one of the first papers I wrote from the project, what hurt them most was nothing substantive in my analysis, but my methodological section, where our relationships were objectified in typical sociological-journal fashion. They were also pained to see, in writing, that my stay in the neighborhood did not make me Orthodox. This remains the case. Although I still learn with a good friend in the neighborhood (though, living in New York, we now learn on Skype), and although my interest in Orthodox thought and life has obviously deepened, I remain personally agnostic.

Some of my best friends, now as then, are from the neighborhood. Many families and individuals not only welcomed me in a superficial way but became part of my life in a way ethnography cannot do justice to. Although they all knew I was conducting ethnographic work, both they and I frequently forgot that was the case. In some cases it was a relief to leave the field, as the relationship between us would be less tainted by the ethnographic.

To a large extent, these personal experiences ended up structuring the focus of the book—the attempt to craft a sociology of summoning. As a doorway into these questions, my own ethnographic entry and exit tales may give an idea of what made sense in the Orthodox neighborhood. When I told Rabbi Chelev-Chittim, a year into the research, that I was thinking of moving in, he was happy to help me out, both as a friend, and because he hoped that being surrounded by Orthodoxy would tip me over in religious terms. His wife, a writer and educator, told me she would try to find me a back-house, a guesthouse for rent, in the neighborhood. She made a few phone calls after Shabbos. The people she knew were booked—they already had tenants in their guesthouses. I went away disappointed. Twenty minutes later, my cell phone rang. One of the people she called knew someone who had a guesthouse that was available within a month. They would be happy to let it. I had found an apartment within twenty-five minutes. I met my landlords-to-be a few days later, and they showed me a spacious one-bedroom guesthouse. They asked me how much I paid at the university housing and said that I could pay the same—the price was about $300 cheaper than that of other apartments in the area, and nobody asked for my credit score. It was, however, important to know "where I *davened* by," where I prayed, and who recommended me to them. When I said that I wasn't sure how I would spend the month before the apartment was ready, they made a few phone calls. A day later they called me to say that another friend with a guesthouse in the neighborhood would let me stay there for a month, completely free of charge.

If the way that many community members in the neighborhood engulfed me and made my move practically effortless is indicative of how membership categorization was translated into action, my exit from the neighborhood was no less telling. Three years after I moved in, at a time when I was vaguely wondering whether it was a good idea to get some kind of analytic and geographical distance, my landlord called me, ominously saying that we had to talk. I thought that perhaps they were frustrated by my level of observance and the fact that I fed far too many stray cats that were fruitful and multiplied, wreaking havoc in the yard and tearing the children's trampoline to shreds. The truth, however, was different. As it turned out, a man whom my landlord knew through one of the Orthodox neighborhood organizations he was active in had died, leaving behind an ill widow and children. As the deceased had wanted his children to live in a religious family, he had asked my landlord if he and his wife would take in his children. My landlord had hoped he would survive, but he didn't. In short, they needed the apartment. A week later, I moved out.[21]

TWO

From Ethnic Enclave to Religious Destination

Coming to Los Angeles from New York in 2003, Rabbi Yitzhok could not at first find much in the way of employment. This was a disappointment, although it didn't seem to be much of a surprise. A tall and willowy redheaded young man with an air of constant optimism, he moved to Los Angeles with his bride, Sheina, whose parents lived in the neighborhood, after his employment as a kosher supervisor on the East Coast was terminated. The couple spent their first few years in Los Angeles with irregular employment. They would sometimes commute to the San Fernando Valley for the Sabbath to help at a Jewish home for the elderly; she worked as a substitute teacher as he worked as a part-time assistant teacher at a private religious primary school or as a kosher supervisor during the High Holidays.

Although Yitzhok was a graduate of a prominent yeshiva, and had his rabbinical degree in hand, he was far from confident in his religious expertise. When conversations moved to education and his rabbinical credentials his usual smile waned. He was often bitter about the Orthodox educational system, saying that he felt he had gone through years of religious schooling only to become semi-literate in four languages—Yiddish, English, Hebrew, and Aramaic. Outspoken in his critique of the Orthodox educational system, which he once said "trains only rabbis and kosher supervisors," he became a teacher's aide in one of the Jewish private schools in the city, hoping to study the system in order to make it better suited for kids who didn't excel academically, and provide students with skills needed in the non-Orthodox world. But like other part-time employment opportunities, the job didn't pan out. Teachers were reluctant to implement the reforms he dreamt up; they treated him, he felt, more like a nuisance than a colleague.

During their fourth year in Los Angeles, after they had had their second child, and as their economic situation became so dire that they needed to apply for food stamps, an opportunity suddenly presented itself. A couple of members of the synagogue that Yitzhok and Sheina usually attended decided to found a new educational institution. Having a teenage boy who was veering toward the secular world, they decided that they would try and create a yeshiva—the Orthodox parallel to an all-boys high school—that catered to teenagers in a similar predicament, kids who were in danger of going "off the path" of Orthodoxy, a place where they could learn religious studies in a relaxed atmosphere. Looking to share this new responsibility, knowing that Yitzhok had ideas about and aspirations in education—and also knowing that he was only partially employed—they asked him about the possibility of becoming the principal and helping them construct this new organization. At first Yitzhok brushed off the idea as madness. He sometimes did not feel competent enough to be a teacher's aide in primary school, much less a yeshiva principal.

Sheina, however, thought that this would be an ideal opportunity. Confident, enthusiastic, and entrepreneurial, she figured that this was precisely the kind of opening Yitzhok needed, both economically and personally, a way for him to realize his potential in a worthwhile religious endeavor. After some convincing, Yitzhok agreed to help build up the yeshiva and serve as its *Rosh*, its principal. Within a matter of weeks, Sheina had constructed an internet site, and families of Orthodox teenagers from as far as New York, Britain, Australia, and South Africa were contacting them, asking for information and negotiating tuition.

The new shoestring yeshiva received no support from any of the leading religious figures in the city. Some prominent rabbis whom Yitzhok and the other founder called for help and endorsement did not even return their calls, and none would let the new yeshiva use their facilities. In private conversations, a couple of rabbis in the neighborhood said they were wary of the budding entrepreneurs' lack of experience. Bringing the Orthodox version of "at risk youth" to such an unstructured situation seemed irresponsible.

The new yeshiva also had no money, counting on incoming students' tuition to defray costs. As the school year started, however, the situation became, in Yitzhok's words, "ridiculous." Students began to fly in before the new school had any teachers except for Yitzhok himself and the other founder, no place to house the students, and no real curriculum. As students arrived, Yitzhok and the other founder managed to rent space from an Orthodox friend in the neighborhood, who sometimes prayed in the same synagogue as they did, and who gave them his place for much below market price, but the funds they had counted on did not come. Eighteen students came in the first year, but families were reluctant to send in the entire year's tuition for a yeshiva about which they knew next to nothing. In many cases, new students meant only more expenses, as students had to be housed and fed before their families paid.

Throughout the first few months of the new yeshiva's life, Yitzhok was working for more than fourteen hours a day: teaching students, bringing them food, frantically trying to raise funds, and having the students over for Sabbath so that they wouldn't be left to their own devices. Although they enlisted another rabbi to do some teaching for very little pay, the teaching was almost entirely up to him. He stayed up at nights to prepare the classes he would teach the next day; most days he improvised. As payments were few and far between, Yitzhok was working for practically nothing, cooking at nights with Sheina and paying from his own pocket to feed the teenagers. As for the students, they seemed to enjoy this state of affairs. They would sleep in late, hang out with their new friends, and spend their time on Facebook or checking emails on the lawn of their "dormitories."

As months went by, things seemed to get a little better. A local synagogue allowed the students to learn in its space for free and thereby implicitly recognized the new organization, and Yitzhok even felt he was gaining some respect from other residents and synagogue goers for his role as principal. And yet he also felt that he was on the verge of a mental breakdown. A thin man to begin with, he looked haggard, and when I sat with him at his small rented apartment, he looked haunted by the constant ringing of his phone. With very little sleep between work, preparations, and cooking, and with almost no money coming in, he applied for other jobs, jobs that paid an actual salary. When he got a temporary position as a religious functionary close to Los Angeles, despite having to commute almost two hours each way to work, he almost immediately left the new yeshiva.

To understand why such a story is possible, a few things about the neighborhood, and the Orthodox Jewish world more generally, should be borne in mind. First, the story underscores the degree to which Orthodox life operates in a laissez-faire organizational environment. Although both founders were not likely candidates to construct their own yeshiva, and no other local network or organization would initially help them set up their organization, they could still do so. There was very little anyone could actually do. And once the organization was in place, it was retro-actively, if begrudgingly, accepted; the founders even reaped some repu-tational dividends.

In such an environment, finding personal meaning through organiza-tional entrepreneurship was an available template for action, especially as prestige and educational attainment and activities are tightly linked in the Orthodox world. The story also illustrates the importance of local ties fostered in local religious organizations—Yitzhok was approached by someone who prayed at his synagogue, found student housing through yet another synagogue member, and finally managed to convince the rabbi at another synagogue he knew to let the students use their space.

But perhaps even more remarkable is the fact that parents from dif-ferent quarters of the world who knew nothing of either of the found-ers or the fledgling yeshiva sent their children to Los Angeles. When I inquired about some of the teenagers who came, I found that most had relatives or other connections in the neighborhood. The Beverly–La Brea neighborhood was not completely terra incognita. The surpris-ing (if modest) success of the new yeshiva in terms of enrollment was predicated on the past successes of neighborhood organizations, and on the migration of Orthodox people into the neighborhood. With a large number of organizations already occupying the neighborhood, some Orthodox people recognized Los Angeles as a Jewish island in a larger imaginary archipelago of livable space. They were sending their children not into a completely unknown situation but rather to a place they already knew had a presence of Orthodox Jewish life, of *yiddishkeit*.[1]

How, then, did such a religious space emerge? Historically, after all, Jews did not come to Los Angeles to find religion. As in New York and Chicago, Jews came for economic opportunities, for the freedom that city life afforded, or, as in the case of Florida, for the weather. There were Orthodox rabbis who came to the city at the turn of the twentieth cen-tury, and there were ritual slaughterers—always religious Jews, at least in appearance. But these were few and far between. Even though many of the Jews who settled in Los Angeles in the early twentieth century came from a traditional religious background, within the span of one gen-eration this form of Orthodoxy was all but gone; whereas Conservative and Reform synagogues flourished, traditional European Orthodoxy de-clined dramatically.[2]

A little over fifty years later, the orientation of Jewish neighborhoods in Los Angeles changed dramatically. To the extent that "Jewish neighborhoods" exist today in Los Angeles, they are all Orthodox. As Jewishness became less and less marked, Jewish neighborhoods lost their distinctiveness. Whereas Fairfax and the Beverly–La Brea neighborhood of the 1930s–70s was recognized as an *ethnically* Jewish neighborhood, at the turn of the century the Beverly–La Brea neighborhood was first and foremost a *religious* destination.[3]

The Neighborhood

Before delineating some of the neighborhood's history, I should describe some of its aspects as it was when I lived there.[4] It is usually hard to locate a neighborhood. The contours of municipal blocks, zip codes, or census tracts seldom have anything to do with the way people experience the space they live in. A neighborhood, in the lived sense, is not simply "there." With a Jewish Orthodox neighborhood, however, this task becomes more manageable. As Orthodox Jews cannot drive on the Sabbath and during religious holidays, they have to be able to walk to their places of worship. Thus, if we draw a walking distance radius surrounding Orthodox synagogues, some kind of living neighborhood space emerges.[5]

These vague contours become more precise after some time spent in the neighborhood. Certain streets are considered boundaries, and although there may be a synagogue or two on the other side, these don't really count. Thus emerges what Orthodox residents often called the "Beverly–La Brea" neighborhood. It was located in the southeast section of Hollywood, bordering West Hollywood on the northwest, the Wilshire area on the south, and Hancock Park on the east (see map 1). It was one of two large Jewish Orthodox residential and institutional hubs in Los Angeles, together with the Pico-Robertson neighborhood a few miles to its southwest, and was widely considered to be the most important Orthodox neighborhood on the West Coast both in organizational and in residential terms.

The neighborhood was relatively prosperous, with expensive single-family houses on the eastern side costing upward of $3 million and a yearly average household income of $72,000 in the census tracts that fell squarely within neighborhood lines.[6] Although Orthodox Jews in the neighborhood were sometimes said to neglect their properties, most

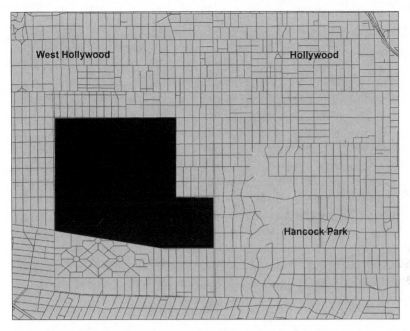

Map 1 The Beverly–La Brea Neighborhood (source: GIS map)

of the houses had neatly manicured lawns, a backyard with some fruit trees, and perhaps a small basketball court or a mini-trampoline for children. The houses themselves represent a hodgepodge of architectural styles. Some of them were the Mission and Bungalow style houses of the 1920s and 1930s, when the first houses in the neighborhood were built, while some were two-story postmodern mansions—single-family homes from the 1920s–40s that were renovated and expanded, eating up as much of their front lawns as legally possible.

The neighborhood also encompassed small areas of rent-controlled apartment complexes at its edges, a fact that allowed for a diversity of class positions, with low-income members in walking distance of the same synagogues as the neighborhood's few millionaires. Moreover, although Orthodox Jews were extremely visible, they comprised only about 15–20 percent of the neighborhood's residents, some 800–900 households,[7] and as others have shown, the area was populated largely by non-Orthodox, white, early adult single and middle-class family residents.[8] Moreover, especially in the north of the neighborhood where the rents were lowest, at least two other groups were very visible: Russian immigrants and young performance artists trying to succeed in the Los Angeles entertainment industry, to make it on Melrose.[9]

The neighborhood was considered by Los Angeles Orthodox Jews, at least in comparison to other neighborhoods on the West Coast, to be religiously exacting.[10] It was home to about twenty-four Orthodox synagogues that spanned the entire range of subaffiliations within the Orthodox world. It housed no Conservative or Reform temples. The neighborhood did, however, boast eight private religious schools, a small academy, a yeshiva, two adult education *kollels*, ritual baths, and numerous semireligious venues such as kosher restaurants, religious bookstores, and so on. Smaller organizations, from welfare organizations to shoestring synagogues and Orthodox family daycare centers, operated from residents' backyards. Walking through La Brea or Beverly Boulevard on a Saturday morning, one was struck by the predominance of Orthodox Jews. Men wearing black garments and long beards, women wearing long skirts and head covers, and small boys with sidelocks seemed to dominate the streets. This had not always been the case.

Forming the Ethnic Enclave: From Boyle Heights to Fairfax

In 1860, ten years after the United States annexed California, there were about one hundred Jews in Los Angeles—a few businessmen who could sense an opportunity, later the county's sheriff. This was far from being an overly zealous bunch. While Jews constructed a cemetery in 1855 and a synagogue that quickly became Reform, and while some Jews took on positions of leadership in the retail and banking sectors in Los Angeles, they did little in terms of religious life. But then, in the beginning of the twentieth century, the small trickle of Jewish arrivals became a deluge. The Jewish population in Los Angeles grew exponentially from 2,500 people in 1900 to 10,000 in 1912, 20,000 in 1917, and 65,000 in 1927.[11] These new immigrants, mostly European immigrants who began their immigration career on the East Coast, moved the center of Jewish settlement from the Downtown area eastward, toward the neighborhood of Boyle Heights.

Although many of these Jewish immigrants came from religious backgrounds, the situation of traditional Orthodoxy in Los Angeles wasn't much improved. Small Orthodox gatherings were held in Jewish neighborhoods, and two Hasidic rabbis settled in Los Angeles during the 1930s (both died within a few years of their arrival), but Reform and Conservative synagogues held sway. The main newsletter of the Jewish community in Los Angeles, the *B'nai B'rith Messenger*, was trying to build rapport between Judaism and Christianity, sometimes deriding the newly arrived Jews for their nonmodern, Old World shtetl ways.

The weakness of traditional European Orthodoxy was overdetermined. Many of the Jews who came to Los Angeles were secular Socialists or Zionists who had little patience with the traditional trappings of religion to begin with; and even those who came to Los Angeles Orthodox did not tend to remain so. In their attempts to secure a living in a largely non-Jewish city, it was hard to observe the Sabbath. The younger generation almost universally shed the "European" religious trappings of its parents. As one young interviewee in Pauline Young's early study of Los Angeles relates when discussing his parents:

My father is Orthodox, European. He wants me to go to *Shahl* (Synagogue) [*sic*]. I see nothing in it, and we begin to fight. Hell and Heaven can't live together, and I keep out of his way as much as possible.[12]

Although the religious mores of the older generation might still be considered as "heaven" by the second generation, Orthodoxy seemed to have slim chances—religious practice and the immigrant identity, at least in this interviewee's pithy response, seemed interchangeable.

Rather than synagogues, the center of Jewish neighborhood life thus tended to be social clubs and mutual help societies. Until the 1940s, small *landsmanschaften*—mutual help organizations for people who came from the same areas in Europe—flourished; Yiddish theater performances were orchestrated by local schools; the vast majority of Jews mentioned in the *Los Angeles Times* in the 1920s and 1930s were popular Boyle Heights boxers and baseball players. Religious leaders who came to Los Angeles were usually sick with "consumption" and had been advised by their doctors to seek out the healthy air and weather on the West Coast.[13] If they were not sick with tuberculosis, they were morally suspect. This state of Orthodoxy in Boyle Heights (and Los Angeles in general) was neatly captured by a joke then told of local rabbis: "Rabbis who come here," the saying went, "either have one lung, or two wives."[14]

This secular bent of Jewish immigrants can also be seen through the scarce resources funneled into religious education. In 1923, out of a Jewish population of 43,000, only an estimated 1,500 children received any form of Jewish education. Jewish schools altogether employed only 11 weekday teachers and 29 Sunday teachers, and had a budget of about $17,000 per year. And even these were not full-time schools but after-school programs and Sunday schools. By 1936, the number of students rose to about 2,319, but the Jewish population in Los Angeles more than doubled at the same time to about 100,000.[15]

Boyle Heights, however, did not stay Jewish for long. Like Jews in other neighborhoods across America, residents were generally eager to take advantage of economic opportunities beyond the confines of the ghetto.[16] And even compared with other mobile immigrant groups in Boyle Heights, Jews had overall higher mobility rates.[17] Middle-class Los Angeles to the west appealed to those immigrants, and especially to their children, more than did a relatively poor immigrant neighborhood. Writing about Boyle Heights as part of his 1946 series of essays on early Los Angeles history, Carey McWilliams noted that the second generation of Jews left the neighborhood as soon as it could:

From the east side, the Jewish second generation has jumped over downtown Los Angeles and located far to the west in the apartment-house district bounded by Santa Monica and Wilshire Boulevards, from Fairfax to La Cienega, which is nowadays a major area of secondary settlement.[18]

Fairfax Boulevard was to become the Jewish ethnic center of Los Angeles for decades—the western edges the Orthodox Jewish neighborhood as it exists today. And as Jews moved to these western areas of "secondary settlement," religion did not seem to be their first priority.

Map 2 shows Los Angeles in 1930. It was constructed using two kinds of data. The Stars of David represent all synagogues listed in the 1930 Los Angeles phone directory and capture all but the smallest synagogues. Not surprisingly, the synagogues are most dense in the east, in the Boyle Heights immigrant neighborhood, and grow sparser as you move west. The dots represent middle-class Jewish households in Los Angeles. These were mapped using the 1930 Jewish New Year greetings in the *B'nai B'rith Messenger*, the largest and most important Jewish bi-weekly, dating from 1898. In a large "greetings" section of this New Year's (Rosh Ha'Shana) issue, many Jews put an advertisement to wish their friends and relatives a happy Jewish New Year. As greetings also included their addresses, I could map where these Jews—a partial sample, to be sure—lived. Two facts are striking about this map. First, the area just east of La Brea was already populated by middle-class Jews. Equally striking from the point of view of the neighborhood's subsequent transformation is the fact that the area, while being the densest concentration of middle-class Jewish households, had *absolutely no synagogues*.[19]

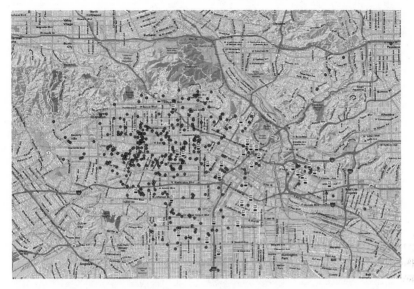

Map 2 Synagogues and Middle Class Jewish Households in 1930 Los Angeles (sources: GIS map, *B'nai B'rith Messenger*, and Los Angeles 1930 phone directory)

The transformation of the area into a Jewish space quickly became visible. In 1939, as part of the large Home Owners Loan Corporation survey, the residential area dubbed "La Brea-Beverly-Fuller," in the middle of the current Beverly–La Brea neighborhood, was described by surveyors as "ethnically harmonious," although an "infiltration of Jewish families is said to be somewhat disrupting."[20] By 1970, with 11,725 Jewish households in the area, they were no longer an "infiltration"; it was a Jewish neighborhood.[21]

Ethnically, Fairfax thus became the undeniable hub of Jewish Los Angeles. In the 1970s, when Los Angeles Jews went to cities they did not know, they would ask where "the Fairfax of the city" was to be found. In fact, in an urban planning survey published in 1982, almost half (48%) of the businesses on Fairfax said they catered to Jewish clientele, with establishments such as Canter's Deli serving Eastern European Jewish food, and a host of other institutions (from homes for the Jewish elderly to two veteran institutions for Jews) operating in the neighborhood.[22] There was also a religious aspect to the performance of ethnicity in the Fairfax area, though this was largely limited to major holy days and festivities. As one elderly resident recalled in a conversation, his Catholic neighbor came running to him one day in the 1950s, in a panic, asking him whether the war with the Soviets had started. All the businesses were closed, and she feared the worst. The reason, however, was less alarming: it was Yom Kippur, the Day of Atonement, one of the few holy days that most Jews in the neighborhood observed.

Of course, between the 1930s and the 1970s some religious organizations did become established in the neighborhood. The first of these, an Orthodox synagogue, was opened already in 1932. Others opened later, many by Holocaust survivors who came to Los Angeles as part of a wave of 185,000 Jews who arrived between 1941 and 1951—another 163 percent growth in the Jewish population of Los Angeles County.[23] The Orthodox organizations in the neighborhood, however, were by and large less exacting in their demands than those of current Orthodoxy. But for a few small storefront synagogues that were created by (and catered to) the few strict Orthodox residents who came post-Holocaust, none of the synagogues had partitions between men and women, the sine qua non of Orthodox services today. They catered to Jews who mainly wanted to celebrate the High Holidays, and they boasted the membership of Hollywood moguls rather than Torah scholars. Similarly, although a few Jewish full-time schools did start operating, they were schools in which a robust secular education was buttressed by religious education, as opposed to the situation nowadays, when strict Orthodox schools focus mostly on religious studies, one of them even teaching in Yiddish as a sign of extreme piety.

Indeed, in 1975, the Toras Emes primary school, the only strict Orthodox school in the neighborhood—founded in 1958 by the few strictly Orthodox families—had 126 students in all grades, including both boys and girls. And in order to reach even this number, different strands of Orthodoxy, which were sharply at odds elsewhere in the Orthodox world, had to overcome their differences so they could give their children a strict religious education. By comparison, in 2008, there were around 900 boys and girls in Toras Emes and its affiliated girls school. And Toras Emes was only one of the neighborhood schools, facing competition from two other strictly Orthodox schools, each of which had about 300 boys and girls.[24] In short, although the Fairfax–La Brea area became an ethnic enclave, up until the late 1970s it was not a religious destination.

Religious Entrepreneurship and Neighborhood Transformation

This story of Jewish Los Angeles has so far proceeded as if the city existed in a social vacuum, as if people came from elsewhere and subsequently lived and prayed in isolation from Jewish life in the United States and beyond. And yet to understand the transformation of the Fairfax–La Brea ethnic enclave into a religious neighborhood, Los Angeles has to be seen in relation to the centers of Orthodoxy on the East Coast. Whereas Los Angeles up until the 1970s had relatively little strict Orthodox organizational infrastructure, New York and New Jersey had by this time already established themselves as some of the most important Orthodox Jewish centers in the post-Holocaust world, with institutions rivaling those in Israel. For a variety of Orthodox subaffiliations, the East Coast became an intellectual and political powerhouse.

From this position, the Orthodox centers of the East Coast surveyed the Jewish geography of the United States with dismay. With a high rate of intermarriage, Jews in America were becoming "assimilated."[25] And although this narrative could be seen as an instance of melting-pot success, the Orthodox in the East saw it as disastrous. Orthodox leaders in the United States began speaking of a spiritual Holocaust, with assimilation succeeding in eliminating Jews where the Nazis had failed. Los Angeles could be considered a prime example of this creeping disaster: here was a large urban center with the second largest Jewish concentration in the Unites States, but with very little Orthodoxy to speak of.

The two organizational clusters I focus on below—two of the largest religious clusters in the neighborhood, accounting for about half of the regular congregants—should be understood within this framework. They were crafted by East Coast-based religious entrepreneurs, attempting to make a difference in what they saw as the heart of the secular world. Whereas place entrepreneurship is usually measured by economic achievement and real estate prices, religious place entrepreneurship is measured in souls.[26]

Real Estate Miracles

Perhaps the most vocal group in the new landscape of Orthodoxy in Los Angeles today, Chabad-Lubavitch entered the scene quite early. A Hasidic group that emerged at the end of the eighteenth century in Belarus, then part of the Russian empire, the movement is now based in Crown Heights, Brooklyn, after Chabad's leader relocated there from Europe in 1940, fleeing the Holocaust.[27] As part of his attempt to recreate the Orthodox world decimated in the Holocaust, its leader at the time, or *rebbe*, began sending emissaries into secular areas to bring Jews to Orthodoxy, to bring light into secular darkness. Los Angeles was one such place. The first arrival took place in 1949, when Rabbi Raichik—a recent immigrant who had survived the Holocaust and joined his rebbe in the United States—was stationed as an emissary. After living for the first six years in Boyle Heights, Raichik followed the movement of the Jewish population and relocated to the Fairfax area in 1955.

Highly regarded well beyond Chabad and active in the neighborhood's small strict Orthodox community—one of the organizers of the first strict Orthodox primary school in the neighborhood—Raichik did not work to sustain a distinctive Chabad presence in Los Angeles. There were few strict Orthodox residents, and they generally banded together, putting the difference between subaffiliations aside to sustain the organizations they shared.

Then, in 1965, the last rebbe of Chabad—Menachem Mendel Schneerson—sent a new emissary to Los Angeles, Rabbi Baruch Cunin. Schneerson became the head of Chabad in 1951 following his father-in-law's death and focused Chabad's efforts on bringing non-Orthodox Jews into the religious fold. Breathing new life in an old strategy, Schneerson started sending emissaries to areas where Jews were present, beginning in major towns and finally covering most places in which Jews could be found, from small U.S. towns to Katmandu. In Los Angeles, Cunin ushered in more assertive attempts to bring Jews back to the fold.[28] First moving into the Fairfax neighborhood, Cunin soon left for Westwood in 1969, where he instated the first "Chabad house" at UCLA, and through large donations and brilliant advertising tactics (such as the Chabad Telethon, a yearly fundraiser that made Chabad and Cunin, "the dancing rabbi," a household name)[29] began to expand the movement's influence.

But although such outreach programs were important, the most important organization in the growth of Chabad within the neighborhood was educational—the installment of Yeshiva Ohr Elchonon acquired by Cunin in 1977. The yeshiva's subsequent move into the neighborhood in 1980 was a "miracle tale" that involved the Chabad authority structure, the dwindling Orthodoxy of the previous generation, and real estate deals.

The Feiner family, an immigrant family with some connections to Chabad dating to its days back in Europe, attempted to operate an old age home in the neighborhood, a business venture that brought other Jewish businessmen in Los Angeles immense fortunes. When the project started losing money, Feiner turned to his rebbe for counsel. As Feiner's son tells it, rather than advising his father to sell and start anew, the rebbe told Feiner to buy as many properties as he could on the block he was on and expand his business. Again and again Feiner bought properties, dwindling his resources and taking loans. But even after he came to own a large part of the block, his business still floundered. When it seemed as if the Feiner family had lost its fortune owing to the rebbe's real estate advice, divine intervention struck in the form of a failed freeway.

The Beverly Hills freeway was supposed to pass through the neighborhood, connecting the area with Westwood and continuing to the San Fernando Valley. As the route was supposed to pass through the area where Feiner's property stood, he (along with other residents) was approached by city engineers and ordered to sell. Although as a home for the elderly it had been a rather dismal failure, as a real estate deal it turned out to be a great success—the transportation authority paid well, a better price than he had paid when he purchased the properties. Then, as if to cement the rebbe's real estate advice, the construction of the highway was canceled in 1976. Following protocol, the property was offered back to the Feiner family. And since land values had fallen in the meantime—mostly *because* of the highway planned to pass through the neighborhood—Feiner was able to buy back his property while making a handsome profit. Now possessing a large property and an aversion to homes for the elderly, and knowing that Chabad needed a lot for a yeshiva, Feiner soon sold his property to Cunin for a low price.

A building and a name already existed: three years earlier, Cunin had taken over an old yeshiva in West Hollywood, a non-Chabad yeshiva that had struggled since its inception in the 1950s, and whose founder decided to try his luck in Israel. As old-time residents like to tell, Cunin promised the founder that he would keep the yeshiva's building and name.[30] He now had a building and a promise in one place, and real estate in another. Cunin proceeded to have the building sawed in three parts and moved it to the new location. In 1980, the Chabad Yeshiva Ohr Elchonon began to operate in the neighborhood.[31]

With the active help of the rebbe from the East Coast, a cadre of teachers arrived on the scene, moving along with their families to the neighborhood and slowly putting Los Angeles on the religious map, with students coming from the East Coast, and as far as Britain and Australia, to join its ranks. The yeshiva also opened a primary school unit largely to cater to the children of staff and of the few affiliated families in Los Angeles.

As the educational system was built up, a synagogue system was simultaneously developed. From the small quorum affiliated with Chabad, a center was first constructed in 1972 on Fairfax Avenue, which then moved to La Brea when one of the congregants capitalized on a real estate deal on a small synagogue whose rabbi also moved to Israel. Subsequently, owing to the influx of emissaries, teachers, and congregants fueled by the yeshiva, the synagogue moved again, to a bigger place a few blocks up the road. Today, one of the sons of the late Rabbi Raichik—the first emissary to Los Angeles—presides over a building on La Brea, about five blocks from the yeshiva. The congregation is the largest Chabad synagogue on the West Coast, with more than two hundred affiliated families and more than three hundred regular congregants on any given Sabbath. Additionally, a host of smaller satellite organizations fanned out: one of Cunin's sons attempted his own outreach program; one of the yeshiva's teachers opened a small synagogue; a recent split between the older and part of the younger generation in the main synagogue drove young Chabad Hasids to start their own place, two blocks away.

The Double Order of Place Entrepreneurship

Two years before the Chabad yeshiva was acquired, a different institution from a very different quarter of the "yeshiva world" of the East Coast made its move into the neighborhood. The Beth Medrash Govoha of Lakewood was constructed in a small town in New Jersey by Rabbi Aharon Kotler in 1943, after his escape from the Holocaust. Kotler was already a well-known scholar in Eastern Europe, and his yeshiva grew to be the largest and most prestigious Orthodox institution outside Israel, dubbed "the Harvard of the yeshiva world" by admirers and cynics alike.[32] By the early 1970s, the Lakewood yeshiva was secure enough in its own position to stretch its influence beyond the East Coast. From Lakewood, Kotler and others drew a work plan—the construction of "community kollels" in locations that held a large number of unaffiliated Jews.[33]

The *kollel*—an institution of higher religious learning designed for men after their marriage—is usually located in the largest and most prestigious centers, where the elite of the yeshiva world live. By moving the kollel into the religious hinterland, Lakewood's leadership planned the neighborhood's transformation. The strategic idea was twofold. First, while kollel students would be involved in their own learning during the day, they would offer classes in the evenings. In this capacity, students could make the lay Jewish population more religious. Second, by moving a part of the elite to the religious periphery, Lakewood would aid in the development of new, autonomous religious centers. Los Angeles was, in this regard, a perfect candidate. When I asked how the kollel came to be constructed in this neighborhood rather than in other locations, its founder looked at me as if I had asked a rather daft question: "This has always been the ethnically Jewish neighborhood in Los Angeles. This *was* the community."[34]

On August 20, 1975, the kollel moved in, renting space in one of the older small storefront synagogues whose rabbi was sympathetic to Lakewood's project. The kollel started with ten families recruited from Lakewood itself, promising students a larger allowance than they would get elsewhere so that they would consider abandoning the Orthodox center. With money secured through donations from Jews in Los Angeles as well as highly affluent Canadian Jews, its founder also bought apartment buildings to house his students' families. Moving from one rented space to another—including one in an old Jewish school—the kollel finally bought a building on Beverly Boulevard. Over the past thirty-three years, the school has produced some seventy alumni—an impressive achievement, taking into account that there were only up to fifteen men studying in the kollel at any given time and that some students stayed for more than eleven years.

The success of the kollel, however, had relatively little to do with neighborhood construction. Although students did offer classes, and some of the Orthodox families that already lived in the neighborhood chose to come to pray and learn, it never became a major draw for laymen in the community. What the kollel did do was to integrate some of the students into the growing Orthodox community of Los Angeles. First, the kollel brought to the city not just men, but families. And as even a relatively generous allowance is not enough to sustain a large family, the wives of the students went to work. As of 2008, about twenty of the wives of the seventy kollel alumni and students held positions as teachers or principals at Orthodox girls schools in Los Angeles. Second, and perhaps more important, the kollel managed to keep around a third of its alumni in greater Los Angeles, both in existing rabbinate positions and in new positions that alumni carved for themselves.

Thus, while most of the kollel's alumni returned to the East Coast, about twenty-five of them stayed in the Los Angeles area. Of these, the majority took positions in the small existing Orthodox world, which was important in turning existing institutions toward a stricter interpretation of Orthodoxy.[35] But even more important, some proceeded to open their own institutions. A member of the first contingent of kollel students started one of the most successful synagogues in the neighborhood, situated directly across from the kollel, and packed full with over two hundred families of regulars, some of whom were older local residents, but most of whom were new Orthodox residents who moved to Los Angeles knowing that there was an established religious presence they could connect to. Other alumni opened outreach programs, schools, yeshivas, and recently another kollel. Without an occupational niche within a religious center, students carved a space that allowed them to make sense of the discrepancy between the prestige afforded them by their learning and the limited possibilities they found in Los Angeles.

The two narratives above outline the rise of two important Orthodox clusters in the neighborhood, which together account for almost half of its congregants, with about 450 families. As these clusters grew, others followed. Thus, as some of the most successful Orthodox businessmen in the neighborhood had ties to non-Chabad Hasidic groups, one of them funded his own kollel, buying property and importing students (with their families) from the East Coast and Israel; a Hasidic-oriented school was soon to follow. In fact, a house that originally held one of the small quorums of Hasidic men became so packed that it ignited a still-unresolved zoning struggle between them and their exasperated neighbors. Another cluster of organizations that developed was "Modern Orthodox," an affiliation more open to the secular world that grew with other forms of strict Orthodoxy in the neighborhood and became more and more exacting as it became organizationally and personally entangled with stricter versions of Orthodoxy.

By the end of the 1980s, strict Orthodox Judaism seemed to take hold of the neighborhood. The Jewish neighborhood was changing, and new residents, the men wearing black and donning hats, the women with head covers and long dresses, emerged in the visual landscape, walking beside the punks and trendy "Melrose Place" youngsters. Spanning the gamut of Orthodox affiliations—from the old-time European immigrant synagogues to new immigrants from Israel and Morocco, from Hasidic to Yeshivish[36]—new organizations dotted the neighborhood. And as these clusters initially shared both the same challenges and some of the same organizations, the Orthodox neighborhood also emerged as a relatively congenial space. People from different affiliations that were at odds in New York or Israel met at the ritual bath and at their children's school,[37] and even if they prayed in separate synagogues, they met at special events and holidays.

The Meaning of Orthodoxy

So far the history of Orthodox Los Angeles has been narrated as the tale of a blossoming social world—from a time in which strict Orthodoxy was scarcely visible, we are now at a point in which Orthodoxy largely defined Jewish space in Los Angeles; to the extent that it is meaningful to speak about Jewish neighborhoods in Los Angeles today, these spaces are largely Orthodox. This narrative has thus been both cohesive and victorious. And yet this neighborhood transformation entails surprising "losers" and "dropouts": those residents who once defined themselves as Orthodox Jews but who came to realize that the new wave of Orthodoxy had rewritten the rules of the Orthodox game.

This flip side of the change in Orthodoxy, and the strict adherence that followed, can be glimpsed through an apparent paradox in the story of Orthodox Judaism in Los Angeles—a survey conundrum. In 1977 the Jewish Federation of Greater Los Angeles conducted a survey of Jews in greater Los Angeles. As part of the survey, the federation tried to ascertain the percentage of Jews who self-identified as "Orthodox." They estimated the Orthodox population to be 5.2 percent of Los Angeles Jews. Twenty years later, in 1997, the federation carried out the same survey.[38] The results of the second survey were a surprise—the number of Orthodox Jews remained more or less the same, and the percent of self-identified Orthodox Jews had actually dwindled, this time to 4.3 percent out of the 519,151 estimated Jews living in greater Los Angeles—22,323 self-identified Orthodox Jews.

For Orthodox residents in Los Angeles, as for a great many others, this stability simply did not make sense. From a situation in which Orthodoxy was largely invisible in the city, there were now at least two neighborhoods where men dressed in black and sported beards and sidelocks, where women wore head covers and long dresses. Both the number of children in Orthodox schools and the number of schools increased dramatically.[39] By any measure they could fathom, this situation was completely at odds with the survey. Orthodox rabbis questioned these results; perhaps, one rabbi mused, Orthodox Jews simply did not answer surveys, as they had too many children to be bothered with long phone conversations.[40] Another rabbi, exasperated by the study, wrote on his blog: "Numbers can lie. People can lie, but pizza shops don't lie." There were simply more kosher restaurants than ever before, catering—obviously—to a booming Orthodox population.

Surveys, however, describe both people and categories. In the movement of people and categories, it is often not the people in question who change their characteristics, but the definition of the categories themselves.[41] In other words, the question may not be whether there were more or less Orthodox people in Los Angeles in 1977 than in 1997, but rather *what Orthodoxy meant* for people who self-identified as such at these two junctures.

The fate of the largest pre-1970s synagogues in the Beverly–La Brea neighborhood illustrates this tension between people and categories. Before the appearance of strict East Coast Orthodoxy in Los Angeles during the mid-1970s, the Beverly area was not bereft of Orthodox synagogues. East of Fairfax there were two large synagogues that had been built early in the neighborhood's history, one in 1932 and the other in 1934. These two congregations still stand today. In fact, these are still the largest and most impressive Orthodox buildings on Beverly Boulevard, taking up over half of two street blocks. Both house lavish halls boasting stained glass and a high dais for the Torah scroll. Indeed, from a passerby's perspective, these buildings would appear to be the center of Orthodoxy on Beverly Boulevard.

But walking into either of these synagogues on a Sabbath morning, a time when most Orthodox men come to pray, shows a striking incongruity. Congregants can be found in the main halls, their high ceilings reminiscent of Gothic cathedrals. But the halls are nearly empty. On one such Sabbath, when I went to both congregations, I found a group of eighteen men and twelve women, mostly elderly, sitting in one; in the other, there were nineteen men and a handful of women. There were no children in attendance in one of the synagogues, two in the other. Despite the claim of the young rabbi at one of the synagogues that more than two hundred families were synagogue members, very few people attended regularly, a far cry from the synagogue's standing in the 1940s as one of the two most important synagogues in the neighborhood, when it was so visible that Benjamin Warner, the father of Hollywood's Warner Brothers, presented it with a Torah scroll in memory of his wife.[42] The rabbi in the other synagogue was much more sober. "The neighborhood has changed," he said, his congregation had obviously declined.

This decline becomes even clearer when one walks through the many halls and rooms in the two synagogues. As both synagogues struggle to pay for their upkeep, they began renting space to other Orthodox groups in the neighborhood. In one, close to Fairfax on the east, where new waves of Persians and Israelis now live, there are two additional prayer quorums, one Persian and one Moroccan, with more than thirty families in each. The other synagogue, closer to the neighborhood's center, seems to have become a Jewish rental hub, with a Hasidic school, a Modern Orthodox welfare organization, and two additional quorums. And in both synagogues, the new quorums outshine the original crowd, with a large contingent of regular attendees and a host of young children running around.[43]

In one conversation, the rabbi at one of the synagogues tried to explain the history of his congregation's decline. Having come from New York, and more strict in observance than most of his congregants, he had always wanted to put a partition between men and women at his synagogue, a *mechitza*. At the time, however, his congregants did not agree to a partition. Orthodox Judaism was a different affair back then. Although many members came to services on the Sabbath, they did not adhere to many of the strictures that now define Orthodoxy. Almost all men shaved; women did not wear head covers or wigs after marriage; some of the members drove on the Sabbath; and even the observance of kosher rules and of other laws was somewhat relaxed. Families wanted to sit together.

But as Orthodoxy began to change, both in the neighborhood and in the wider American context, the *mechitza* became a powerful symbol.[44] In the 1980s, he finally decided to adhere to the new norms of Orthodoxy and insisted on a partition between men and women in services. Most congregants were vehemently opposed, but he pressed on until he eventually had his way. As a result, however, half his congregation left, opting to pray at a Conservative synagogue farther away where they would be able to continue to sit together. As religious practices connected to the categorization of residents as Orthodox changed, then, people had few choices: they could accept the greater strictness in everyday practices that the shifting categories implied, or they could retain their practices and switch their affiliation, as half of the congregation chose to do.

What this redefinition meant for individuals can be glimpsed in an interview with a woman in her nineties, the daughter of a European Orthodox rabbi, who still went to one of the two "old" Orthodox congregations in the neighborhood and who identified herself as Orthodox. At the beginning of the interview, she described her move to Los Angeles, trying to find a better climate for her son's health:

So when I came out to Los Angeles, it was very hard to get kosher food, it was flown in by plane. And then . . . so we ate dairy, we ate a lot of dairy, and I wanted to have a *shokhet* [ritual slaughterer] to slaughter a chicken, and I went there on Santa Monica and they said, "oh [there is an] Israeli *shokhet* . . . and he can *shekht* [slaughter] the chicken . . ." and I know something about chicken. And I said, "Do you come from Israel? Do you slaughter the chickens?" He says, "Yeah." So I says, "What do you do? Chop off their heads? Because I want to know the *Halakha* [religious law]." So he can't tell whether I'm Orthodox, if I'm Jewish or anything like that. And he says, "Sure, come in." So he pulls out the hair [the soft feathers on the chicken's neck] a bit, and cuts this way, and goes back again [making two cuts]. I say, "Thank you very much, but I can't eat your *hashgacha* [supervision]." "What do you mean?" I says, "I happen to know that you only go one time and not twice, so goodbye." So that's the way it was here, very hard to get kosher things.

However, even as she told me of her early exploits as an Orthodox Jewess in mid-century Los Angeles, she added that there were certain things that she did *not* do: she did not cover her hair after marriage, and she dressed "like everybody." Then, at the end of the interview, she remarked on how the neighborhood—and her own status—had changed:

When I bought the house in the beginning of 1959, and I moved in the end of 1959 . . . So my neighbor and her husband were the only frum [religious-Orthodox] people living on this street over here. And now I'm the biggest *shiksa* [Yiddish derogatory term for non-Jewish woman] living here. But I'm strictly Orthodox.

Orthodoxy had obviously changed, and the woman lamented her status shift, having gone from being a self-fashioned symbol of Orthodoxy to being a shiksa, figuratively a "non-Jew" in the new constellation of Orthodoxy.

An Orthodox Island

In summary, the history of the emergence of strict Orthodoxy in the Beverly–La Brea neighborhood presents two interlocking stories. One story, victorious, tells of the rise of a new form of Orthodoxy in Los Angeles since the late 1970s, a new institutional and residential island that erupted into the ethno-cartography of Orthodox Jewish space in the United States and beyond. This is the story that many Orthodox friends I talked to were fond of telling, a story of organizational construction and of a transformation of ethnic space into a religious destination.

It is also a story that elucidates some aspects of everyday life in Beverly–La Brea. The different entry and immigration stories set the stage for a neighborhood in which multiple Orthodoxies construct their own organizations, and in which emerging entrepreneurs are able to construct their own niches—partly answering the question of why so many organizations exist in a space where a few would suffice.[45] Thus, the neighborhood slowly emerged as an organizationally and residentially dense Jewish space. Whereas the area was once considered uninhabitable, beyond the pale of settlement, it increasingly appeared on the horizon of possible residential space for Orthodox Jews around the world. Finally, it now makes sense to send a child from Australia or New York to a newly minted yeshiva in the Beverly–La Brea neighborhood. Even if it is far from being a center of Orthodoxy, it is a recognizable Jewish Island.

Additionally, that strict Orthodox life first found its organizational expression in a few shoestring organizations shared among multiple subaffiliations helps make sense of the cordial, often warm, relationship among different Orthodox subaffiliations today. Although with numbers comes differentiation, and subaffiliations in the neighborhood increasingly have their "own" organizations, affiliation-based distinctions are not as clear-cut as in Orthodox centers such as New York or Israel. When two Hasidic groups—Satmar and Chabad—were at each other's throats in New York, they were sharing the same building and ritual bath in Los Angeles; when non-Hasidic Orthodox rabbis derisively called Chabad "the closest religion to Judaism" in Israel, they sent their children to the same primary school in Beverly–La Brea.[46] Many residents still remember a time when they shared organizations, and many have cemented friendships and organizational ties that transcend their specific Orthodox affiliation.

While this story sets up much of the discussion in the following chapters, the transformation of the neighborhood into a strict Orthodox space also presents a window into the changing nature of Orthodoxy as a membership categorization. Thus, the other story, more subdued, is about the way in which the very categorization of Orthodox Judaism changed, so that people who defined themselves as Orthodox in pre-1970s Los Angeles were either pushed away or accepted a movement to stricter practice. Through this dual process, a new and much stricter Orthodox Los Angeles has emerged. And although this new Orthodoxy may now still rent space in the synagogues of old, their version of Orthodoxy simultaneously pushes this "immigrant religion" into oblivion.

THREE

Organizational Entanglements

The history of the Beverly–La Brea neighborhood begins to make the texture of its organizational life legible. Orthodox families were able to move in precisely because there was enough of an organizational presence in the neighborhood to sustain an Orthodox life within the space they inhabited, enough for an island to emerge within the imaginary archipelago of the Orthodox world. And once different Orthodox groups came into the neighborhood, multiple logics of action made for a rich proliferation of organizations. This chapter begins to lay out the processes of summoning through which the web of organizations in the neighborhood sustained and drew residents into Orthodox life. I focus on the way in which the dizzying array of neighborhood organizations exerted pressures on residents to participate and spend their money and time, entangling residents in the dense social web that surrounded them.[1] And by doing so, I show the organizational rhythms and syncopations that residents came to expect—the intersituational patterns of action.

The Structure of Organizational Belonging

On a walk through the neighborhood, the sheer number of religious organizations on its main thoroughfares was striking. There were about twenty-four synagogues in the neighborhood, all of them Orthodox. For about 800–900 families, this means that there was approximately one synagogue per 37 families. And this was not counting schools, kollels for adult higher learning, welfare societies, ritual baths, and shops that catered specifically to the Orthodox. There were no fewer than seven Orthodox synagogues within a single mile of Beverly Boulevard. Counting the smaller groups renting space within them, there were eleven quorums sharing the same street. Even more synagogues could be found on La Brea. In one block there were three contiguous synagogues that belonged to different Orthodox subaffiliations (what one rabbi living in the area referred to as the "*shul*-plex"). Synagogues were in a state of constant flux: there were always new *minyans*[2] popping up, while others closed down or were incorporated into existing ones. In Chabad alone, there were three quorums when I started my study. When I left the community five years later, there were five.

The large number of organizations does not, in itself, explain the experienced density of summoning in everyday life. Noting that there are many religious organizations tells us little about *how* residents are tied to them—the same number of organizations could each cater to a small number of loyal members, or all constantly vie for the participation of all the residents. In the former scenario people are snugly located in a small network of membership, in the latter they are constantly summoned by a plethora of organizations.

In order to approach this question, I return to the notion of the network, the multiple ties that bind people to each other and bridge different organizations. Of course, the structure of ties in itself is ambiguous: people can have a few intense ties that take up much of their time and effort, or many casual ones they whizz through in daily life.[3] But despite its limitations, when organizations constantly summon members into interaction and participation, to sacrifice both time and money, the structure of organizational ties is telling.

Using fieldnotes and interview transcripts from my five years in the neighborhood, I mapped ties among members and organizations, describing how members bridged twenty-seven different organizations in the neighborhood.[4] Looking at patterns of organizational participation allows us to see how organizations are tied to each other. No less important, it also gives an (admittedly impressionist) picture of the way neighborhood residents are tied to each other. When most organizations are relatively small, participating in an organization almost inevitably means knowing other members. A map showing how members bridge different organizations is also a proxy for the networks of acquaintance and friendships residents sustain across the neighborhood.

Including only relatively straightforward relationships, four kinds of ties are mapped here: (1) *Where members worked*: Both personnel and members of one organization sometimes also worked or were otherwise professionally active in other organizations, thus becoming a conduit of information and gossip, as well as pulling others they knew into their wider social circle. (2) *Where members schooled their children*: Residents who prayed at different places often sent their children to the same school. Parents often carpooled across subaffiliations to the same schools and further gathered and interacted at parent-child events. Children, of course, interacted and sustained friendships at school, through which parents got to know each other. (3) *Where members prayed*: Although members usually had one synagogue with which they saw themselves as primarily affiliated, what they called their *Shabbos shul* (their Sabbath synagogue), they also prayed at other synagogues on special occasions, or simply if going to a different synagogue was sometimes easier. In these cases, individuals within subaffiliations effectively "bridged" different congregations. (4) *Co-use of space*: Some organizations, especially large ones, rented their space to other organizations, which provided members of different organizations ample opportunity to meet. Organizing this rudimentary network map by types of organizations, their affiliations within Orthodoxy, their size, and the ties among them, produced the heuristic mapping shown in figure 1.

Even before we look at the structure of ties in the network, their density is striking. As sociologists have long observed, different lives and identities may be sustained simply by limiting interaction to a specific category of people.[5] Thus, for example, as Rogers Brubaker argued in a study of Romanians and Hungarians in a Romanian town, members of different ethnicities often need to do very little in order to sustain the boundaries between them—simply going to different schools and churches did the trick. As long as residents are nestled in an "institutionally complete" environment, where most organizations are designed for and catered to a specific set of people defined by criteria of group membership, the boundaries between them and the outside world can be kept by interactional default.

Viewing the Orthodox residents through such lenses of institutional completeness is useful. With the important exception of most residents' work lives,[6] people's organizational lives were almost purely Orthodox Jewish. Orthodox schools catered only to Jews, and almost only to strict Orthodox families; synagogues were obviously Orthodox, as were ritual baths, and even welfare societies catered only to less fortunate Jews.

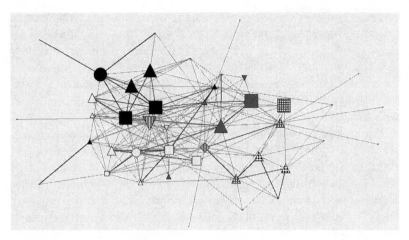

1 **Black:** Yeshivish   **Circle:** Kollel   **Thick line:** Layering of   **Large:** Over 70 families
White: Hasidic   **Square:** School   tie-forms   **Medium:** 40–70 families
Grey: Chabad   **Diamond:** Volunteering   **Thin line:** Single tie-form   **Small:** Up to 40 families
Dotted: Sephardic   **Triangle:** Synagogue
Checkered: Traditional   **Upside-down triangle:** Ritual bath
Striped: Interaffiliation
The organizations on the periphery that are not marked by a shape are either outside the neighborhood or
small organizations within the neighborhood that I did not have enough data on.

As Erving Goffman concisely put it, one of the most interesting things about a dinner is who was not invited.[7]

And yet it is also essential to know what happens around the table. A quick look at the map reveals a number of structural dynamics. First, there are denser ties among organizations that belong to the same Orthodox subaffiliation—marked graphically by the clustering of nodes of the same color. People tended to go to schools that "belonged" to their affiliation, and to pray in affiliated synagogues; synagogue rabbis often taught in schools sharing the same tradition, lectured at affiliated synagogues, and so on. The rabbi in a non-Hasidic Orthodox ("Yeshivish") synagogue, for example, was also the principal of a large Yeshivish school in the neighborhood; the head of the Chabad yeshiva intermittently lectured in all other Chabad operations in the neighborhood, and advanced yeshiva students offered free classes to lay members during the summer months. In fact, the network of relationships among residents belonging to the same subaffiliation is significantly underplayed in this mapping, as residents belonging to the same Orthodox affiliation also met each other on special occasions and affiliation-wide events that are not captured in it. But even discounting these affiliation-wide events, residents belonging to the same Orthodox affiliation would almost inevitably meet each other in different capacities: when they sent their children to school, at synagogue, when they went to the ritual bath.[8] Even though not all people within a subaffiliation knew each other intimately, they usually knew something of each other, who they were, and where they prayed.

But another look at the map shows that ties were not limited to people belonging to the same Orthodox subaffiliation. For example, the few nonaffiliated organizations in the neighborhood drew people from all affiliations. The volunteering organization for people suffering economic hardship in the neighborhood, which prepared and delivered Saturday meals to the homes of residents, had a sign on its door with pictures of different hats, representing different strands of Judaism—from the nonaffiliated baseball cap to the Hasidic *shtreimel* fur hat. The point was simple, as the text underneath it made clear, "it doesn't matter which hat you wear, we are all Jews." And indeed, although it had more people coming from modern and traditional Orthodoxy, the organization was headed by a Hasidic Jew, and men with long beards and sidelocks worked side by side with Modern Orthodox youth. Even more striking, the women's ritual bath in the neighborhood, housed on the property of a Hasidic synagogue, catered to all Orthodox women in the neighborhood (though a smaller, fancier, interaffiliation ritual bath was constructed near the end of my stay). Women from all different affiliations came to the ritual bath following their menstrual period, making it a place where women (of a certain age) would at least see each other, irrespective of their affiliation.

Ties connecting different residents and organizations, however, were not limited to those that existed within affiliations or to nonaffiliated Orthodox organizations. Residents also bridged organizations from different affiliations, tying them tightly together. Thus, for example, although each affiliation had a set of schools that were considered "theirs," these were not hermetic, and parents often sent their children to other Orthodox schools, beyond their affiliation. Two of the oldest schools in the neighborhood, considered strictly Orthodox, but non-Hasidic, were some of the first organizations in the neighborhood and were considered excellent schools on a national scale, academically better than most other Orthodox schools. Some Chabad and other Hasidic parents thus sent their children to those schools, making them more central— better connected to more organizations and to different Orthodox affiliations—than they would have been if only people from a specific affiliation had sent their children there.[9] Similarly, synagogue rabbis or teachers were often invited to lecture in other institutions. Residents sometimes found themselves working at an organization that did not line up with their specific affiliation—a Hasidic-trained rabbi headed a Sephardic congregation; a teacher at a Yeshivish school was personally affiliated with Chabad but often prayed at a traditional synagogue that was simply on his way to work.[10]

Of course, such mapping has its limitations. Some residents managed to remain more or less ensconced within their particular subaffiliation, rarely venturing to any other events or organizations. Although in my five years of fieldwork in the neighborhood, I almost never met someone who didn't occasionally venture outside affiliated organizations, residents did so to varying degrees. In other words, the fact that some residents bridged different affiliations does not mean they all did, at least not often. But the bridging of organizations affected even the most single-minded (or simply shy) followers of a particular subaffiliation. The ties described resulted in acquaintances, often friendships. This in turn, meant that even if some people weren't organizationally tied to multiple affiliations, most people they knew were. They then tended to meet people outside their affiliation, and to be drawn into different social and organizational circles through their acquaintances within their affiliation. People found themselves seated with relative strangers at weddings, bar mitzvahs, or circumcisions, for example, or simply when people from outside their affiliation came to pray in their synagogue, or sent their children to their schools.

In short, Orthodox residents in the Beverly–La Brea neighborhood tended to be simultaneously tied to multiple organizations and to have ties to residents across different affiliations of Orthodoxy. The sheer amount of ties between members and organizations—both within and beyond their own subaffiliation—meant that individuals were almost constantly summoned. They were spread thin among a plethora of competing demands for their time, energy, and money. This condition of *overlapping belonging* to neighborhood Orthodoxy not only linked them through information flows but sustained the neighborhood and, to a lesser degree, the Los Angeles Jewish Orthodox population as a *social world* they all belonged to. That is, Orthodox life in the neighborhood operated as a set of institutions, processes, and organizations that were engaged in a mutually defined activity, organizationally rooted and connected to each other. As such, it formed what Tamotsu Shibutani termed "a universe of regularized mutual response."[11] As I later show, people acted in anticipation of how others in the neighborhood—both within their affiliation and across other Orthodox affiliations—would understand their actions.[12]

Organizational Rhythms: Schools, Panhandlers, and Patterns of Summoning

The condition of *overlapping belonging* that characterized almost all of the Orthodox residents I knew sustained a social world in which residents were almost bound to bump into, and create ties with, other Orthodox residents in the neighborhood. But even more striking is what being tied to an organization meant in everyday life, how organizations insinuated themselves into people's lives—pulling them into interaction, affecting the kinds of situations they could expect to find themselves in, and shaping members' lives even when they were away. Organizations linked residents not only by serving as conduits of information, the favorite flows in the ties network analysts tend to describe, but by constituting the social world they belonged to, how they saw both Orthodox Judaism and, ultimately, themselves.[13]

Not all organizational attachments are the same. Some have relatively modest demands on the self, while others may be termed "greedy institutions," to use a metaphor offered by Lewis Coser. Such institutions are greedy not in the monetary sense, but "insofar as they seek exclusive and undivided loyalty and they attempt to reduce the claims of competing roles and status positions on those they wish to encompass within their boundaries."[14] The examples Coser uses to make his case are diverse—from the housewife for whom the family is a greedy institution, to members of utopian communities, subjects of dictatorships, and uprooted Jews serving in seventeenth-century European courts. And whereas Coser's sampling may be omnivorous, the basic logic is similar—in each case the institutions demand the time and participation of members and emphasize a specific identification within members' web of group affiliations, while downplaying other affiliations and identifications they may have, both symbolically and practically locking them into a particular self and a specific social world.[15]

Seen from this vantage point, it was the entire Orthodox *neighborhood* that could be considered "greedy." It was precisely through the layering of demands that it was meaningful to speak of a greedy institution, through multiple practices of summoning of multiple organizations and acquaintances.

One way to capture what this layering of interactional summoning means is by thinking about organizations as comprising rhythms of action. Each of the organizations that members were tied to had its religious and practical rhythms. The schools, the synagogues, the ritual baths, and the classes offered all had a set of predictable temporalities— from the morning prayers to the school schedules, from the yearly fundraisers in the synagogues to the High Holidays. As residents were drawn into these organizations, their lives were beholden to the organizations' different (and often overlapping) rhythms. And from an organizational perspective, rhythms were actualized precisely through the summoning of members into participation. Thus, not including work hours, residents spent a large part of their waking time in organizationally structured activity, so that the cadence of their own lives was shaped through organizational rhythms.[16]

As a way to flesh out how institutions made demands on people's time and patterns of action, it is useful to linger for a while on one set of demands—those issued by educational organizations, perhaps the most obviously greedy of Orthodox institutions.[17]

Like schools anywhere, Orthodox schools made demands on both students' and parents' patterns of action. School hours were generally long, students were usually expected to study 13–14 years (after high school, there was a continuation of the yeshiva for boys and a seminary for girls), and parent involvement was often required. But in comparison with most schools, Orthodox schools made surprising demands on parents, drawing them into their rhythms and entering their lives in ways that are rare in other educational contexts.

Partly, it was a matter of economics: Orthodox schools are private and cost between $11,000 (for most Orthodox primary schools in the neighborhood) and $25,000 (in the case of at least one Modern Orthodox high school in the Pico-Robertson neighborhood). Although residents were, by and large, comfortably middle class, they also tended to have a large number of children, with five children being the norm rather than an outlier, and families with seven children being quite common.[18] In such a context, school fees became one of the most pressing issues in the lives of members, a topic of constant discussion. A few residents told me that they had dished out more than $500,000 for children's schooling throughout the years.

In fact, however, few people actually paid full school fees—even those who ended up paying around half a million got large discounts for some of their children.[19] Families with five or six school-age children—which often happens in large families, where the differences between children's ages are usually not more than two years—could not be expected to pay full tuition for all of them and received some form of discount. Children of teachers usually secured large discounts (sometimes in the form of deductions from their parents' pretax income), and children from less affluent families almost universally received some kind of financial aid. Engaged in a moral project, schools also enrolled students who could not pay *at all*, either by redirecting some of the money paid by full-tuition families or through fundraising. In interviews with principals of two of the largest schools in the neighborhood, they both noted that they were receiving less than full tuition for about two-thirds of the students.

These economic arrangements are important both because of the kind of commitment they entail, and since they channel money into Orthodox organizations. Money flowed into the neighborhood—from residents' salaries in "the non-Jewish world" to the Orthodox organizations that they belonged to, as well as from families outside the neighborhood who sent their children to be schooled in the neighborhood's prestigious schools. But they also fostered commitment and participation by pulling parents into interaction. Thus, parents who received discounts were often nudged to contribute to the school in other ways. One parent I knew organized "pizza lunches"; a few others volunteered to drive children to school, taking more than their share of the carpool, and thus meeting other families in the neighborhood; parents in two families I knew actually acted as fundraisers for the school, as they had the skills to do so. Through such activities, parents, and especially those who received discounts, were drawn into greater involvement in the school's affairs, fusing their own rhythms with those of the school, while also interacting more with other parents with whom they collaborated.

But, to return to the metaphor of summoning, it is not only about being pulled into network ties, but also about being summoned into particular ways of being. And it is here that Orthodox schools are markedly different from most others. To begin with, strict Orthodox schools have entry requirements for children's *parents*. To be admitted into the major strict Orthodox schools in the neighborhood—those that were central in the network map presented above—parents needed to sign a document stating they were observant Jews; parents needed to attest that they did not have a television and that they kept the laws of the Sabbath; married mothers signed a statement that attested that their hair was covered. Other aspects of family life were also monitored, though less strictly. Thus, for example, one family I knew well had a small poodle, something usually frowned upon in Orthodox circles, as dogs are connected to profanity in Kabbalistic literature, as well as being considered a *goy-ishe* (non-Jewish) thing to have. The strict Orthodox school that two of the boys attended warned the family a few times that if they did not get rid of the dog it would expel their children. This particular family resisted, and the school backed down and did not ultimately expel their children—probably because the family was one of the few that paid full tuition—but the fact that such a threat was even possible is telling.

Beyond these "background requirements" of practical piety, schools also steered interactions in the home, setting up family institutions crafted by the school and practically structuring family rhythms. Every weekend primary schools sent parents a series of questions. The questions concerned the portion of the Torah read during the week, the *parshah,* with the questions thus dubbed "parshah questions." As adult residents were assumed to be following the weekly portion in synagogue, where it was read during Sabbath morning services, they were also assumed to be able to quiz their children. Parents received the questions from the school on Friday, and after Sabbath they had to sign a form indicating that they had indeed quizzed their children. At every Sabbath meal I shared with families that had school-age children, this quizzing was an integral part of the gathering. And although some children were not thrilled at the prospect of answering the questions and sometimes managed to artfully dodge them, the process became a site for raising religious topics at the Sabbath table, a family tradition, and—for many children—an opportunity to become the center of attention in a large family, if only for a few minutes.

Schools thus shaped both students' and parents' rhythms and activities. In a sense, they temporally "invaded" family time. Controlling both the level of practical observance and family activities, these practices blurred the boundaries between school and family. This blurring of both spheres and time was even more pronounced in high schools, and especially girls high schools.[20] As strict Orthodox women marry very young, often when they are 18–21, and as marriage is made through matchmaking, the high school becomes crucial for a simple reason: one of the most important "recommendations" in the marriage market—and as in the job market, recommendations are crucial for finding a good match—is that of the school's principal. Graduates of a large girls school in the neighborhood often told me they were positively in awe of their headmaster. As he was intimately involved in their future matches, the sword he had over his students' heads was truly powerful. What if they misbehaved, and consequently botched their entire married lives? One student told me that a few years after she had graduated, as she was driving in her car with a man, she saw her old principal walking down the street. She immediately ducked "so he won't see me with a man." The thing was, the man in her car was her husband; she was terrified out of habit.

Especially when the school installed a panopticon-like closed-circuit television and a speaker system in the hallways, girls felt they must constantly be on their best behavior. During an interview I had with the principal, he occasionally asked a student he saw on the closed-circuit television what she was up to, giving her a little jolt. But perhaps even more striking, when I asked what happened to students who had finished the school years ago, trying to figure out where teenagers who grew up in the neighborhood ended up, he took a yearbook from the 1990s, and looking at the pictures, he effortlessly told me where each of them lived, whom they had married, and what they and their husbands did today. As opposed to most educational institutions, girls high schools (and especially this one) intervened in residents' lives in a way that transcended what we think of as the school's jurisdiction, both spatially and temporally.

And although schools were indeed the "most greedy" institutions within the Orthodox neighborhood, other organizations did not lag far behind. As I further develop in the next chapter, synagogues made multiple demands on members' identification, time, and money; residents were bombarded with mail from Orthodox organizations asking for their donations (no one was really sure how these organizations, many of them in Israel, got their addresses; "divine providence" was the bemused, and sometimes exasperated, answer some residents gave as they emptied overflowing mailboxes); members were asked to pay dues and participate in fundraising dinners; they were called up for evening classes such as the one this book begins with.[21]

The condition of overlapping belonging that Orthodox residents found themselves in was thus translated into multiple layers of summoning to both organizational participation and action in the "private sphere" (or rather, the blurring of the presumed differences between spheres). And although different organizations indirectly competed with each other for both time and money, they shared the same moral project. The reason, for example, that *every* Sabbath meal in a house with children I went to (and there were over a hundred such occasions) included parshah questions—that no one "rebelled" against the intrusion of schools into the family—was that it was part of the same larger project. Schools, family, and synagogue life were a cluster of institutions that cohered around the sustaining and crafting of Orthodox life.

Rhythms, as the example of Orthodox schools in the neighborhood makes clear, also bled into the working of other institutions. The school invaded the intimate "private" sphere of the family; the worries of the marriage market meant that summoning affected not only the rhythms of the present but also those of an imagined future. The rhythms of Orthodox life were thus complex—there were the rhythms of religious practice (the prayer times, the Sabbath, or the holidays) as well as organizational rhythms that only partly matched those of religious practice.

And even beyond this symphony of rhythms, residents had to learn to expect the summoning of institutions and organizations at every point. Rhythms were usually predictable, but residents needed to attend also to the syncopations of their social world—to the possibility of being summoned at a moment's notice.

Perhaps the most stunning example of the way the Orthodox neighborhood literally "knocked on residents' doors" was how religious edicts directed money flows *away* from the neighborhood. In general, all Orthodox families are supposed to tithe. However, in contrast to groups that control the funds congregants tithe (as does the Church of Latter Day Saints, for example), there is no central authority to which Orthodox people are obligated to tithe. Tithing is a relatively personal affair, with people finding their own causes and organizations. Although this obviously relaxed controls on tithing, residents I knew often discussed its details among themselves: Do you tithe 10 percent of your salary before or after taxes? Should you have to tithe if you do not have enough money to live comfortably? Could you go to your rabbi and get an exemption from tithing until you put your finances in shape? What does "living comfortably" even mean? In Los Angeles, are you comfortable if you have only one car in the household, or does a minimal level of comfort presume two cars? If you are sending your children to an Orthodox school and paying full tuition, which then gets partly redistributed to less affluent students, does that count?

Nevertheless, life in the neighborhood presented a set of pressures that enforced at least part of the tithing structure, sometimes getting residents to pay even more than 10 percent of their income. The organizations that people frequented and saw themselves as a part of needed to generate operating costs. A synagogue, for example, needed money. If the building was not owned, rent had to be paid, along with utilities, salaries for janitors, the costs of sponsoring a light *kiddush* meal after the Sabbath morning service, and perhaps a salary and even a house for the rabbi in the case of very large synagogues. Members usually deducted the money they gave to synagogues from their tithing obligations, but they were constantly bombarded with requests—from other synagogues they were connected to, from schools, welfare organizations, or from other institutions in the United States and Israel in need of donations.

The neighborhood also supported a large number of Jewish panhandlers. Some of them were "regular" synagogue *schnorrers* who came every morning to ask for some money, and to whom most people gave no more than a dollar (even though there were usually a few schnorrers coming every morning, so the amount added up). Others, however, were part of a phenomenon unique to the Orthodox world. Every year, hundreds of poor Orthodox Jews come from Israel to collect money for institutions in Israel—but mostly for themselves—in Orthodox communities throughout the United States. Usually traveling in small groups, these transnational panhandlers, *meshulachim* (singular: *meshulach*), rent a car together, going from city to city, from neighborhood to neighborhood, from door to door, either by referring to address books painstakingly collected by themselves and other meshulachim who preceded them, or simply by spotting the *mezuzah* on the doorpost.[22]

Throughout the year, Orthodox residents in the neighborhood could expect to hear a knock on their door and to be greeted by a pious-looking bearded Israeli asking them for money. And residents, by and large, played along, often writing a number of checks at the beginning of the month, so that a portion of tithing money went toward these fundraisers-panhandlers. Checks were usually written out for $18, as in *gematria*, a numerological system of switching numbers to letters, 18 could be translated as "alive" and was thus a popular sum (multiplications of $18 were also a good amount to give for other tithing purposes, as well as for gifts at weddings, bar mitzvahs, and so on, where $180 was a popular check).

The meshulachim phenomenon also generated its own organizations. Orthodox residents in Los Angeles and elsewhere wanted to know whether the meshulachim that showed up at their door were genuinely poor and pious individuals who needed the money for legitimate reasons. There were both urban legends of, and personal encounters with, people dressing up as pious Jews but turning up later in Las Vegas to spend their earnings, or simply meshulachim turning out to be non-Jews who had grown a beard and learned a few words of Hebrew and Yiddish for the role. One resident told me of a meshulach who came to his door but seemed somehow off. Rather than giving him the money and ending the interaction quickly, my friend began quizzing him about

Jewish life and law. After a few questions, the "meshulach" broke down. He was a poor secular Jew from Vancouver, an alcoholic who realized that he could make some money if he grew a beard and sidelocks.

Moreover, residents also wanted the money they gave to be tax-deductible, which was not easy to do with checks written out to individuals. Thus, a new organization has appeared throughout the American Orthodox world; Va'ad ha'Zedaka ve'ha'Hessed, roughly translated as the Committee for Alms and Grace, with its headquarters in Lakewood, New Jersey, had a local branch in the neighborhood, renting a space in the expanses of one of the traditional Orthodox synagogues.

The Beverly–La Brea branch of the organization—connected to the organization in Lakewood, but operated and funded by a local Orthodox man—employed two people tasked with interviewing the meshulachim. Operating from a large synagogue, these employees would then send the meshulachim's story to Lakewood by fax, where people verified it with institutions in Israel. If the verification went smoothly, they gave the meshulachim a certification that allowed them to collect money in the neighborhood for two weeks. At the same time, the organization also made it easier for people to make their donations to meshulachim tax-deductible. Instead of making checks out to the person at the door, people wrote the checks to the Va'ad ha'Zedaka ve'ha'Hessed. The meshulachim then handed over all the checks they had collected to the organization (sometimes as many as a hundred checks), who consolidated it into one check in their name. Every weekday, meshulachim lined the hallways leading to the office, sharing stories, telling each other about the best doors to knock on, and preparing either for their "examination" in the offices or to receive their checks.

While fascinating in its own right, the phenomenon of the meshulachim is especially revealing once we attend to the way it created a shared experience of neighborhood life, as well as when we attend to its interactional details. The meshulachim provided endless material for commiseration. The following fieldnotes excerpt, taken after a large Saturday dinner with over ten guests at a house of a prominent neighborhood rabbi, was one opportunity, among many, where the topic of the meshulachim came up:

Talking about his synagogue, the rabbi says that there are so many meshulachim that come that it is unbelievable. His wife laughs, and says that this is probably good, there is another minyan—yet another quorum in his overflowing synagogue. Everybody laughs at that image, but then the rabbi says that this would have been nice, but that the meshulachim usually don't even pray, they just come to collect money. He says that they have become very demanding as well, he handed one of them a $1 bill a couple of days ago and the guy told him that he doesn't take $1 bills, only $5s or $10s . . .

The wife says that things are "not like they used to be," there are more and more meshulachim, and they just come one after the other, without end. She also doesn't trust them like she used to, "you can't know what is going on these days." One day she came home and there was a meshulach waiting for her in her own kitchen, as she apparently forgot to lock her door; she escorted him outside and said she is willing to talk to him, but only outside. "There are so many of them, sometimes there is a carful, and they just go, one after the other, after the other . . ." One of the guests chimes in, says that this is the way a lot of them do it, get together as a group and then rent a car together, park in a neighborhood, take different directions, and then switch. People nod in exasperation . . .

One of the rabbi's daughters adds that once, when she was young, she was alone at the house, and a meshulach came and asked for money. She only had one dollar as her allowance and she gave it to him, but he started shouting at her, that this was too little. Another of his daughters adds that everyone she knows is preparing envelopes and trying to cut short conversations with the meshulachim, otherwise it would be endless. One of her friends' parents simply put a set number of checks in sealed envelopes in the beginning of the month and slips them under the door when a meshulach comes. The thing is that once she came to visit her friend and knocked on the door, when, instead of answering her, she was slipped a check.

Although it was exasperating, there was a joy to complaining together, in the opportunity for a good *kvetch*. The meshulachim provided a shared experience, a way to bond over the absurdities of everyday life that both cemented a shared world together and afforded moments of neighborhood humor that can be shared only among the Orthodox. It was a way to form a space of sociability and commonality, one that created a world within a world in the Beverly–La Brea neighborhood.

And although everybody around the table commiserated about the meshulachim, none of them actually proposed to deter them from coming. Instead, they still gave them money (albeit sometimes not as much as the meshulachim would have liked). Indeed, another resident told me of a plan to have a free motel constructed for the meshulachim who came to the neighborhood, so they wouldn't have to pay for their accommodations, after an apartment building they had previously used was taken over by a school.

In order to get a handle on this de facto international welfare system that makes it worthwhile for men to come all the way from Israel on a kind of reverse pilgrimage, summoning becomes, again, crucial. When the meshulachim knocked on the Orthodox door, they didn't simply ask for money: they presented a narrative, an Orthodox story of suffering and Torah learning, of need and piety. Meshulachim often started by talking about an Israeli institution they fundraised for, or their personal travails—usually their attempt to find a good match for their daughter while lacking money for the wedding, or an illness of a relative. This set of narratives, whether or not they were true, echoed popular religious tales in which the righteous man or woman (the *tzaddik* or *tsadekket*) goes out of his or her way to help poor Jews in need, thus already casting the interaction in the hues of Orthodoxy.

Meshulachim often, however, added "a word of Torah"—a short talk about religious matters that they prepared beforehand. Thus, for example, sitting in the house of a resident who wrote Torah scrolls for a living, as well as the text written in mezuzahs and Orthodox men's phylacteries, the meshulach started talking about Jewish calligraphy and the differences between European and Middle Eastern styles of writing the Hebrew. And although my host seemed a bit impatient, he could not stop the meshulach, and they entered into a short conversation about writing styles. By showing his knowledge and starting a conversation on the writing of scrolls, the meshulach was creating a practical commonality, as well as positing himself as a deserving, pious Jew.

Even more striking is the fact that many meshulachim see themselves as coming from a sacred space (Israel) to the heart of the profane (Los Angeles, Hollywood). One meshulach whom I spoke to while he was waiting to cash his checks at the Va'ad headquarters told me he didn't like Los Angeles, it was a "shell" of a place (a Kabbalistic category denoting profanity, the lack of godliness), while another said he thought the neighborhood was obscene—it was a place where dogs were treated like human beings and human beings like dogs. As they interacted with the families, they did so not only as panhandlers asking for alms, but also as fellow Jews in need of a religiously prescribed act of kindness, and even as emissaries of holiness, descending into the profane.

One of the most striking interactions I was part of in the neighborhood occurred as I was writing fieldnotes in a small café. Going out for a cigarette, I saw a slightly shabby Orthodox-dressed man waiting at the bus station. As I wore a yarmulke, he approached me and began talking Hebrew, complaining that he was probably the only Jew in Los Angeles taking a bus (and was quite skeptical when I said I too took the bus). As I reentered the café, he walked in after me and started talking about his need, asking for money. Since people were staring, I got up and took the conversation outside. Trying to end the interaction quickly, I gave him three dollars. He took them, put them in his pocket, and then gave me a dollar back from a different pocket, asking me to give it to charity for his sake. I nodded, confused. We shook hands, and I walked back into the café.

The incident was both puzzling and emotionally stirring. Giving me money, the meshulach turned the tables on the interaction. From a panhandler he became a fellow Jew, even a benefactor of sorts. When I asked an Orthodox friend in the neighborhood what he made of it, he laughed and said that it seemed that the Messiah had finally come. However, he quickly added, the incident did actually make sense. Perhaps someone had given the panhandler money to give to charity, something that Orthodox people often do when friends or relatives go on a trip abroad (every time I went abroad I was given money to distribute to the poor). Perhaps, they conjectured, he had somehow been reminded of the money somebody gave him and decided that this was a good time to give the money. Moreover, as other acquaintances pointed out, Orthodox panhandlers are also obligated to tithe. And though it was rare for a schnorrer to give money to the very person from whom he had just taken money, it was common for a schnorrer to go through the synagogue collecting money and then put one dollar in the donation box, tithing as he left.

The interaction with meshulachim thus summoned residents in a few ways. First, even in cases like that of the crafty resident described in the fieldnotes who would slip a check under the door, the knock on the door summoned residents as Orthodox Jews—the kind of people who would be expected to both listen to the meshulach and donate money to him and his alleged cause. But, moreover, it summoned them through the interactional performance of the meshulachim. By stressing their own religiosity, the meshulachim posited themselves as religiously equal to residents. This obviously helped them transcend their status as poverty-stricken men asking for money but simultaneously defined their benefactor as the "the kind of Jew" who would appreciate a word of Torah, who would tithe to the poor, who supported the holy land of Israel.

Neighborhood Organizations and Patterns of Summoning

Living in the Orthodox neighborhood, residents found themselves constantly entangled in a web of ties and interactions with organizations, acquaintances, even people at their doorstep. With a plethora of organizations and the overlapping patterns of belonging that characterized them, they found themselves being constantly invited into participation and interaction. The *viscosity* or density of the lives of residents in the Orthodox Beverly–La Brea neighborhood was partly structured through this layering of summons.

This layering also blurred the usual distinction between private and public spheres. Is the interaction with meshulachim private or public? Are parshah questions the ultimate family ritual or an infringement of the school upon personal life? This blurring of spheres and rhythms of life, in turn, was predicated on the taken for granted: that even if people were exasperated, strapped for money, or simply tired of the constant bombardment of summoning, these moments were part and parcel of the same general project. It was hard to resist them precisely because each summons was seen as consequential for the entirety of the Orthodox project. In that sense, summoning had a moral dimension: rooted in a religious project with transcendent undertones, each interaction posited the question "What kind of person are you?," "What kind of Jew?"

These patterns of summoning gained their potency from the intersection between pragmatic challenges of Orthodox organizations vying for money and participation and the interactional pressures of members who were approached by organizations, acquaintances, and complete strangers. But the success of organizations in summoning residents was also predicated on the fact that they were based on a largely codified structure of Jewish law. To take the last example, residents gave money to the meshulachim because they genuinely wanted to help them, but also because they were religiously obligated to tithe. The next chapter focuses on this intersection, how codified religious and liturgical edicts shaped the ways residents were drawn into sustaining an interactionally dense social world.

FOUR

Edicts and Interaction in Synagogue Life

The men praying in morning quorum were moved. They had just read the daily portion of Psalms at the end of the service in the synagogue and were conversing in hushed tones before they dispersed to work. One of the kids in the local yeshiva had been critically ill for two weeks, hovering between life and death in the hospital, a victim of a larger E. coli outbreak.

A couple of weeks beforehand—at the beginning of the Sabbath speech he usually gave just after the reading of the Torah—Rabbi Chelev Chittim had told congregants of this student. It was a teenager he knew well, and he urged them to "keep him in mind" when reading the daily portion of Psalms. During the kiddush meal, after prayers ended, he told them the story as best he knew it: the student had probably been poisoned by prewashed spinach, part of a series of incidents of E. coli poisoning across the United States. Other students from his yeshiva were holding vigils in the hospital, reading psalms, but it was important for people in the synagogue to keep him in mind. Since that Sabbath, almost every morning reading of psalms elicited a short conversation about the student's situation, congregants asking each other if there were any news or just saying they hoped he would pull through.

More than any other text, and especially in Hasidic and Sephardic circles, reading psalms is supposed to have an actual effect on the goings-on of the world. Although in most speeches and religious texts the hidden miracles of everyday life are far more important than "open miracles" in the form of explicit divine intervention, the reading of psalms has an almost talismanic quality. Each day of the Jewish lunar calendar was assigned corresponding chapters in the Book of Psalms, so that through the month congregants read the entire book. And whereas "the psalms of the day" are uniform across much of the Orthodox world, more personalized recitations of chapters are routinely added—congregants in some sub-affiliations of Orthodoxy read psalms corresponding to their age, their children, spouse, and others who they consider in need of prayers.

As the case of the poisoned student makes clear, reading psalms is not only a way to tie religious duties to intimate relationships. When psalms for a child, spouse, or anyone else are read "with the person in mind," it can affect the outcome of the condition prayed for—either helping keep a loved one safe and prosperous or acting as a powerful supplication for the health or deliverance of someone in need. Having someone in mind, in turn, can be a result of prodding from friends, religious authorities, or even chain emails. One short email I received on a congregational listserv simply read, "Rachel Silverstein needs our *tefillos* [prayers]. Please say *Tehillim* [Psalms] for Rachel bat Ester [Rachel, daughter of Ester] for a *refuah shelaima b'karov* [speedy and full recovery]. May we hear *bsuros tovos* [good tidings]!"[1]

Although it didn't happen too often, rabbis would thus ask members of their congregation to have someone in mind, mobilizing the congregation into adding this person to the list of people they already prayed for. These could range from large-scale political causes to personal matters. Some Orthodox men and women I knew, for example, recited psalms for the safety of Israeli soldiers during the Gaza incursion of 2008; others whom I knew in Chabad-Hasidic circles read psalms when Chabad emissaries were attacked by terrorists in Mumbai, India, early in 2009, before the news of their death was released.

Which brings us back to the yeshiva kid lying in the hospital with severe E. coli poisoning. At the beginning of the student's hospitalization, congregants would ask the rabbi, and each other, if they knew of any news. Were there any new developments? How was he feeling? Although it never became a central theme in synagogue life, the student's condition became etched into their everyday routines. Members spoke about E. coli in other settings, weighing different theories regarding the spread of food poisoning in the modern world, discussing the hidden dangers of organic food. At one Saturday kiddush meal following morning prayers, congregants discussed the possible connection between pigs defecating in organic spinach fields and the outbreak of

E. coli poisoning. The religious connotation was clear: pigs, the most impure of beasts in Judaism, became suspects in the case of a poisoned Jew.

The small synagogue I usually prayed at wasn't the only one in which congregants recited psalms for the sick teenager, or where spinach and E. coli became topics of conversation. The news spread through Chabad and beyond almost instantaneously. Since Orthodox organizations are tightly connected through networks of work, school, and participation,[2] congregants throughout Beverly–La Brea as well as in other neighborhoods in Los Angeles were soon reciting psalms with the yeshiva student "in mind."

Psalms thus provided a way to insert congregants—the vast majority of whom didn't know the yeshiva student—into a communal affair. Although we can safely assume that not all "had him in mind" every time they recited psalms, they sometimes did. And even if they didn't, somebody in the synagogue often did and brought the situation of the poisoned yeshiva student to their awareness. But more important, since reciting psalms was widely considered to have a practical effect, congregants became active protagonists in the affair. Much like residents who may join search parties when someone goes missing in rural communities, members felt that they too took part in the action.

The consequence of the insertion of congregants into this social drama was palpably visible when finally, after weeks in the hospital, the young man was released and held a thanksgiving meal (*seudat hoda'a*) for what everyone I knew termed his miraculous recovery. The meal was not widely publicized. And yet when I went to the event with another congregant, we could see people milling about the yeshiva from more than a block away. Over two hundred men came. All the yeshiva students were there, as were many members of the Chabad synagogues in the neighborhood, and quite a few I had seen in other synagogues in the neighborhood and other neighborhoods, such as Pico-Robertson.

The atmosphere was festive; the large hall in the basement of the yeshiva was brimming with people. Latino caterers brought more and more trays of food in one of the halls of the yeshiva and placed them on a few additional tables in a back row near the wall. Pineapples, chocolate fountains, marshmallows, strawberries, neatly stacked pieces of cake. Some men sat at long rows of tables; others walked around, stopping to chat with friends and acquaintances.

As I entered, the yeshiva student who had been sick was wrapping up his speech. He still looked ill, almost disappearing in black clothes that seemed much too large for his current size. He was speaking quietly, with effort. He almost lost faith, he said, while he was in the hospital.

He was scared, but then, when he saw what everybody was doing for him, praying and saying psalms, his faith was strengthened. People applauded and hummed a Hasidic tune. Later, the principal of the yeshiva gave his speech: "The psalms that everybody read . . . Psalms helped the kid . . . maybe . . ." The crowd laughed incredulously while the headmaster smiled and continued, "The yeshiva boys asked me what they can do, and I told them that the only thing they are really masters of was their time, so a lot of them sat and learned an extra portion of Talmud every day, another speech of the rebbe. Each one did what he can . . . I want to thank everybody for what they did." After his speech was over, I heard one of my friends talking to another, laughing and saying that the *Rosh* (headmaster) really likes to be controversial, repeating his words, "Psalms helped the kid . . . maybe . . ."

Both the recovering yeshiva boy and the head of the yeshiva, like other speakers throughout the evening, crystallized the stages of the narrative as a unity.[3] For the yeshiva boy, the narrative was unproblematic: the psalm reading and prayers helped him recover. Congregants' role in the drama was retroactively ratified by its main protagonist.[4] When the head of the yeshiva seemed to cast doubt on the effectiveness of psalm reading, the residents who attended actively "repaired" this transgression, laughing incredulously and mentioning how he "likes to be controversial." But even while striking a more rationalist theological tone, the principal too thanked everyone for "what they did." The interactional insertion of congregants into the communal narrative was vindicated.

Complementing the organizational rhythms of summoning outlined in the previous two chapters, there is a distinct processual structure to the narrative above.[5] Religious observances propel congregants into specific forms of action, especially in the context of synagogue life. These, then, are etched into their everyday lives in ways that propel them into each other's lives. The religious and the social are intertwined as people interactionally flesh out their religious life. This chapter takes the layering of religious observances and sociality as a starting point and traces some ways in which edicts give rise to forms of summoning.

Interactional Summoning and Synagogue Life

To an important extent, Orthodox life is defined through its relationship to the synagogue. More than any other single institution (with the possible exception of the educational system), the synagogue organizes patterns of residence and occupies the time and imaginations of residents.

Most Orthodox men visited a synagogue twice a day for their morning and evening prayers, making even the most noisy and messy of synagogues into an intimately inhabited place.[6] Men and women brought toys to put in the back to distract bored children; men brought their own prayer shawls and laid claim to spaces or desks.

The relationship to the synagogue also shaped the neighborhood in its most physical sense. Since Orthodoxy interprets religious law to proscribe the manipulation of electricity on the Sabbath, members cannot drive on Saturday. This, then, means that they need to live within walking distance of their synagogue, easy walking distance if their children are to come. And, in turn, living next to a synagogue implies that they need to live within walking distance of other congregants. Over time, as the history of the neighborhood demonstrates, more and more synagogues and other organizations are built around the same space. Even in a city such as Los Angeles in the era of the automobile, when religious worship and residence in the city are largely decoupled, religious law and synagogue life result in a space where organizations and members' residences are layered upon each other.

The synagogue is also more than a place in which men and women come to pray on the Sabbath and on holidays, and where men pray daily. It is where congregants learn together, either informally or in classes; where special occasion dinners and holiday celebrations take place; where some people have their children's first haircut at age three (the *upshernish*), circumcision, and bar mitzvah; where people gossip on the Sabbath; where men may informally organize "whiskey clubs" to make learning more congenial. As sociologist Samuel Heilman put it,[7] there is a "synagogue life" that goes well beyond strictly religious activities. As in any social club, people develop styles of participation and tend to develop personal friendships.

And as in any other social club, patterns of summoning take shape and thicken over time. They emerge simply by dint of having a group of people meet regularly, so that when somebody does not come, others wonder where he is. They emerge as particular events become inscribed in collective memory, and as gossip is naturally exchanged where personal lives regularly intersect.[8] Summoning also arises through organizational necessities—as rabbis and other religious functionaries call upon congregants to attend fundraising dinners and pay membership fees, for instance.

While this is true for any social club—from people who regularly hang out on a street corner, to regulars in a bar, or mushroom collectors who meet to go hunting for fungi in the forest[9]—the patterns of summoning that arise in the context of synagogue life also emerge out of religious exigencies. Orthodoxy, as some sociologists of Judaism have noted, is somewhat of a misnomer. Although belief—*doxa*—is important, Orthodox life revolves around a set of *practices*. Ortho*praxy* would have been a more accurate name.[10] This chapter thus presents some moments in which the intersection of religious law and interactional patterns of summoning provides synagogue life with its unique social texture.

Although the opening vignette and the structure of psalm reading is dramatic, life is usually not so epic. I thus present three routine processes through which uniquely Orthodox spaces of interactional summoning are opened by religious edicts and liturgical structures, from the ways in which the call for hospitality on the Sabbath crystallizes relationships between residents, through the personalization of participation and the ways in which personal lives are implicated in the liturgical structure of prayer itself. These processes, then, produce moments of summoning that are based equally on religious law and on interactional necessities, giving rise to a predictable form of summoning and sociality.

Sabbath Meals and Entangled Lives

In retrospect, one of the most striking aspects of my fieldwork was that for five years I was invited to *every* single Friday evening meal and Saturday lunch. Excluding summers, when I tended to be elsewhere, I was probably invited to some three hundred such meals in congregants' homes. Indeed, I often fielded multiple calls and inquiries as to whether I would like to come over. More remarkable still was that since I am vegetarian, the households I was invited to usually cooked especially to cater to my diet. At some point, it dawned upon me that it might not all be attributable to my charm, or even to the personal generosity of my hosts (though they were incredibly generous).

Rather, retirees, single people who had moved from elsewhere, young married couples who didn't yet have children, or visitors to Los Angeles who happened to come to the synagogue were all invariably invited. Both in the synagogue I usually attended and in others, there was often a kind of friendly contest to see who would get visitors first, with lighthearted jokes about people who were quick to move on such "opportunities" and "stole all the guests." In one Sephardic synagogue I visited, one of the people I met told me that I was welcome any time and didn't even need an invitation, since he usually had more than ten guests over for the meals.

Friends I have spoken to about the inviting of guests noted that it was a *mitzvah*—a religiously prescribed act of hospitality to one's fellow Jew who may otherwise be left alone on the day of the Sabbath. Especially in the case of strangers coming through who may not have a place to "spend the Sabbath," it is an important religious act. But rather than an onerous obligation, as friends also told me, it was also, usually, fun. Having a guest over for the Sabbath was somewhat of an adventure. It was a way to enliven the Sabbath table, either by having an acquaintance come over or simply by bringing a new and unknown voice to the table. And invitees who lived in the neighborhood, like myself, cemented friendships with those who invited them.

Having guests over, or in a Yiddishism, "eating by" someone, was so widespread as to become both habitual and invisible. Going over fieldnotes, I found few meals where I was the only guest invited. And, of course, even in these cases, there was me. Moreover, except for the cases of visitors flitting through the neighborhood, people were not randomly assigned to households. Over time, and as friendships were made, people tended to come to specific households. Much like the infiltration of schools into family rhythms described in the previous chapter, the expectation of hospitality meant that Jewish others were integrated into family life.

In most cases, Sabbath guests situationally reciprocated in predictable ways. They held up their side of the conversations, they generally did their best to be pleasant, as well as going a bit beyond the expectations of guests in helping in the kitchen, and so on. And yet people who were quite awkward interactionally were still invited. Joel, for example, was an elderly guy who almost never spoke a word. A resident of one of the neighborhood's old people's homes, he sported a long gray-streaked beard and a long beige overcoat he wore throughout the five years I knew him when he came on Fridays and Saturdays for prayer. He would pray quietly in a corner he laid claim to and invariably would be invited over by one of the congregants. He would say a short thank you and join his hosts, walking slowly.

On numerous occasions, when I ended up eating in the same household with him, he never spoke a word. He would answer in one or two words when asked something, and I slowly assembled some flashes of his life (he went to a prestigious college but dropped out; his family lived nearby, but they weren't very close). But even the little I knew of him was after years of note taking. Most often he simply ate without saying a single word and went home after saying a short thank you. For all that,

I never saw him come to synagogue and not be invited. Mostly, during the prayer service, one of the congregants or the rabbi himself would approach him and ask if he would come for a meal. Usually he came, but many times he was already "booked"; somebody had snatched him first.

Perhaps even more striking was Ezra, a homeless man who came for months at a time, then disappeared suddenly, then reappeared as suddenly as he had disappeared. A lanky young man in his thirties, with a sweet and vivid sense of humor when he was well, he drank too much and may have abused other substances. He lived in his car for a while, holding irregular odd jobs, until he sold it when he wanted to travel to Israel. He hoped beyond hope to find a religious utopia (and perhaps personal deliverance), only to return discouraged, telling me it was "just another country," and with stories about his largely failed attempts to hitchhike through the country. After his return, and without a car, he lived on the streets of the neighborhood. A man prone to highs and lows, he had a hard time living on the streets, and his situation seemed to deteriorate. He was mild-mannered at times, but at other times suffered sudden bouts of anxiety, where he would become agitated, sometimes shouting at other congregants.

Ezra, however, was not only welcome at the synagogue but routinely invited for meals. He had some religious learning from his childhood and could read Hebrew. When he was well, he could, and often did, contribute to the conversation when it pertained to religion. But at other times he would just sit quietly, only to suddenly start on an unrelated topic in a loud and frantic voice. On a number of occasions, as the meal drew to an end, he became increasingly restless, starting to sing religious songs at the top of his voice, seeming to try and prolong the meal as much as he could, dreading the moment in which he would transition from the warmth and conversation of a middle-class household to the streets.

Although Ezra was welcomed in the synagogue, his visits were not always smooth. For someone with alcohol consumption problems, the kiddush meal following Saturday morning prayers was often a challenge. Bottles of whiskey and vodka invariably accompanied the meal, and although most people drank only one little shot to accompany the "words of Torah" spoken around the table, Ezra often downed more than his share. At one point, when he quietly monopolized a bottle of whiskey, one of the other congregants decided to take action:

We all hum a Hasidic tune and raise a toast. As we sing, I suddenly see Mr. Orbach standing by Ezra, pulling something. They get up, and Orbach pushes Ezra. Ezra says,

"It's only water, relax," but Orbach pushes Ezra and walks away; then, returning, he says something to Ezra in a stern voice. Everybody else is trying to quietly ignore what is going on. Ezra says loudly, "Take it easy, why do you have to be so stuck up?" He looks as if he is going to cry. Orbach walks to the closet and grabs a prayer booklet. His movements are quick, jerky. He prays quickly and walks out, almost slamming the door.

People are quiet, not sure what to do. Some people try to restart the conversations they had, but the sentences hang in the air uncomfortably. Then Rabbi Chelev-Chittim says we should make the ending prayer for the meal. We all pray and leave the syna-gogue. I walk out and ask a friend who was sitting next to Ezra what had happened. He says that Orbach was trying to yank a bottle of spirits from Ezra, who wouldn't let him take it . . . Ezra was quietly downing the bottle at his table, taking shot after shot. He nods his head, "put an alcoholic near a bottle . . ."

And yet even after this incident of public shaming, Ezra was still invited over to both the synagogue and people's homes (though not Orbach's). In the following week, Ezra was back at the synagogue and invited to the rabbi's house for the Sabbath lunch. Jewish and alone, Ezra seemed to be entitled to sociality and hospitality even when aspects of his behavior seemed quite problematic.

And whereas dinner invitations can be thought of as exchanges in a "gift economy" that cement and structure relationships, invitations in the Orthodox neighborhood were anomalous in a number of ways. First, there was little equivalent reciprocation. True, some people tried to bring a bottle of wine to their hosts before the Sabbath, and there were situational obligations of deference and demeanor that people generally kept: some guests even prepared "a word of Torah" they could share with their hosts. But these were relatively minor forms of reciprocity. And even they, as the cases of Joel and Ezra show, were often breached. Religiously prescribed, the invitations seemed to create fewer obliga-tions than they otherwise would have. Inviting the guest was a religious "opportunity" that did not create the same reciprocal obligations.

For the same reason, unequal exchanges did not create strong hier-archical structures. Whereas unequal reciprocation of gifts is supposed to form a hierarchy between giver and receiver—it is assumed that if the giver cannot "return the gift," he loses a status match—in the meals I attended invitees simply did not act like unequal parties. They were usually polite and thankful, but not more than any other guest in a well-reciprocated relationship, often less so. Indeed, invitees were of-ten actively courted and seemed to choose whom they would bestow the pleasures of their company on. Embedding hospitality in a religious context neutralized some of the interactional obligations and pressures of the gift while constructing and cementing a thick world of social ties.[11]

"A Cohen for Hire": Pragmatic Concerns, Religious Edicts, and Sociality Patterns

Whereas the general call for hospitality sustains interactions and relationships that emerge in and through the synagogue, they are not directly necessary for the ongoing functioning of the organization. In a roundabout manner, the expectation of hospitality may bring singles or lonely retirees to the synagogue, and thus, perhaps, bring in more people who then pay their dues and sustain it. But even if this is true, this form of congregational summoning is both weak and indirect.

There are, however, more direct ways in which religious edicts personalize congregants and directly summon them into the organization while fostering a specific form of sociality and interaction patterns. Thus, in order to have a viable daily prayer, a minyan is necessary, a quorum of ten adult male Jews (over bar mitzvah age) praying together. In some synagogues, this is far from being a problem; dozens of congregants flock to the synagogue every morning, afternoon, and evening. In fact, in the large Cohen Avraham synagogue a few blocks down the road from the synagogue I usually attended, so many people came every morning that the synagogue held at least three morning minyans at different times, for the early birds, the not so early, and those who could afford to start their day at 9:00 a.m. In the smaller Chibat Yaacov synagogue, however, amassing ten adult men at 6:30 on weekday mornings was sometimes a challenge. On quite a few occasions, coming at 6:30, members had to wait, with about seven or eight other sleepy congregants, for the tenth, if not the ninth, man to appear.

This was a problem on a few different levels. First, since this was a strict Orthodox synagogue, the rabbi preferred to start the morning prayer precisely at sunrise when it fell more or less during regular prayer times (around 6:30 a.m.), which happened especially during the autumn months.[12] A much more pressing problem, however, was less theological in nature: congregants needed to get to work on time. A fifty-minute prayer that started at 6:30 still allowed congregants to be on their way to work by 7:30, which for many was already a challenge, with Los Angeles traffic to contend with. Beginning the prayer any later would have practically meant being late for work.

In order to avoid such situations as much as possible, the congregation rabbi had to keep track of the men who usually came to the morning minyan. When one congregant had to go for a few days to visit relatives, or when another went on a business trip abroad, the rabbi reminded others that, at least for the next week, they should make an extra effort to make it on time. In my first year in the neighborhood I was surprised to receive a short phone call from the rabbi: "Dov-Ber is leaving for Europe. Can you try and arrive on time for the next few days?" Surprised, I agreed. "If you can't come, just tell me before so I can call somebody else to make sure we have a minyan." On occasions when a minyan was still lacking, there was no choice but to nudge a sleepy (or sleeping) congregant. A couple of the men who had most of the congregants' numbers on their cell phones would go out of the room and call congregation members whom they knew. On several occasions, when I didn't arrive at the morning prayer, I received text messages at about 6:36, when congregants became antsy. One read, "Hi; would you like to join us for our almost minion [sic]? Big rewards ;)", while another, a couple of months later, simply read "Short on minion; help!"

This picture points toward the emergence of a very predictable form of interaction. As actors have to solve pragmatic problems in a predictably institutionalized context, recurring social forms and collective solutions to these problems arise. Congregants who arrived to pray at 6:30 a.m. wanted to make it on time to work; the rabbi wanted the congregational work to proceed smoothly. These relations between institutionalized liturgical structures and actors' pragmatic projects then fostered a specific form of interaction—the rabbi needed to know and find out where congregants were almost on a daily basis and expected congregants to notify him when they were away; congregants knew quite a lot about each other's movements; phone calls and text messages became a recurrent feature of the morning rituals. Even the little jokes and proposed solutions shared between the antsy congregants became predictable: how they should simply go outside to the street and kidnap an unsuspecting passerby, or run to the local yeshiva to bring a couple of high schools kids.

The intersection of institutionalized religious edicts and pragmatic projects, however, did more than necessitate certain forms of interaction. It also elicited a specific form of commitment from members, beyond that generated by the social pressure to arrive on time. The calls for participation were not simply a generalized summoning but had a particular flavor. In a very real sense, religious practice became a team effort, and members of the congregation developed a "team spirit." That is, they felt that they and others in the congregation were involved in a shared project and were partly responsible for the success of the project as a whole.[13] Though it is reasonable to assume that members sometimes didn't answer their phone although they were actually awake, they always came if they answered the phone, and if they were annoyed, they did not show their annoyance publicly. They couldn't loudly complain even if they would have under other circumstances: the religious obligation to join the morning prayers whenever feasible could not be taken lightly, even if it was not absolutely binding.

The minyan was not the only occasion for the personalization of religious edicts in the synagogue. There were also other, even more personalized situations in which religious edicts similarly summoned congregants into interaction and participation. One such case concerns the religious roles of the Levite and the Cohen. Belonging to a Cohen or Levite family denotes special religious proscriptions and requirements in Orthodox Judaism. A Cohen is, literally, a member of the ancient priestly class; a Levite, in turn, is a member of the tribe of Levi from which the Cohens were chosen, and which also has special religious obligations.[14] Although today Cohens and Levites have roughly the same set of religious observances as the rest of the community (since, in the absence of a temple, ritual slaughter handled by the Cohens has been replaced with common prayer), there are still small differences between their obligations and those of other members. Thus, for example, when the Torah scroll is read—on Saturdays, religious holy days, and Monday and Thursday mornings—Cohens and Levites are called first to stand for the reading of the scroll. The rabbi or his helper first calls a Cohen, both mentioning him by name and stating that he is a Cohen, and then the Levite. When a Cohen is not available the rabbi must state that there is no Cohen present and proceed to call a non-Cohen to take his place.

As in the case of the minyan above, the intersections between institutionalized religious structures and actors' pragmatic projects produce predictable patterns of summoning. Thus, in a small congregation, the absence of a Cohen—especially on the High Holidays, when he performs an extra blessing—could denote a serious religious personnel problem. In small congregations, Cohens are thus actively sought. As one "Cohen" Orthodox Jew humorously narrated, living in the Valley he often acted as "Cohen for hire" for the religious holidays, receiving phone invitations weeks in advance from local rabbis to make sure he could attend their services.

In the Chibat Yaakov congregation, where I usually prayed, there were only a few Cohens. On most Saturdays there were two, but quite often only one. Thus, the "Cohen" role was personalized to the utmost degree. It was not simply "a Cohen" that was sought; it was either Jeremy Cohen or Jeff Katz. One Saturday, when both failed to show up, the rabbi looked around before calling for a replacement (prefaced by the necessary incantation "there is no Cohen here"), not scanning the crowd randomly, but specifically searching, looking for either Jeremy or Jeff. When I told Jeff one Saturday morning that he looked like he could use some sleep, he retorted, resigned, "Well, I am a Cohen, I've got to come."[15]

Although the comment was humorous, there were other similar moments in which people lightly complained about how they had to come, like it or not. And ever so rarely, people would admit that they sometimes "played the system" and decided not to go to synagogue altogether. As one friend told me mysteriously when I asked him where he was on Saturday, he was "by the other synagogue." In a large neighborhood, there were strategic cracks through which one could take time off. With many synagogues to choose from, residents could trust that if they didn't show up, others would assume that they went elsewhere rather than slept in.

But as this comment also makes evident, although congregants were relatively willing to come, and very seldom voiced their exasperation, we should not equate summoning to a warm and positive feeling of communal belonging. Being summoned meant, practically, that one had to wake up early in the morning whether he wanted to or not; that people would exert subtle (and not so subtle) pressures to participate. The thickness of summoning was a double-edged sword.

Liturgical Gaps and Interactional Necessities

The forms of interactional summoning that emerge in the context of the synagogue are multilayered: they range from the kinds of ties that emerge in all social clubs, to specific forms of sociality that are predicated on the interactional interpretation of religious edicts; from specific forms of hospitality supported by religious injunctions, to the inscription of personal troubles in semipublic psalm readings, and the personalized pulls of prayer.

On an even more minute level, interactional summoning was etched in the very structure of liturgy. While common prayer may be important in providing an arena that produces shared emotion and meaning, it is also a shared form of practical choreography that members learned to read and participate in over time. For the initiated, the daily liturgy of Jewish Orthodox prayer is occupied by a plethora of personally specific interactional meaning, with clues to the lives of their fellow congregants. These "clues" are not randomly distributed but form an important part of the prayer structure.

One example can be seen in the part of the prayer called the Kaddish Yatom, the orphan's supplication. In every one of the three major daily prayers there is a section that is to be said either when one has lost a parent in the past year or on the yearly day of the parent's death—the *yahrzeit*. This prayer, in a mix of Hebrew and Aramaic, is said aloud, punctuated by the congregants' ritual amens. To the newcomer, this is just another part of the prayer, another incantation among others. Yet this prayer is a highly personalized affair performed in front of a large audience. The way in which this kind of personal-public performance becomes interactionally relevant can be seen in the next fieldnotes excerpt, where a visitor to the synagogue, living in another part of LA, came after a few years of absence:

After prayers, we all go to the adjoining room for the light kiddush meal. Sitting quite close to Malchiel, the visitor asks him how he is. Malchiel smiles and says he is well, asks what the visitor is doing here, "to what do we owe the pleasure?" The visitor says he was invited by a friend for Saturday, he "just had to come." After a brief silence, he asks Malchiel, concerned, "The Kaddish you said, is this a yahrzeit, or did something happen?" Malchiel says it isn't, his father died in January. The visitor nods and says he is sorry, asks Malchiel if his mother is still alive and how she is holding on.

To the synagogue members, Malchiel's Kaddish had become almost invisible, inaudible as a statement about his personal life. After all, his father died almost a year beforehand, and they had heard his daily recitations of the orphan's Kaddish for so long that it had ceased to mean much; no one had approached him to talk of his deceased father in the last few months. Yet for a visitor who knew Malchiel, the Kaddish was news—either he had chanced to come for a visit on a yahrzeit, or else . . .

The structure of liturgy thus comes to mean that an interactional gap is created. Malchiel's acquaintance knew that something might be terribly amiss, but he couldn't be sure—it could be simply a commemoration ritual, or could have signaled the death of a close family member (but, then, who?). Even if the visitor knew Malchiel only superficially, such information requires some kind of reaction. After all, if something terrible had happened, then not offering even nominal condolences could be construed as extremely rude. Encountering this situation didn't mean the visitor had to approach Malchiel himself, and in similar situations members first asked others in the congregation rather than the potentially bereaved, but some sort of interaction became necessary.

The Kaddish is far from being the only such site in the prayer. A look at the Siddur, the common prayerbook that includes the necessary prayers for everyday ritual and the holidays, shows it is peppered with passages that are read "only if," and thus catapult congregants into each other's lives:

In the morning, I hear Rabbi Chelev-Chittim chant an unusual prayer after the reading of the daily Monday Torah portion. I don't remember this prayer being recited on other days so I flip over to the right place in the Siddur and see it is a prayer said when a birth occurred. As he finishes the prayer a chorus of mazal tovs ensues. I turn to Zelikowski, standing behind me. "Who had a birth?" He smiles, "Chelev-Chittim's daughter-in-law just had twins in London." Later that day, meeting Dov-Ber for our evening Talmud session, I ask him if he knew about it. He says he didn't. "I knew she was pregnant but found out she gave birth only this morning, when Chelev-Chittim said the prayer."

The news, of course, would have reached the congregants sooner or later. After all, the rabbi was bound to sponsor one of the kiddush meals in honor of the birth. He did, actually, a few days afterward, explaining that the kiddush was sponsored by his wife, as "she got two new grandsons," which made for a second round of mazal tov exclamations. And yet the prayer recited at the Torah reading, a prayer he was religiously obliged to recite, evoked interaction. Even those members who did not expect it knew that somebody in the congregation had given birth, and in a small congregation this was noteworthy news to pursue.

These private-public prayers are not limited to the marking of central rites of passage—birth, bar mitzvah, marriage, death—but also said on other central occasions. Thus, when one of the congregants returned from a short family trip, he unexpectedly went up to the Torah during the morning prayers and recited the Gomel, the prayer said when one crosses the ocean, gets well after life-threatening illness, or survives a life-threatening experience. As he recited the prayer people looked up from their prayerbooks, and some exchanged glances. After the prayer, a flurry of congregants approached the congregant, asking what had happened. Relishing his becoming the center of attention, he said that as he was coming back from the vacation with his wife, the plane's wheels wouldn't drop, leaving him and his wife circling the airport for almost two hours. The situation got more and more tense, until the gasoline was so low that the choice was land or drop, and the pilot decided to take his chances and descend. In the end, the wheels were actually operational, it just didn't show up on the pilot's screens, but these were two tense hours. Both he and his wife were thoroughly shaken; she kissed the ground when they were finally taken off the plane.

These interactions all share a similar structure. A prayer connoting an important private incident is recited in public. The prayer, however, leaves a gap. Others in the congregation know that something has happened but either don't know what that might be or know only a part of the story. Indeed, these little mysteries of everyday life share some features with works of literature. In the field of comparative literature, some writers have described similar gaps as some of the most important devices in storytelling.[16] Narratives, according to such a reading, are inherently incomplete and require the reader to fill in the gaps peppered through them. These gaps, as literary critics note, have some common characteristics: they are not automatically visible but need a proficient reader who is attentive to the text in front of her; filling these gaps is mandatory for understanding the situation; gaps are positioned at key points in the narrative, when the details obscured are most important.[17]

The interactional gaps in the liturgy do not function in the same way as those described in literature. In literature, the gaps are filled with readers' untestable "hypotheses." The pleasure of the text is then partly derived from the personalized answers the reader provides and discovers while reading. In liturgy, gaps are more predictable, and partly solved in interaction. However, there is a striking similarity between the gaps literary critics find encoded in literary works, and the gaps encoded in liturgical practice. In fact, liturgical gaps have all of the three characteristics they describe: they can be detected only when one "knows" the structure of the liturgy well enough to decode the meaning of different prayers (thus, for example, although I read and understand Hebrew, it took me about a year before I started "hearing" these interactional gaps in prayers); the gaps cannot be filled automatically; the prayers containing those gaps denote key occurrences in the congregants' lives. The combination of the structure of liturgy and everyday civility rituals thus makes it almost a moral obligation to interact with others and find out just what has happened. The gaps are filled, indeed must be filled, through social interaction.[18]

Effervescence, Meaning, Interaction

It may seem that by focusing on the patterned moments of interactional summoning embedded in liturgical practice and synagogue life, we are treating them like an ethnographic cabinet of curiosities. But thinking seriously about such patterns shifts some of the discussion of meaning and ritual and their place in sustaining the participation and identification of actors.

For, after all, religious practices, and especially situations of public worship, have long been the staple of social analyses. Ritual situations form the fulcrum of a whole tradition that stresses the formation and reaffirmation of ties through the excitement of shared ritual—the "effervescence" of collective action.[19] Meanwhile, a complementary analytic move in the study of religion sees religious texts and rituals primarily as narrative structures.[20] Here the webs of meaning within which people are located, and which they themselves spin, are the focus of analysis. Such meanings are not necessarily collectively held: ethnographers of religious meaning have moved from the collective level of congregations, faiths, or civilizations to increasingly look at religious meaning as a meeting ground between texts and lives, biography and practice.[21]

These traditions are still crucial for understanding religious participation and experience. As studies of effervescence and emotion highlight, shared action and time is a powerful engine for solidarity formation.[22] Like a mass demonstration or a military parade, there is something emotionally stirring about large prayer meetings, or even sometimes in the shared songs of the Sabbath rituals and the tunes hummed over dinner or the kiddush meal. In some moments, the synchronization of sound and movement allows people to lose themselves in the act, while simultaneously creating emotional attachments to both the situation and the collectivity.

In another key, meaning is not a "variable" that adds flavor to social life. Meaning infuses any action or causal sequence.[23] Joint action simply cannot become exciting without some form of sense-making. (A negative case would be someone who accidentally finds herself in a demonstration for a cause she finds abhorrent; even the best performance of joint action would probably not sway her.) Similarly, the arts of summoning described here cannot be understood without recourse to meaning. For someone to call an acquaintance at 6:30 a.m. and expect this acquaintance to remain on friendly terms with him, the caller needs to assume something about the call's meaning—both in relation to the other people waiting, and in terms of the importance of prayer.

To see how meaning is evoked, and how moments of summoning emerge in predictable, mechanism-like regularities, requires the sociologist to think not only of *action* and subjects' *projects*, but of *interaction*—the collective act and the social worlds through which such meanings are made consequential. Rather than thinking about the way religious meaning plays into people's understanding of their lives and how they conceptualize their futures and pasts (whether in narrative or in inter-action), zeroing in on acts of summoning requires us to think about the ways in which such meanings are made consequential in drawing actors into a social world—giving rise to unexpected moments of tran-scendence such as the cathartic praise meal for the poisoned student, situations in which actors feel unpredictably needed for collective ac-tion to proceed, but also to moments of unwanted attention, pressure, exasperation, and irony.

In other words, it is not only that people form relationships and real-ize their projects through religious narratives and structures. It is also that they find themselves implicated in other personal and organiza-tional projects. Meaning is not only mobilized in interaction: it is in-voked, negotiated, and shapes the ways in which actors become part of a shared world.

Such patterns of summoning are also, much like the organizational rhythms and pulls described in the previous chapter, predictable. In this case, they are predicated on the layering of religious edicts and everyday routines and civilities. Indeed, Orthodox men and women of different stripes and from different localities would probably recognize these dy-namics as a variation on a well-known theme.[24] In this sense, the per-sonalization of religious participation is scripted into the institution, an "institutional fingerprint" of interaction—patterns of interaction that are produced and reproduced within certain settings as a result of the re-current pragmatic aims of actors and institutionally codified practices.[25]

FIVE

The Buzz of Difference

To become a certain kind of self, people do more than act in socially recognized ways, enacting who they *are* as they are summoned in interaction. There is an accompanying harmony to the theme of summoning and the constitution of selfhood and social worlds. Rather than being reminded only of who they are, people enact, and are reminded, also of who they *are not*. This chapter and the next take this semiotic insight as their point of departure, showing how specific Orthodox selves were evoked and invoked within a shifting structure of differences.[1]

The density of everyday life in the Orthodox neighborhood afforded residents ways to locate themselves within an array of biographical patterns and subaffiliations. To be Orthodox was to be constantly differentiated, constantly positioned as a particular kind of Jew and not another.[2] As one of the oldest jokes in the Jewish arsenal goes, when an Orthodox Jew arrives on a desert island he immediately builds two synagogues, one for prayer, and the other to never set foot in.

These divisions included axes of distinctions—totem poles of status that people generally understood as shared, even if they didn't like them. But they also clustered people in some subaffiliations that were not obviously considered "better" than others (though some people within each affiliation sometimes claimed they were). Tracing these distinctions and the ways that they were both held and situationally traversed provides a crucial insight that categorical generalizations risk missing: that to be summoned as an Orthodox Jew is also to be defined as a particular *kind* of

Orthodox Jew. The Orthodox neighborhood was a social world, a universe of regularized mutual response—but that was because people were aware of their own and others' positions in relation both to groups in the neighborhood and to the Orthodox world more generally.

Being More (or Less) Frum

Being *frum*, literally meaning "devout" in Yiddish, is perhaps one of the most widely used terms of evaluation and distinction in conversations with Orthodox residents of European descent (which included the great majority of Orthodox Jews in the neighborhood). Most residents I talked to simultaneously talked about it in two ways: in one sense, it was a synonym for "Orthodox Jew." An Orthodox Jew was *frum* whereas a non-Orthodox Jew was *frei* (or "free"); non-Jews were not even part of the categorization. In another sense, however, and especially in the stricter subaffiliations of Orthodoxy, it also put people of different subaffiliations on a totem pole of prestige, where people were not simply either *frum* or *frei*, but rather more or less frum, based on the levels of strictness of observation of religious law and external signs such as the beard, married women's head cover, men's sidelocks, or the black hat.

In one sense, geography already did some of the work. Living in the Beverly–La Brea neighborhood was already a mark of frumness, located within the symbolic cartography of the Orthodox world. Thus, within Los Angeles, the neighborhood was considered to be the most religiously exacting. Although Pico-Robertson and North Hollywood a few miles away both had large Orthodox communities, these neighborhoods had more variation in the level of observance of residents, whereas Beverly–La Brea was considered to be strict overall. This notion was reflected in an article in the *Jewish Journal*, a Los Angeles Orthodox monthly, that detailed the case of people who didn't feel religious enough for Beverly–La Brea and therefore moved to Pico-Robertson, while others, first residing in Pico-Robertson, saw their move to Beverly–La Brea as a step in their deepening commitment to religiosity, as a geographic correlate to a religious career.[3] As one woman, witnessing the change in the neighborhood put it:

You go down Beverly and La Brea, and you don't know what country you're in—there's every kind of shtreimel and *peyos* [Hasidic fur hat and sidelocks] . . . It's hard for me to go out on Saturday in normal clothes. I feel that I'm being disrespectful to who knows whom. I feel out of place.

Orthodox Jews both inside and outside the neighborhood often referred to this fact, though in a more victorious tenor. Within the Beverly–La Brea neighborhood, I was often told that this was *the* Orthodox neighborhood in Los Angeles. When one of my friends spotted an acquaintance from Pico-Robertson in his synagogue, he approached him, shook his hand, and teased him by asking: "What are you doing on the Jewish side of town?" Similarly, a married woman who had grown up in La Brea but later moved to Pico-Robertson told me, in a matter-of-fact tone, that she was not as religiously strict as she had been brought up to be: "After all, I moved to Pico."

At the same time, however, members readily admitted that this was, after all, Los Angeles. This was not Jerusalem, not Bnei Brak, not Crown Heights, New Square, Williamsburg, Lakewood, or Monsey, the centers of the Jewish Orthodox world in Israel and the United States. They sometimes commented that, in relation to these centers, Orthodox life in Los Angeles was diluted, that it was not as religious as it could or should be. And indeed, some Orthodox Jews I met in New York referred to Los Angeles as a *midbor shmoma*, a desert of desolation. Beverly–La Brea may be "the Jewish side of town," but not "the Jewish side of the United States." Where people lived shaped the ways in which they could be summoned—not simply as "an Orthodox Jew," but as someone who inhabits a space that then defines how they are evaluated, understood, and defined.

Beyond such residential signs, however, perhaps the most salient categorical indication of frumness is the observance of the Sabbath. As the Orthodox interpretation of Jewish law postulates that a Jew may not drive on the Sabbath, use electricity, or listen to music—and that men should, if at all feasible, go to synagogue for the three daily prayers—such observance is a highly visible and restrictive indication. Alongside the dietary rules of *kashrus*, Orthodox residents thus spoke about these laws as a general indication of frumness, synonymous with Orthodoxy. As one Chabad interviewee said when talking about a different community's shift toward stricter religious practice since the 1970s:

That's also a community that . . . there were no frum Jews there. I don't want to say there were no frum Jews there because the rebbe says "only God knows who is frum," let's say *shomer Shabbos*.

Shomer Shabbos, the Hebrew term for someone who keeps the Sabbath strictures, is seen here to be a substitute for the category of frum. Only

God can see devotion, but the external signs of keeping the rules of the Sabbath are clearly visible. And, of course, the actual and the proxy are, for all extents and purposes, indistinguishable.

Even children attended to these signs of religiosity, seeing them as important, moral, definitions of self. At one point, a friend of mine, an Israeli Jew, arrived in Los Angeles from Berkeley for a visit. As he already sported a beard (though more of the hipster variety), I thought he looked perfectly Orthodox when he put on a yarmulke. But his sketchy knowledge of religious law outed him:

I bring Tom for a Sabbath meal at the Rubins'. One of the Rubins' little girls, five years old, asks me quietly, when Tom is in the bathroom, "How is he your friend? He isn't frum . . ." I ask her how she knew that he wasn't frum. "I told him I play piano, and he asked me to show him," she answers. "I didn't want to tell him, so I said that my mom doesn't allow me."

Playing a musical instrument on the Sabbath is prohibited in Orthodox circles, a proscribed form of work.[4] By asking the child to show him how she played, in effect encouraging her to break religious law, the visitor thus exposed himself as "non-frum" in the girl's eyes. The anecdote would appear to be straightforward: the gaffe showed him for what he was. But two things about this interaction bring the moral salience of frumness to the fore: First, the child inquired how this man, being non-frum, could possibly be my friend. Understanding me to be frum (as she saw me often in her parents' synagogue, and over the course of many Sabbath dinners and lunches), she couldn't fathom how this could be. Second, the tactful avoidance of the clear gaffe is telling.[5] Since not being frum was an obvious moral failing, she did not want to embarrass my non-Orthodox friend and expose his failure. To tell him that she couldn't play because it would break the laws of the Sabbath would make him, ipso facto, not only ignorant but morally tainted. Whereas adults might perhaps educate him about religious law, as he "didn't know any better," the girl tried to protect his selfhood, to save face for him, and told a partial truth: her mother wouldn't let her play the piano.

While the basic observance of Sabbath and kosher rules are acknowledged throughout the Orthodox world—no one who self-defines as Orthodox would say it is religiously admissible to eat pork, mix meat and dairy, or light a fire or drive a car on the Sabbath—not all observances are as clear-cut. In many cases, it wasn't universally agreed upon what was a sign of devotion, and what was going unnecessarily, perhaps fanatically, beyond the letter of religious law. Like most categorical evaluations, frumness was not a simple totem pole, on which everyone accepted that certain groups were higher up than others.

Thus, for example, Modern Orthodox men who did not have beards did not usually think of themselves as any less frum than Hasidic Jews, with their long beards and sidelocks. After all, Torah law directly forbids only putting a blade to the skin of one's face. Electric shavers, which cut the hair rather than shaving it, are thus permissible. Similarly, religious law forbids men only to shave the area around their ears: nowhere does it say that men should sport long sidelocks. These and many other interpretations of law were later customs or rabbinical strictures that explicitly went beyond the letter of the law as a way to extend the religious edict to its logical extreme. But the status of such customs and rabbinical decrees is not as ironclad as Talmudic interpretation of Torah law, and the relation between such "strictnesses" (*chumros*) and being a frum Jew was thus subject to question.

It was, however, still understood that some subaffiliations were stricter than others. This stratification can most clearly be seen in the marriage market. An Orthodox matchmaking website tellingly called *Frumster*, which some people I knew in the neighborhood used, gave the following categories in the section dedicated to a user's "religious profile": Modern Orthodox Liberal; Modern Orthodox *Machmir* [strict]; Yeshivish [non-Hasidic strict Orthodox] Modern; Yeshivish black hat; Hasidic. Not only were different subaffiliations neatly marked from each other, but they were stacked "up" in ascending order of observance—how frum the profile on *Frumster* was. And, what is more, as the category "black hat" makes clear, the ascending order of frumness is tied to external markers.

For strict subaffiliations of Orthodoxy, this ascending order was often taken quite literally. Being frum was not simply a dichotomous division between those who kept basic dietary and Sabbath laws and those who did not. Rather, there were gradations of frumness, signified by practical observance or by visible markers. For example, one of the signs that a novice was becoming "more frum" at Chabad synagogues was his starting to grow a beard. The beard, according to most Hasids, should be worn long and should not be cut at all, a prescription that gives it a rather disheveled look. Thus, a clear indication of growing frumness was either that members had stopped attending to their short and well-trimmed beards and let them grow wild, or that they had started growing them. When I failed to shave for a week, one synagogue member approached me and asked if I was growing a beard. When I said I just forgot to shave, he patted me on the shoulder and said, "Keep forget-ting." And although the comment was humorous, it pointed to an im-portant consideration: as external markers enabled the summoning of a resident as a particular kind of Jew, playing with these markers could thus help constitute the kind of person one was becoming.

The symbolic importance of the beard as a sign of frumness emerged during a conversation with a man from a small Hasidic group in the neighborhood, when he described the religious rigor of his parents-in-law. Fearful of incurring his wife's wrath, he tried to explain:

Her parents are a little bit more . . . they don't look like me, they don't have a beard. A little bit different, a little bit less . . . I don't want to call them less religious, because she would be very angry with me . . . more of a Modern Orthodox approach. I don't judge, God knows.

He caught himself in time and engaged in a series of self-repair se-quences, affirming—like the man in the excerpt above—that only God really knows who is more and who is less frum. But the sign that came immediately to his mind was his father-in-law's close shave. It was obvi-ous to him, though apparently not to his wife, that without a beard, his father-in-law was "a little bit less . . ."[6]

Much like the beard, the black hat, the sidelocks, and other markers were considered in some circles to be markers of frumness. Moreover, signs of frumness weren't located only on the body. They were mani-fested in the organization of the house, where no TVs were visible; where only the most abstract art and important rabbis' portraits adorned the walls; where the living room was inevitably lined with religious books (*sforim*). Browsing through the living-room library of one friend, I found that out of fifteen shelves, the top twelve were dedicated to sforim, while the bottom three had literary classics such as Dostoyevsky, Homer, and so on. As he was an academic, I asked him where he kept his professional books. He said he kept them in the bedroom, adding with a wry smile, "these here are the show books."

The maintenance of these signs required ongoing work. While resi-dents' level of observance was often marked and stabilized through organizational belonging, they still needed to consciously enact their frumness, as they expected others to be interpreting their actions. Thus, for example, although none of the strict Orthodox households I went to had TVs in their living rooms, many residents I knew did have either a television or another device for viewing media in their homes. After all, the viewing of wedding videos, religious films, or the televised speeches of prominent rabbis was not only allowed but often encouraged. Yet this fact gave rise to a complex set of pragmatic-cum-moral questions: Where to put the television? How to screen media? As the following excerpt shows, the solution to these questions was far from obvious, and managing them sometimes became a site for enacting religious observance:

> I sit in the Cohen family's living room to see a video of their wedding movie on their wedding anniversary. The DVD is viewed on the wall of their room, which has a few windows at street level. Before viewing, Cohen goes to the window on the side, a small window that looks right onto the screening wall. There is no curtain, but he improvises one. He looks at me, "I don't want people to think I have a huge TV."

Although we were preparing to watch a wedding, undoubtedly "kosher" viewing material, the screening had to be managed with care. At least from Cohen's point of view, anyone walking down the street could potentially see that a movie was being screened inside, thereby getting the wrong impression regarding the family's level of religiosity. In order to be "correctly summoned" by other Orthodox Jews, residents had to manage appearances.

Last, work was similarly stratified according to its relationship with the religious world.[7] Secular lines of work were often referred to as *parnasah* in strict Orthodox circles: ways to make money that should be secondary to members' religious lives. Having a "Jewish job," on the other hand—working as a rabbi, teacher, or kosher supervisor—was considered more prestigious, though it usually meant earning much less than other Orthodox residents who had white-collar "secular" jobs. When I dared to ask a twenty-one-year-old man whether he wanted to go to college after receiving the rabbinical ordination toward which he was studying, he icily remarked, "Being a rabbi is good enough."

One of the ways in which a Jewish job was differentiated from a non-Jewish job was through its adherence to different time cycles from those of secular jobs. Whereas Orthodox residents working in secular jobs had days off on Christian holidays such as Christmas, and on civil holidays such as Veterans Day and Presidents Day, holding a Jewish job meant that holidays and daily work schedules were constructed along the Jewish calendar. Instead of clashing, the rhythms of organizations and of individual observance were complemented by the rhythms of work life.[8] In the next excerpt, although having a secular job actually entitled a member to join a Jewish learning retreat, it was still taken by one congregant as an indicator of less intense involvement in Jewish life:

I come to Rabbi Chelev-Chittim's synagogue on Friday around Christmas-time. The synagogue is relatively empty, as many of the congregants didn't show up, using their vacation from work to organize a *Shabbaton*, a Torah-study retreat in the Valley. As the Shabbaton was organized by Russian congregants, almost all the Russian-born men aren't there, except for Rabbi Kortzky, a teacher in one of the Orthodox schools in the neighborhood. After prayers are over, Rabbi Chelev-Chittim asks Kortzky, jokingly, "What are you doing here? Aren't you supposed to be in the Valley?" Kortzky shrugs, "I have a Jewish job, you know . . ."

Although his work schedule barred Kortzky from going on the religious retreat, his response resignifies his absence. Being on "Jewish time," he was not able to participate in a religious activity. By reminding the rabbi why he could not make it to the religious gathering, he presented himself as one of the few who must abide by a different time structure. Where a shared temporal landscape is socially significant in the construction of a shared world,[9] Kortzky's absence from the religious retreat was transformed into a sign of religious adherence. Like the rabbi, he was bound by a different, specifically Jewish time structure. This differentiation between goyishe (non-Jewish) and Jewish time was perhaps best crystallized in the praise that one of the congregants heaped on one exalted religious figure: "he doesn't even know the goyishe date." The ultimate sign of frumness was that the rabbi was bound solely by the Jewish lunar calendar, did not even know the secular date, did not share the basic unit of timekeeping with the world outside the Jewish Orthodox world.

Different Orthodoxies: On How Not to Eat a Kosher Pizza

The practical meaning of frumness shifted across situations: it was used to distinguish Orthodox Jews from non-Orthodox; it was wielded by members of strict subaffiliations as a way to distinguish themselves from members of what they saw as more lenient subaffiliations; and, just as important, it appeared as an internal structure of difference and constant enactment *within* congregations. Frumness thus provided residents with a flexible signifier, a language through which to imagine a stratified social space.[10] But locating residents' identification within Orthodoxy was made not only hierarchically but also "horizontally," through residents' relationship to specific subaffiliations of Orthodoxy. Even among the strictly Orthodox—those who saw themselves as "more" than Modern Orthodox, "more" than traditional—subaffiliations further located residents. And, in this case, differentiations connoted not who was more or less frum but rather differences in outlook, observances, and attitude that were much more akin to character stereotypes than to a stratified moral space.[11]

Perhaps the most important distinction within the strict Orthodox world is that dividing the *Hasidic* from the *Yeshivish* (sometimes also termed *Litvish* or *Misnagdic*)[12] world. This split originated in the late eighteenth century, when the Hasidic movement—an Eastern European religious movement within Orthodoxy that stressed simplicity, experiential devotion, and a form of approachable mysticism—first appeared. The established religious authorities within European Jewish life of the time, especially the centers of learning in Vilnius, Lithuania, were strongly opposed to the movement. Both the emphasis on experience and the personalistic adherence to a dynasty of rabbis (or rebbes) that emerged in Hasidism were seen as heretical. Instead of pietistic ecstasy, entrenched Orthodoxy further emphasized legalistic studies of the Talmud; rather than the Hasidic dynastic court they emphasized the relative meritocracy of the yeshiva world (hence "Yeshivish").

Despite the early resistance of religious authorities, Hasidism was successful, composing about half of strict Orthodoxy today. Whereas in the nineteenth and early twentieth century Hasidim were often considered heretics by their Yeshivish brethren, they have since been "accepted" and have even made theological inroads into Yeshivish Orthodoxy, with the Hasidic language of experience seeping into the yeshiva world. But this blending is far from complete. There are still both theological and organizational differences between the camps. There are also still some noticeable differences in appearance between Hasids and Yeshivish Orthodox Jews: most Hasidic groups grow extremely long sidelocks, whereas Yeshivish men generally do not; on the Sabbath Yeshivish men tend to wear ties and suits, as well as black hats, whereas their Hasidic counterparts wear a long black coat tied with a silk belt (the *bekishe* and the *gertl*) and most wear large and extremely visible *shtreimel* fur hats.

Beyond the difference between Hasidic and Yeshivish, there was a dizzying array of internal differences. Within the Hasidic world itself, there are a multitude of groups that emerged in different places in Eastern Europe and usually take their name from the town in which the rabbinical dynasty was located in the nineteenth century—Satmar and Munkacz (hailing from Hungary), Lubavitch (from Belarus and then Russia), Gur and Vizhnitz (from Poland), Breslov and Skver (from what is now Ukraine), and many, many more. Although these groups share a history and some theological similarities, they have different core texts, usually written by the rebbes of the group, different customs, observances, and even ways of dress, with slightly different shaped hats, slightly different ways of wearing one's garb.

And as with any other politics of small differences, Hasidic groups are sometimes bitterly opposed to one another. One of the most publicized tensions within the Hasidic world occurred in New York City between Chabad and Satmar Hasids. Originating from different corners of Eastern Europe, the two Hasidic courts developed different philosophies and organizations: Satmar is anti-Zionist whereas Chabad are right-wing supporters of both Israel and the settlement movement; whereas some Chabad Hasids believe that the late Chabad rebbe, who died in 1994, was potentially (or, as some maintain, actually is) the Messiah, Satmar sees this as heresy bordering on idolatry. Whereas Chabad focuses, organizationally, on drawing nonaffiliated Jews to Orthodoxy, Satmar is known for trying to secure its boundaries and not mingling with the non-Orthodox. In terms of appearance, Satmar men don shtreimels on the Sabbath and wear long sidelocks; Chabad generally keep their sidelocks short and, following the example of the last Chabad rebbe, wear not shtreimel fur hats but wide-brimmed black Borsalinos.

The differences among subaffiliations of strict Orthodoxy were usually not understood in terms of status distinctions, with no clear hierarchy among the subaffiliations. People made jokes about "other" subaffiliations, whether poking fun at learned and "soulless" observances (in the case of Hasids joking about the Yeshivish), making light of the miracle tales of the rebbe and nonpunctuality in prayer times (in the case of Chabad), or noting uncompromising strictness of character (when joking about Satmar). These jokes did not, usually, denote a religious failure. It was more as if different subaffiliations denoted character traits rather than distinctions of observance.[13]

This translation of Orthodoxy's subaffiliations into character traits can be seen in the following excerpt, which was probably a personal low point in my fieldwork in the neighborhood. It was a dinner at the home of a Chabad family, with whom I had a close relationship, a week after I had given them one of the first papers I had written from my fieldwork—a paper in which, in true methods-section manner, I wrote that I was not religious and objectified our relationship in what I thought was a "correct" sociological fashion.[14] Feeling hurt and betrayed by what she had read, my hostess decided to raise the issue around the Sabbath dinner table, with about seven other guests present:

As we are sitting, Mrs. Borstein asks me, in front of everyone, how my "spying" was going. I try to deflect what she said by saying that I do enjoy the Hasidus and Talmud classes I am taking. She then says: "You know, there is a saying in the Talmud: 'Whoever is learning not for God's sake, it would have been better that his mother would have had a miscarriage.'" People around the table become extremely quiet for a few seconds, when her husband bursts out, "You should have been born Satmar . . . ," at which everybody laughs (if a little tensely).

Trying to mitigate Mrs. Borstein's sharp comment regarding my status as a none too observant Jew and my betrayal as an ethnographer, her husband assigned her to a different subaffiliation of Orthodoxy—whereas Chabad Hasids are known for their outreach and patience with non-observant Jews, Satmar Hasids do not have outreach programs and are considered much less understanding regarding nonobservant Jews. By assigning his wife to Satmar, Mr. Borstein was, in effect, suggesting that she was being somewhat unforgiving. In this sense, the question that the assignment of an Orthodox subaffiliation answered was not "Are you a better or worse Jew?" Rather, the question was: "What kind of (unerringly Jewish) person are you?"

The differences between Yeshivish and Hasids were understood in similar terms, despite the history of tension between Hasidic and Yeshivish Orthodoxy. Hasidim often spoke of Yeshivish Jews (or "Misnagdim," as they often called them) as meticulous and exact regarding prayer time (much more so than Hasids) and religious law. Though this exactness in the realm of law was sometimes ridiculed by Hasidim as a quality that came at the expense of piety, it was—again—not seen in the stark colors of previous generations. One Hasidic rabbi, who was known for starting prayers on time, and who had little patience for the miracle tales that Hasids often tell, once told me jokingly that he was "an extremely *Misnagdic* Hasid."

Another joke that crystallizes this religious-cum-personality-trait divide, which I have heard on both sides of the Hasidic-Yeshivish divide, tells of a Talmudic sage who prayed with such devotion and zeal that a column of fire rose from where he stood, reaching up to the heavens, burning a few unlucky birds that happened to fly by. A Hasidic Jew, upon hearing this story, starts dancing in ecstasy, contemplating the great devotion of the sage. The Yeshivish person, upon hearing this story, immediately goes to the law books, trying to determine to whom the fried birds belong and who would be liable for damages.

These distinctions, as I show later, were often transcended. They did, however, translate into organizational boundaries. Although on weekdays the boundaries were often crossed, on the Sabbath residents belonging to different subaffiliations almost inevitably prayed at different synagogues. Additionally, in the case of Chabad, many children went to specialized Chabad schools in the Pico-Robertson neighborhood, away from other strictly Orthodox schools. And even when people prayed in the same synagogues and their children attended the same schools, some pragmatic boundaries were still present. Thus, although both Yeshivish and Hasidic strands of Orthodoxy are extremely strict in matters of religious practice, different strands emphasize different religious laws and are more lenient on others. This, in turn, may come to mean that relationships between families belonging to different sides of the divide may be jeopardized. Children attending the same strictly Orthodox school may play and learn together, but they cannot easily eat at each other's houses if they adhere to different strictnesses with regard to the laws of kashrus.

This boundary is embodied in a humorous story I heard in the neighborhood, one about two children—one Chabad-Hasidic and one Yeshivish—who warily approach a kosher pizzeria. The Chabad kid cannot eat the pizza because the cheese is kosher but not to the strict standards of Cholov Yisroel kosher.[15] The Yeshivish kid cannot eat it because the wheat has to be left standing for a year (a law that Chabad Hasids do not hold by outside of Israel but that Yeshivish in the neighborhood took extremely seriously). The kosher pizza remains untouched.[16]

Intersecting Distinctions: A *Purimshpil*

In a relatively small neighborhood, the distinctions between "more" and "less" frum and between different subaffiliations within Orthodoxy— with all the gradations and subgroupings these entail—meant that people often felt they could locate themselves and summon each other in very precise detail. Although these distinctions were situational, in many cases being overlooked and practically ceasing to exist, they were important ways to understand how residents fit into the social world of Orthodoxy in the neighborhood. One incident in which these distinctions were brought into relief involved a Purim play (*Purimshpil*) written and performed at one of the synagogues that I visited. The light-hearted play was performed in front of the whole congregation, aimed especially at the children, and this year's theme was the importance of Jews' loving each other. The message was clear: Jews should overcome the distinctions that separate them and remember that they are all Jews.

Their differences, after all, are not as essential as that which brings them together.

The plot was simple. Satan tries to sow seeds of discontent and separate Jews from each other. He sends "the evil inclination," baseless hatred, to egg on any argument between Jews that he witnesses. Each time, Mordechai, the exemplary Jew, emerges to foil the attempts of the evil inclination. It was a bare-bones production. The "cast" had met a couple of times to read the script written by the rabbi. I played the evil inclination and wore plastic horns.

The three arguments the rabbi depicted were between a Chabad-Hasidic Jew and a Yeshivish Jew; a nonreligious and a religious Jew; and a Modern Orthodox and a strict Orthodox person. As this humorous play embodies much of what I have written about earlier, I quote it at length:

Scene II: A typical Chabad Hasid and a typical Yeshivish guy are sitting. The evil inclination stands at their side, encouraging their argument by pantomime.

Yeshivish: You're Chabad, aren't you?

Chabadnik: Yeah, so what?!

Yeshivish: How come you guys never learn a word except for Tanya [a Hasidic book written by the founder of Chabad]? You drink all the time. You should be ashamed of yourselves!

[I smile, jumping up and down.]

Chabadnik: What are you talking about, you snag [short for "Misnaged"]? You may learn a little, but you never think of G-d. Everything you do is mechanical. You have no idea of spirituality.

Yeshivish: You simpleton!

Chabadnik: You heretic!

[Enter the good Jew, telling them to love each other, that the Chabadnik learns the Talmud a lot, and that "plenty of non-Hasidim pray with kavanah *(intention) and try to get closer to G-d."]*

Scene III: A nonreligious guy is sitting near a religious guy.

NR: Pardon me, are you Jewish?

R: Nu . . . do I look like a Muslim?

NR: I thought maybe you were Amish . . .

R: I am *heimish* [Yiddish for homelike, sometimes used as a synonym for Orthodox], not Amish!

NR: Well, I'm Jewish too, and I think it is terrible that you still keep those outmoded laws! You can't eat this, you can't eat that. You can't even turn on the lights on Saturday. You treat women as second-class citizens.

R: How dare you?! If I was Amish (whispers to the audience, "God forbid") you wouldn't have criticized me. You're just a self-hating Jew! You don't even have the self-respect to stand up for our religion because you want to assimilate and be like everyone else!

[Enter the good Jew; he tells the nonreligious person, "Even if you're not observant, you should respect religious people. They have a deep commitment to love G-d and their fellow man." Turning to the religious Jew: "You shouldn't be harsh with a nonreligious Jew. He's never been exposed to Torah. And it's no fault of his own. He's entirely ignorant. He doesn't know any better."]

Scene IV: A Modern Orthodox type and a strictly Orthodox type [a Charedi] are sitting on a bench.

Charedi: Do you call yourself a religious Jew?

Modern Orthodox: What do you mean *call myself*? I am a religious Jew.

Charedi: Religious? You've got to be kidding. With a yarmulke the size of a Pepsi-Cola cap? You wear the same clothing like any *shaygetz* [derogatory word for non-Jew]! Instead of yeshiva, you go to college. Instead of learning Torah, you watch TV.

[I jump in obvious joy.]

Modern Orthodox: You are religious fanatics. You make me sick. You give all the rest of us a bad name. You're ignorant of the world. You look for one *chumra* [strict observance beyond the letter of the law] after another. You dress like a hundred years ago, and, besides, you have dandruff and bad breath!

[Enter the good Jew; he tells the Charedi: "You should know that most Modern Orthodox Jews take religious law very seriously. Don't be fooled by external appearances." Then he turns to the Modern Orthodox Jew: "You know the Charedim love Torah and Jewishness so much, their higher standards elevate all the community."]

The play lightly satirizes the internal distinctions between different Jews—the religious and the nonreligious, the Chabad and the Yeshivish, the Modern and the strict Orthodox. But, of course, this depiction of differences, held in a strict Orthodox synagogue, was partisan. Both the outline of the arguments and the way these were resolved by the figure of the good Jew were telling.

The conciliation between Jews in the first scene minimizes the differences among strict subaffiliations along the lines outlined above. Stereotypically, Chabad Hasids (and Hasids more generally) don't learn as seriously as those in the yeshiva world, focusing on their own Hasidic texts; the Yeshivish are too dry and formalistic in their adherence to law. But these, as the good Jew notes, are stereotypes. Although there may be some difference in outlook, Hasids do learn the Talmud seriously, and Yeshivish do pray with spiritual zeal. What is most interesting in this scene is not the stereotypes but that, as opposed to the resolution of other scenes in the play, differences are not bridged but practically erased.

The conciliation is very different, however, in the sketches featuring the Modern Orthodox and the nonreligious Jew. In these two cases, conciliation is achieved from a position of superiority. Although the Modern Orthodox Jew may be serious about his Judaism and the observance of religious law, he must nonetheless understand that the strictly Orthodox have "higher" standards that "elevate" the community. The sketch featuring the nonreligious Jew is more striking still. The nonreligious can say what he does only because he doesn't know any better; in the words of the play, "He's never been exposed to Torah. And it's no fault of his own. He's entirely ignorant. He doesn't know any better."[17]

"FFBs" and "BTs": Biography and Distinction

The Purim play was telling as an exercise in communal auto-ethnography.[18] But perhaps as interesting as the distinctions that were brought to the fore and satirized were the distinctions that were left unmarked. For frumness is not democratically distributed, and it was interesting that a synagogue that catered to many Jews who became Orthodox later in their lives did not note one of the most salient distinctions: that between Orthodox Jews who were born to Orthodox families (especially from illustrious rabbinical families) and those who came from a secular background and became Orthodox later in their lives.

Many residents I talked to mentioned that people who became Orthodox later in their lives were even more meritorious than people born religious, often quoting the Talmudic passage proclaiming that "in a place where a repentant Jew holds by, even the righteous cannot stand." After all, they had to choose what was taken for granted for others.[19] But the repetition of this phrase actually highlighted the importance that most people accorded to the question "Were you born into a religious family?" That is, are you "frum from birth," an FFB (as both Orthodox Jews in the neighborhood and beyond called it)? Or were you raised in a non-Orthodox environment, a Jew who has "come back" to the fold, a *ba'al tshuva*, or BT?

The differentiation between FFB and BT was prominent throughout Orthodox subaffiliations but was probably most visible in one subgroup in the neighborhood—Chabad. One element that has made the

Chabad Hasidic group a particularly salient and visible group in American Orthodoxy is its emphasis on drawing secular Jews around the world into Orthodoxy.[20] And in the Beverly–La Brea neighborhood, the Chabad contingent was largely made up of such "returned" Jews, in addition to some residents who had moved from Chabad's stronghold on the East Coast.

Despite being sought out by Chabad members, BTs occupy a problematic position. Although they observe religious edicts, this observance is sometimes perceived as strained or unnatural. Not having studied Hebrew, Aramaic, or Yiddish from childhood, BTs usually have strong American accents when reading the Torah, botching the *r* and *ch* sounds in prayer; they speak with an American accent rather than with the Yiddish undulating yeshiva inflection; they are almost invariably perceived to miss some items on the never-ending list of observances.

And as with the gradations of frumness, being BT was also a possible liability in the marriage market. Within the same "religious profile" on the matchmaking website described above, one of the categories is "family background," which includes the options: "from a secular family"; "from a traditional family"; "from a religious family"; "convert."[21] In one instance, a woman asked me for details about a mutual acquaintance for whom she was trying to find a match. After finding out that he had become religious at the age of sixteen after having grown up secular, she pensively noted, "It is all right for this match [the girl came from a Modern Orthodox family]. If it were a frum family that had been frum for five generations or something, things would have been different." There is a subtle arithmetic of distinction at work. Since he was a good Hasidic Jew, she saw him as "more frum" than a woman from a Modern Orthodox family; but being a BT, he was something less—especially in the eyes of those who were frum "for generations." In the end it added up, and a match seemed like it would be possible.[22]

The observation that BTs occupy a problematic status in the Orthodox world is not new.[23] When BTs first sought to enter the yeshiva system in Israel, they were turned down for fear that their earlier contact with the secular world could not be erased, and that the FFB students would be adversely influenced by them.[24] But the distinctions between BTs and FFBs do not emerge only in organizational settings and in the marriage market. FFBs and BTs alike attended to minute indications in practice and to embodied indications of religious ability. Although new BTs tried to emulate both the FFBs' embodied and external indications of frumness, at certain points their performance would fall apart.

In one household where the couple was newly religious, having become frum only a few years before my visit, a large bookcase with over forty shelves was paraded in the living room. But this indication of Orthodoxy was offset by one simple fact—almost all the books were written in Aramaic, Hebrew, or Yiddish, languages that neither husband nor wife could read or understand. When I asked about the books, the owner seemed a little embarrassed and admitted he could not read them at present. He added that he hoped to be able to read them one day, and that—most important—his children might be able to read them even if he never did. Like the nouveau riche in their consumption of art, he consumed goods that he did not have the skills to appreciate.[25]

The ways in which the biographical backgrounds of BT members were understood and negotiated by FFBs were also apparent in quips and jokes. In one instance, while waiting for some guests to arrive for a meal at one rabbi's house, the host decided to lighten up the atmosphere by telling a joke:

There was a BT woman who had a mentor that was walking her through the process, teaching her how to perform the *mitzvos* [religiously prescribed observances]. After many years they met again by chance, and the newly religious woman asked her old mentor to come for Sabbath to her home. Coming to the house, the mentor was impressed by the beautiful Jewish home the woman had, how meticulously she performed the mitzvos. But one question kept nagging at her—after lighting the Sabbath candles, the newly religious woman dramatically moved her hand across her forehead and then shook it in the air. It was a custom she had never seen before. When she asked her old student about it, the student said, confused, "But that's the way you always did it." Taken aback, the mentor thought for a minute, and then started laughing. "It was a hot summer, I was sweaty."

Faced with an almost endless number of edicts and customs, BTs must imitate everything they see and learn by watching their rabbis and FFB friends. BTs must learn to follow not only the letter of the law, but also elements such as hand movements and ways of holding one's body while praying—embodied knowledge tacitly held by those raised in religious homes, or those who have been religious for a long time.[26] In such an atmosphere, mistakes are almost inevitable and, from the point of view of those raised religious, quite humorous.

The humor of distinction, however, was not innocent. It was a reminder that BTs carried a secular past and that they were in some sense passing as "real" Orthodox Jews. In many encounters, members made sense of each other's actions not only according to embodied action but also according to their perceived biographical path. They were summoned not simply as "Jews" or as "Jews of a particular affiliation," but precisely as BTs. This, in effect, was the most jarring aspect of being a newly religious member. A BT resident once told me he tried for years to be "as good as" those raised Orthodox. One Sabbath, he went to a dinner at a friend's house, who happened to be an FFB. As they were sitting at the table, they started to hum Hasidic tunes, *nigunim*. They were humming different tunes when the FFB turned to my friend and jokingly said, "And you learnt all that from cassettes?!" It was at this point, my friend said, that he realized that he could never really be completely "in." What bothered him was not only the unanticipated jab of distinction, but the fact that he *had* indeed learned the Hasidic tunes from cassettes. The joke was demeaning not simply because it subverted the identification he had worked so hard to achieve, but because it was irresistibly accurate.

Another example of the ways in which people "read" actions through biographical knowledge can be seen in an interview excerpt with one Orthodox resident. When we spoke about the neighborhood, the interviewee, an FFB who considered himself particularly exacting, talked at length about how he attempted to avoid certain parts of the neighborhood, as well as his reactions to the routes that other residents and fellow synagogue members took, particularly with regard to a hotdog stand that sold nonkosher food:

I never go by there, when I come to synagogue I make sure I come from the other side. I don't want this kind of impurity when I go to pray. But sometimes I see these people, newly religious, going by Moe's on Shabbos, going past it . . . and I know their mouth is watering. And I ask myself, can they stand in the way of temptation, or do they go home and have a little one?

What is striking about this excerpt is the extent to which different ways of walking, ways of seeing, and biographical knowledge all come together to form distinctions. Simply walking past the nonkosher hotdog stand seemed to make one suspect of being less frum than others. But such markers alone were not enough. Thus, when the synagogue rabbi himself walked daily past the store, nobody implied that he was less frum for it. It was only when the knowledge of a person's biographical pattern was combined with an observation of his way of walking that the observer knew "their mouth is watering."[27] As they carry their past with them, BTs are suspected of continuing to also carry, in spite of everything, their secular being.

The Shifting Sands of Distinction

The forms of distinction described here were ways to locate oneself and others in a social space. Although residents were summoned as Orthodox Jews, they were also summoned as *specific kinds* of Orthodox Jews— as more or less frum, as members of different subaffiliations, as BT or FFB. Distinctions were often made in hierarchical terms, but they also narrated in concise terms what kind of Jew one was. When people told me, and each other, about Orthodox residents I didn't know, they inevitably said which subaffiliation they belonged to, usually before telling me any other biographical details about them (what they did for a living, for example).

These distinctions, however, were not stable. They were predictably modulated and transcended through a host of organizational, ritual, and narrative situations. Much as people were summoned into being through different organizational rhythms, they were also located in social space differently in different times. Status hierarchies and distinctions were not simply located but organized as a patterned set of situations.

First, as organizations summoned residents into Orthodoxy, they were also important sites for sustaining distinctions. Schools in the neighborhood were partly distinguished by their ties to specific subaffiliations;[28] synagogues were inevitably tied to specific subaffiliations, and a few catered specifically to the newly religious, thus reproducing the BT/FFB distinction; some classes catered mostly to specific subaffiliations. However, organizations also allowed—sometimes even pressured—residents to transcend these very distinctions.

Thus, families sometimes sent their children to a school that "belonged" to a different subaffiliation, and many classes and special events drew people from different quarters of the neighborhood's Orthodox micro-cosmos. Additionally, some organizations, such as local welfare organization and the main women's ritual bath, explicitly defined themselves as interaffiliation organizations, catering to residents from all affiliations, biographical careers, and levels of observance. In all these instances, distinctions were at least partly transcended in organizational action.

The specific history of the Beverly–La Brea neighborhood sometimes created pressure to transcend subaffiliations on an organizational level. To return to a point I made earlier, the prominence of one boys primary school (as well as the local girls high school) until the 1990s meant that there was practically only one school that strict Orthodox parents sent their children to.[29] Families that usually prayed in different synagogues thus met through their children or through their involvement in the school. These inconsistent connections between members' strands of Orthodoxy and the educational system continued even after new affiliation-specific competing organizations were constructed.

These organizational pressures also arose through the control of real estate. Thus, for example, since the (non-Chabad) Hasidic kollel rented space from a Chabad synagogue, non-Chabad Hasids could often be seen praying and attending special events in the Chabad synagogue, something that is much rarer in places like New York. Similarly, since the old immigrant–European Orthodox synagogues rented out space to Sephardic congregants, minyans of old Ashkenazi and younger Sephardic Jews were quite common.[30]

Although organizations sustained distinctions, the pragmatics of members' participation, organizational actors' desire to keep their organizations afloat, and the organizational history of Orthodoxy in Los Angeles provided for moments of transcendence. These forms of transcendence might be based on necessity or comfort, but this didn't make them any less important.

Taking a longer time frame, organizations also allowed for more enduring movements among affiliations and categories. The strict Orthodox schools in the neighborhood, for instance, supported a pattern of religious upward mobility of sorts. Going to a strict Orthodox school, for example, positioned children of BTs as bona fide Orthodox Jewish members. This meant that they could be relatively sure that people would not see them as carrying with them the secular past of their parents, and they could often marry into "old" Orthodox families.[31] It also meant that children were able to call the shots at home—recreating the FFB/BT distinctions as an intergenerational dynamic. On a few occasions, in families of newly religious members, children corrected their parents' observance. Some of the teenagers I saw would tell their parents that they were getting aspects of religious law wrong, that they should say a different blessing from the one they had just uttered, or would simply treat their parents' often-strained mumbling of Hebrew prayers impatiently.[32]

Beyond the school, members also moved between synagogues and affiliations when they went for afternoon and evening classes. When prominent speakers came to town, for example, congregants from different synagogues, as well as from other parts of town, would come to hear them. Although a Hasidic rebbe would attract more Hasids than Modern Orthodox residents, the audiences were usually heterogeneous.

The same was true for the many free classes offered throughout the week, where residents of different subaffiliations often studied together, as well as for participation in other interaffiliation institutions.

Complementing the organizational patterns of transcendence, distinctions and categorizations were situationally crossed also in ritual. At least in certain situations, it seemed to make no difference what "kind" of Jew one was; it mattered only that one was Jewish and Orthodox. Distinctions, from this perspective, should be understood not as a rarified mental construct but rather as a loose structure of situations and interactional sequences along with the specific processes of summoning such situations entail. Whereas people could expect to be reminded, in certain situations, that they were a specific kind of Jew, in other contexts no such reminders existed, and people performed roughly the same situational role.

One such situation was the quorum (*minyan*) of men needed for the three daily prayers to commence. Ten men over the age of thirteen are required for these prayers. In this context, it was generally irrelevant what "kind" of Jew one was. The only relevant thing was that the person in question was Jewish, meaning that he asserted that he had been born to a Jewish mother. At one small synagogue where gathering a quorum of men was a challenge, a nearby synagogue would often supply the men, as they had men to spare. It did not matter that the needy synagogue was Modern Orthodox, whereas the supply synagogue was Hasidic. The same was also true in the opposite direction—from "more" to "less" frum. At another synagogue, a homeless man who came for prayers—a man who had started off far from being Orthodox, though he was undoubtedly Jewish—was happily counted for the minyan, and other schnorrers, who actually came in the morning in order to get donations, were sometimes roped into the minyan—a "professional hazard" since staying for the minyan often meant that they couldn't go to other synagogues on time to ask for donations.

Since the minyan was ritually blind to distinction, and especially during the weekdays, neighborhood residents often did not walk all the way to their favorite synagogue if it was too far. Instead, many of them would go to the nearest synagogue or to the one that was on their way to work, whether or not it was the "right" kind of synagogue. This was especially evident during the summer months, when sunrise was very early. Some of the residents who had to commute to work would pray at sunrise, sometimes at 5:00, whereas others could pray much later; pragmatics trumped distinctions. Which synagogue a given person went to was predicated on his work schedule more than on his subaffiliation.

During certain times of the year, moreover, the distinctions between different Orthodoxies were explicitly and concertedly made irrelevant, or at least porous. On the day of Simhat Torah, signaling the end of the one-year cycle for reading the Torah, Orthodox families would walk between different synagogues in the neighborhood, walking into each synagogue to dance with the Torah scroll and with each other, albeit separately and with women mostly watching the dancing. This practice, called *tahaluchos* (literally, "parades"), allowed members of different synagogues to have a taste of synagogues they would not normally frequent. Members thus went from Hasidic synagogues to Modern Orthodox, from Yeshivish to Sephardic, dancing and singing in each—a wide array of Orthodox dress and subaffiliations temporarily joined together in revelry. Some of my friends in the community waited for this "shul hopping" to get a sense, if only once a year, of the Orthodox spectrum that the neighborhood supported.

Again, distinctions were thus situationally transcended and intersituationally patterned. There were specific places and times at which they were meaningful, but others at which people did not act as if they were separated. Rather than thinking of the different strands of Orthodoxy as ever-apparent internal fissures, it would be much more precise to think of them as rhythmically shifting sets of social distances. People in different groups could anticipate when distances would grow and when they would be rendered irrelevant. The distances also differed depending on the strands of Orthodoxy—strict Orthodox subaffiliations seemed to have more opportunities to traverse social boundaries among themselves, even though these were apparent in dress and institutional affiliation, than did, for example, Sephardic Orthodox and Yeshivish residents.

One of the things that made the FFB/BT distinction painful for many of the BTs I talked to was precisely that one could never know when exactly the distinction would crop up. As opposed to other forms of distinction, which provided situationally predictable rhythms of distance, the distinctions between BTs and FFBs could be brought to the fore quite suddenly. People who had become Orthodox had often expected this distinction to be transcended—and had experienced it as already transcended in their everyday lives—only to encounter the distinction when they did not expect it.

Finally, it is important to note the common features that characterized the situations in which internal distinctions were transcended. They were transcended precisely on those occasions that most defined the people in the neighborhood as part of a collective project of "Jewishness"—during prayer, at religious festivals, in many of the schools, and in the internal welfare system. In these cases, pragmatics served to underline the more pervasive rhetoric of inclusion and exclusion—in which Jews were pitted mostly against the non-Jewish "other." As I show in the next chapter, this is precisely the difference between the situational transcendence of internal distinctions and the boundaries separating Jews from non-Jews.

Situational Boundaries and Balancing Acts

So far, the book has focused largely on the pulls of the Orthodox social world in the Beverly–La Brea neighborhood. One reason for this is theoretical—my purpose is to trace the moments of summoning through which an Orthodox self and social world are sustained and constructed. But another is pragmatic. As the fieldwork was demarcated by the space of the neighborhood and the places in which people congregated within it—synagogues, classes, Sabbath meals, and so on—the interactions between Jews were almost the only ones visible to me. Non-Jews were rare, and if they found themselves present they were usually waiters, cleaners, an occasional guest sitting quietly on the sidelines at a wedding.

This invisibility, however, was partly an artifact of the ethnographer's location. For many of the Orthodox in the neighborhood, the day was punctuated by "Jewish" and "non-Jewish" times and situations. The day might certainly begin Jewish, with the morning quorum of men praying and perhaps reading a few pages of Psalms before work; but then most men (and many of the women) would go on to work in non-Orthodox, non-Jewish environments, with non-Jewish colleagues, speaking about "non-Jewish" topics. If the map of organizational summoning I outlined before presents an important part of Orthodox residents' lives, it is also partial. It is a picture that makes non-Orthodox organizations and social worlds invisible; Jewish neighborhood residents weren't *only* Orthodox Jews. The picture of summoning ignores other arenas and forms of summoning that may potentially pull residents away from their identification as Orthodox Jews.

For some social worlds such an oversight may not require elaboration. As a host of sociologists have argued, we live in a world made of increasingly complex and varied networks, and our identifications are pulled and reshaped in a multitude of ways as we navigate different social contexts.[1] Since most of these social worlds make only situationally circumscribed demands on our selves, the question of other affiliations would not, perhaps, be crucial. But the summoning of Orthodox residents in the Beverly–La Brea neighborhood was not so forgiving. Part of what made the summons as an Orthodox Jew powerful was precisely that it was considered a primary category of identification that could not be considered on a par with other available definitions of self. As a highly moralized definition of self it could not be neatly circumscribed to a set of situations.[2]

How, then, was this choreography of difference sustained? How did residents simultaneously move between Orthodox and non-Orthodox social worlds, while disavowing the pulls these other social worlds exerted? How do Orthodox Jews discursively and organizationally work to undo possible and actual identifications with and relationships to non-Jews?

Situational Boundaries

The way the non-Jewish world was cut off was most easily visible when the subject of intermarriage was invoked. At one of the first events that I attended during my first year of fieldwork, the rabbi leading the services spoke about the situation of American Jewry. Speaking to a crowd made up of both Orthodox and non-Orthodox Jews who had come to observe the Day of Atonement, the rabbi spoke of Orthodoxy as the last bulwark of Jewish defense in a landscape of assimilation. In his address, time after time, he referred to intermarriage as the white Holocaust. Where the Nazis had failed, intermarriage might yet succeed. In fact, others with whom I have since discussed this issue have gone further, affirming that if all the non-Jews born of intermarriage are counted, the souls lost by Judaism are actually more numerous than those murdered in Europe. Against the physical Holocaust of the Nazis, there was a spiritual threat, a "spiritual Holocaust."[3]

Jewish education was often explicitly seen through these lenses. Orthodox schools ensured that children did not have friends who were nonreligious or—much worse—non-Jewish. This, in turn, would also translate into a smaller chance of "marrying out."[4] Thus, for example, posted in Hebrew on the walls of one of the neighborhood synagogues, an advertisement for an Orthodox school in the neighborhood crystallized this function not only as the latent by-product of a religious choice but as the raison d'être of Jewish schooling. Large letters at the top of the ad made the message clear: "Mother, I think congratulations are due," and then, immediately below, "The heart of a mother cries: the bride is not Jewish." The message was clear—if Jewish parents wanted to avoid the tragedy of intermarriage, they should send their children to a Jewish school.[5]

This fear of assimilation was not exclusive to Orthodox residents of Los Angeles. On a broader scale, the possibility of the "disappearance" of Judaism, effected precisely through the process of becoming "white" in America,[6] is a concern shared by some Conservative and Reform Jews in the Unites States, and is a salient issue for many who study the demography of Judaism.[7] Not surprisingly, however, the urgency of the question, and the definition of Orthodoxy as an answer to such a threat, were both lively topics of discussion among Orthodox Jews, and generated studies showing Orthodoxy to be the only viable option against assimilation, at least so far as demographics were concerned. The projection shown in figure 2, published in a Jewish journal, is based on the 2000 Jewish census. It captures both the threat of assimilation and the moral position that Orthodox residents perceive themselves to occupy.[8] Treating "Judaism" through the lens of religious law—where Judaism is matrilineal, passed on and defined through the mother—the projection makes two points. First, it asserts that secular, Reform, and Conservative Judaism lose their populations through low birth rates and intermarriage. Accordingly, the three left-hand columns show Jews to be disappearing. Within two generations, there is only "half a Jew" if you are secular, one if Reform, two and a half if Conservative. Against this disastrous outcome, Centrist (Modern) Orthodox and strict Orthodox families (both Hasidic and Yeshivish) proliferate, thereby effectively "saving" American Judaism from dissipating into undefined whiteness.

But whereas the idea of the "white Holocaust" and the view of assimilation as a threat to Judaism did not denigrate the other as much as it used hyperbole in the attempt to fence in those within the in-group, it was often accompanied by narrative tropes that were less easily explained away. Perhaps it was a result of generations of persecution, during which the only outlet for threatened Jews was to make snide comments about

WILL YOUR GRANDCHILD BE JEWISH ?
(REVISITED)

= 10 people

	SECULAR	REFORM	CONSERVATIVE	CENTRIST ORTHODOX *	HASIDIC / YESHIVA ORTHODOX *
First Generation	100	100	100	100	100
Second Generation	41	46	66	163	324
Third Generation	17	21	44	266	1,050
Fourth Generation	7	10	29	434	3,401
Intermarriage Rate (NJPS 2000)	49%	46%	32%	6% *	6% *
Average Number of Children Per Woman (NAJDB based on NJPS 2000)	1.29	1.36	1.74	3.39 **	6.72 **

2   Report on Assimilation (Gordon and Horowitz 2006)

the coarseness of non-Jews and to tell miracle tales about Jews over-coming an evil Russian landlord; perhaps it was a corollary of the self-definition of a strict religious group that sees itself as chosen. Whatever the case may be, the strictly Orthodox residents I met—more often in Hasidic circles that in Yeshivish and Modern Orthodox ones—spoke of non-Jews in a manner that can only be described as anti-goyishe, an uncomfortable mirror image of anti-Semitism.

Thus, some rabbinical teachings hold that non-Jews do not have a "godly soul" but rather only an "animal soul" of physical desires; that they are indeed human but cannot surpass their nature to connect to godliness, unable to nullify themselves before their creator. Non-Jews are, in Kabbalistic terms, "shell." When I asked a few residents about this aspect of Jewish theology, I was told that it was wrong to interpret it as "anti-goyishe"—everyone had an animal soul, Jews included. Jews merely had the potential to become vessels of God, a rare occasion in itself; Jews were not necessarily "better," but simply "different."

Even if such an interpretation makes the shell metaphor seem somewhat less demeaning, this was not the way in which residents appropriated the term. Near the end of my fieldwork, when I was less timid about being confrontational, and when I felt enough of an insider to become personally hurt by the fact that people I cared about talked in these terms about non-Jews, I argued about this question with a young Hasidic man I was studying with, telling him that I found this depiction of non-Jews hard to swallow. As others had done, he told me that I had misunderstood the meaning of the text and asserted that Jews were merely different, though they did have a more important job to do in drawing the world back into godliness. I then asked him whether he had heard on any occasion that goyim were better than Jews. After all, if they were merely different, perhaps, on some level, they would be better. At first not able to find any example of such usage, the young yeshiva student finally triumphantly declared that he had in fact heard such statements when the head of the yeshiva he studied in would say to the students, "You are worse than goyim," understanding the irony of this answer only a few seconds after he had uttered it.

Indeed, the notion that goyim have no soul was evoked as a readily available way to organize a narrative. In the following fieldnotes excerpt, a woman in the neighborhood was telling me over Sabbath lunch about her family life in Russia:

Mrs. M. tells me that when the family lived in Russia, they stayed in a communal apartment, partly sharing it with a non-Jewish family. The family seemed nice enough, and was always very polite to them, but because it was communal, she knew that the wife was cheating on the husband when he was away. When the husband came home she was always extremely sweet, but when he wasn't, she had a "friend." She says she learnt from it that goyim are always two-faced. On the one hand they will be nice and polite, but you never know what they are up to when you are gone. She told about the neighbor's situation to some other woman she worked with, who was also non-Jewish, and before she got to tell her that the woman had had an affair, the co-worker told Mrs. M. that the reason she might have had problems with the husband was that she was having an affair. "Goyim know goyim," she tells me, "I didn't know what was happening because I am Jewish. This is the soul of the goy." Her husband chimes in, "Goyim don't have *neshama* [godly soul]."

The story was essentially a piece of gossip illustrating their old life in Soviet Russia. But as she narrated her travails, what became readily available to her and her husband was an anti-goyishe trope. Lacking the spark of Jewish holiness, the adulterous neighbor was explained away.

Originally a theological category, it becomes a characteristic used to denigrate the non-Jewish "other." The wife's infidelity is understandable in light of her not being imbued with "a soul."

These narrative tropes were usually wielded as a way to emphasize the superiority of Jews, as a symbolic boundary marker.[9] It was a genre tied to specific situations—when speaking to a small crowd about the importance of Orthodox Judaism as a bulwark of morality, for example, or when making sense (in the company of other Orthodox Jews) of residents' experiences with non-Jews. In the next prolonged episode in the field, during which I actively pushed this speech genre beyond its circumscribed situational niche, the ways in which such boundaries are performed comes to the fore:

At synagogue, a few people were having a postprayer gathering commemorating a yahrzeit, honoring the day on which the father of one of the synagogue members passed away. A few congregants put tables together in the main hall of the synagogue. Salads, lox and bagels are dished out, with some whiskey and vodka for obligatory toasts. And, as part of the occasion, the man who held the yahrzeit told a Hasidic tale:

In a town in Russia, in the nineteenth century, there was a Jewish guy who delved into secular knowledge and soon enough became a doctor. He was becoming less and less frum, though, and ended up marrying a non-Jewish woman and having two kids by her. Soon after his marriage, he started having dreams of his father. In his dreams, his father would come and plead that he return to his faith, return to the right path. The doctor ignored the dreams, but it proved too much for him. At a party one day, he suddenly saw an apparition of his dead father, pleading with him to forgo his evil ways. Mad with terror, the doctor took a little handgun he had and tried to shoot at the apparition, firing wildly into thin air.

Understanding then and there that he could not escape his true faith, the faith of his father, he ran from the party, away from his family. He took the first train out of town, and leaving his old life behind him, decided to become a simple, religious man. Moving far away, he became a Hasid. But though he knew he was doing the right thing, he felt that the sins of his past wouldn't let go. The goyishe children he had with the non-Jewish woman were constant reminders, for which there was no forgiveness. After a few years, devoured by his sense of guilt, the ex-doctor decided to see what had happened to his old life. He returned to the town he had lived in, though nobody recognized him, sporting a beard and long sidelocks and dressed in Hasidic garb. At the train station, he asked someone if they knew of the doctor that used to live there a while ago. The man knew who he was talking about, "Oh, the mad Jewish doctor, yes . . . He ran away, and two years ago, in a fire at his old house, his wife and children were killed." Then and there, the ex-doctor knew his sins were forgiven.

As the speaker ended his story, people around the table lifted their drinks, said *yeshar koyach* [roughly translated as "good job," and usually said when someone tells a "Jewish" story or is called up to perform some aspect of religious service], drank a toast, and went on to the next story, about the good deeds of the organizer's father. No one in the audience seemed to object to a moral tale in which the happy ending was brought about by a woman and two children being consumed by fire, dying for the sin of marrying a Jew, or being born.

Since I didn't want to interrupt the gathering, I kept my mouth shut. But later I had the opportunity to pursue this further.

That evening, I was invited to Joseph and Chaya's house, for a dinner with the couple, their young children, and Chaya's parents. After the children were put to sleep, I raised the topic, saying that a story told at synagogue bothered me deeply, but without saying that Joseph had been one of the people sitting around the table as the story was told. As I began telling the story, Chaya's father nodded. He knew the story and could tell in advance why I would find it offensive. And I was not the only one who found it so. When I finished telling the tale, Chaya was livid, saying that it was terrible, that she couldn't believe it was told at a religious gathering, telling me that I should not think for a moment that this was representative of Judaism. Joseph was very quiet, seemingly embarrassed, hoping that I would not "out" him as one of the people who had heard the story and said nothing.

The story added fuel to a longstanding discussion we had about Orthodoxy and the way Orthodox residents talked about the figure of the non-Jew. Joseph, a rabbi, tried to defend the Orthodox view. He usually said, as did other residents I spoke to, that the idea was not that Jews were better, but that we were different and had a different relation to God. We had a different role to play; we were "a kingdom of priests, a holy nation." Other nations and peoples had their own job to do on earth, the seven Noachide laws, for example. He said that in yeshiva his teachers often told him that the best analogy was that of a corporation. In a corporation you need both the executives and the janitors, he explained. It was just like that. I inquired if Jews were the janitors or the executives. No surprises there.

The debate was split three ways. Joseph protected the interpretation of Orthodoxy I was questioning. Chaya argued forcefully that I was misunderstanding Jewish theology, and that if I wanted to understand Judaism I should look not at what people *actually* say and do, but at what they are *supposed* to do—after all, we are still in exile, and it isn't a perfect world. Chaya's father took a more distanced stance, unsure why I was getting so upset with the story when it was clearly a social dynamic that I could find more or less in any group. But, at the same time, he enjoyed seeing his son-in-law squirm and countered his daughter's claim that this wasn't the true meaning of Jewish theology. Chaya's mother was mostly exasperated with her husband's cynicism.

On my way back home, I walked slowly with Chaya's father. In an introspective mood, he commented about the conversation we had just had, saying that he sometimes thought he could never be really frum. He had become religious later in life, and some of his best friends growing up, and still today at work, were non-Jews. Maybe he couldn't be "the real thing," he mused, without unreflexively assuming his own superiority as his son-in-law did.

I thought this episode was over, when, two weeks later, I got a phone call from Chaya. She called to tell me that she was so bothered by our conversation that she decided to check how other Orthodox people would react to the story. As she was a substitute teacher in one of the girls high schools in the neighborhood, she decided to bring it up in her eleventh-grade class and to spend a good chunk of the class discussing it. Though she needed to prod the girls a little, and she did start the class by asking what was wrong with the story, she said that some of the girls were appalled; one of them told her that the goyim in the story were treated as if they were simply "props" that have no life of their own, as if they were there only as background.

This case's meandering trajectory—beginning as a religious gathering in synagogue, morphing into a heated Sabbath dinner conversation, and ending up as a classroom discussion—specifies the way in which boundaries are treated in varying situations. In the appropriate situations (at a religious gathering, for example, or while telling other Orthodox Jews a tale in which non-Jews happened to be the protagonists), anti-goyishe remarks were not uncommon. In fact, although they were not a weekly occurrence, I heard dozens of remarks about non-Jews throughout my stay. From passing comments about the perceived immorality of Melrose as the "goyim's pleasure" (*goyishe naches*), to stories in which non-Jews represented impurity, these remarks constitute a situationally circumscribed genre.[10] But in a different context, the very people who made these remarks felt embarrassed about them, especially when the issue was scrutinized and not merely treated as the background for self-glorification. The schoolgirls who were offered the story as a "problem" had no trouble in understanding and articulating the dehumanization of non-Jews, their erasure qua people.

In the situational context of the speech genre, however, it would be difficult to stand against these remarks. As with sexist comments on a "boys' night out," it would be hard to raise objections without destroying a moment of togetherness, defined by the denigration of others. The religious connotation of these remarks made resistance within the situation more difficult still. Thus, for example, in another religious gathering a few months after the one above, the speaker (who had come from one of the centers of Orthodoxy on the East Coast) told a story with a similar narrative structure: a Jew becomes so assimilated that he marries a non-Jewish woman but later remembers who he really is and runs away. In this version of the story, however, the woman starts looking for him. The story was told to a large crowd of over a hundred men. At that point somebody remarked from the back, "*Nu*, a good wife." Everybody burst out laughing. The juxtaposition of the circumscribed genre with everyday marital expectations sustained a tension that made for a potent moment of humor.[11] The speaker, however, did not relinquish his authority and sharply remarked: "No! Profanity [*tum'a*] is always trying to corrupt us." In this moment, there was no place to playfully put the genre in abeyance.

It was once again striking that within the crowd, there were at least a few people who had told me in private conversations that they thought one of the biggest challenges facing the strict Orthodox Jewish world today was this sort of "anti-goyism." None of them said a word. And if they did notice that anything was amiss, it did not ultimately seem like an appropriate place to intervene, either out of respect for the guest or because it would destroy the mood of the occasion. The degradation of non-Jews was situationally circumscribed but within these confines hard to resist.

To return to the extended fieldnotes entry above, another revealing episode was Chaya's father's rumination about his inability to truly be "in." Weaving in and out of Orthodoxy—because of both his biography and his work in the "non-Jewish" world—was a challenge he had to face. In moments of problematization (such as those brought about by ethnographic interference), he couldn't so easily defend the superiority of Jews. In order to be summoned into a social world that makes deep moral claims on those summoned, the ties of summoning coming from other social worlds need to be at least temporarily cut.

Part of what makes the anti-goyishe genre so striking is that it is a situational genre that makes intersituational claims on actors' selfhood. And yet for almost all residents this necessitated a complex choreography of difference. Most residents had goyishe occupations where they worked with goyim and had goyim friends; it was hard to sustain such boundaries when the very way they lived their lives was often indistinguishable from that of their non-Jewish, middle-class neighbors.[12]

To do so, most residents I knew carefully cordoned off their non-Orthodox working lives when they were in religious situations—around the Sabbath table, in the synagogue, during religious get-togethers. It wasn't that people spoke only about religious matters in these situations. There was quite a bit of gossip, talk about personal lives, even (though more rarely) talk of what they actually did at work. What was elided was the social world that pulled them into this other world, *who they did it with*. As I went through my notes of almost five years, I realized that after all this time I knew almost nothing about these relationships. The interactional work environment, which in other contexts is the most salient aspect of work-life narratives, was completely obscured. Not only were non-Jews never invited to the Sabbath meal or to High Holidays, but they were also discursively dropped from the scene.[13] The general sensibility that governed the Orthodox neighborhood life as a speech genre determined not only what to talk about and how to talk about it but also what remained in the conversational shadows.[14]

In fact, one of the only prolonged conversations I heard about my friends' co-workers in a religious situation took place when, at one Sabbath meal, a few of them started to talk about the problems they had with handshaking in the workplace. Strict Orthodox men are not supposed to touch women who are not their immediate family members (and vice versa). But in some work situations, a handshake with someone of the opposite sex is expected, and failing to shake the hand of a female colleague—or worse, a boss—could be taken as an affront:

Moishe was telling how he was interviewed for a new position in the organization he worked for, and at the end of what he thought was a very successful interview, the woman interviewing him extended her hand to shake it. He didn't extend his hand, and after an awkward pause she retracted her hand. "This was the end of this job," he mused, although he knew that some of his non-Jewish co-workers later told the interviewer that he was a good worker. Another man sitting around the table said that he really tried not to get into a situation where he would offend a woman by refusing to shake her hand. He said that when he knew that he would be in a situation where a handshake with a woman would be expected, he made sure to hold something in both his hands—a book and a bottle of water, for example. Handshakes were expected only at the first second of introduction, or at the very end of the meeting, so simply having his hands occupied for this brief part of the situation would do the trick.

Again, the mention of non-Jewish co-workers here is not leveraged to tell a tale of work companionship. The topic of the discussion is the pragmatic challenges facing Jews in their everyday lives outside the confines of Jewish life—the interactional potholes of the non-Jewish world. It was only in writing up my fieldnotes that I realized that at least some relationships with Moishe's co-workers had to be more meaningful—some people did, after all, vouch for him.

Indeed, on one rare occasion when non-Jews were discussed on a Sabbath, the speaker had to "repair" his own story:

At the Alstein family, the husband—an engineer—talks about a conversation he had with a non-Jewish colleague. The guy was an Egyptian-born engineer who works in his department. They started talking about religion, and his co-worker reminisced about his childhood in Egypt, and about the Jewish friends he used to have. Around the table, sitting with us, is another man from the synagogue, Mrs. Alstein, and their daughter, a teenage girl, now going to seminary [the girls' post-high-school equivalent of a yeshiva]. As he is talking about his conversation, his daughter asks, aghast, "You were talking to this Arab?!" Performing a double-take, Mr. Alstein quickly says something like "Yeah, I was talking to him, and then I got into my car and sped out of there as fast as I could." Everybody laughs, and the conversation turns to another topic.

It is obvious, of course, that the end of the story is made up, tacked onto the actual story as a form of social repair.[15] The question, then, is: what exactly is being repaired here? There is nothing in the conversation itself that is unbecoming—the conversation concerned Jewish life, and Jews were presented in a flattering light. It was thus "utterable" within the coordinates of Orthodox life. The problem was rather the very possibility of a Jew conversing with a non-Jew—and an Arab to boot—simply as two co-workers would. The daughter none too subtly criticized her father for having even taken part in such an interaction with an Arab, who is presumably deemed worse than other non-Jews.[16] When the father jokingly insisted that he had done his utmost to escape the situation, he retroactively represented a friendly interaction with a co-worker as a dangerous encounter. Situationally, the topic was "diffused," and the dinner could continue.

It was only when speaking to my best friends in the neighborhood, and then only when I inquired about their working lives, that I heard about office jokes, about friendships in the workplace, or how one of my friends regularly went with a few office friends to a shooting range. But these friendships were almost always kept quiet. The same people who might, in one situation, mention their friendships with non-Jews would in other contexts either silently listen to the kind of anti-goyishe remarks I described earlier or even actively produce such remarks on their own.

The way Orthodox residents spoke, or didn't speak, of the non-Jews they interacted with allowed them to enact their undivided belonging. Although it may indeed be the case that for some—those who work "Jewish jobs" and perhaps a few others—this speech genre actually reflected the way they experienced their lives across situations, this is highly unlikely. But, whether or not it reflected their experience, it was a collective act that sustained the illusion of an intersituational purity of self. By discursively erasing or degrading the non-Jew, residents could treat the circumscribed set of Orthodox situations as if they defined their entire being. It was in this sense that the boundary between Jews and non-Jews often seemed so dramatic.

Shabbos Goys and Neighborly Relations

The relationship between the summoning of an Orthodox Jewish self and interaction with non-Jews, however, is not completely captured by the dynamics I outlined above. At least in one set of situations, Orthodox residents were *more* likely to interact with non-Jews. It was the case of the *Shabbos goy*—the Sabbath Gentile.

Thus, the fact that Orthodox Jews are not allowed to perform specific actions on the Sabbath—mundane actions such as turning electric switches on and off—is often a recipe for minor crises. One incident that happened to me more than once, and at one point or another to almost everybody else I knew in the neighborhood, was to forget to turn off the lights in the bedroom before the Sabbath. When this happened, the usual thing to do was to sleep with the lights turned on, burying one's head under the blankets or the pillow.[17] There was, however, another option. Although Jews could not perform these actions themselves, they could conceivably ask non-Jews to perform the actions for them. Jewish theology does not require non-Jews to follow most religious commandments that Jews should ideally abide by. Indeed, according to the common interpretation of religious law, non-Jews are *not* allowed to keep the Sabbath. Hence the institution of the Shabbos goy: a non-Jew who is asked to perform actions for the benefit of Orthodox Jews on the Sabbath—and in the Beverly–La Brea neighborhood this was inevitably a non-Jewish neighbor.

Residents I knew did not often ask their non-Jewish neighbors to perform such actions for them and usually simply suffered the inconvenience. Sometimes, however, the inconvenience was deemed bothersome enough for them to ask a non-Jewish neighbor for help. To take one example, a Hasidic friend told me that he had first gotten to know his neighbors when he came home with his wife one Friday night and realized that they had both forgotten to turn off the lights in the refrigerator. This meant that opening the refrigerator would cause the light to turn on, thereby violating the laws of Sabbath. As all of their Sabbath food was in the fridge, this also meant that they were stuck with food just out of reach. On this occasion, my friend went to his neighbors' house and tried to explain to them what had happened—that he needed them to open the fridge and turn off the light switch in it so that they could eat their Friday night meal and their Saturday lunch.

What makes these interactions initially even more awkward is that, in compliance with religious edicts, Orthodox Jews cannot directly ask the non-Jew to perform the action. This, in effect, would amount to performing the action oneself. Instead, they have to ask in a roundabout manner. As my friend joked while narrating the incident, he had to go next door, introduce himself, and then explain to his bewildered neighbors that Orthodox Jews could not perform certain actions on the Sabbath and that he had forgotten to turn off the refrigerator lights. He could not, however, explicitly say that he needed their help, instead being forced to say something like: "Isn't it a shame that the food is there, but I can't open the fridge? It would be nice if someone opened the fridge and turned off the lights . . ." He had to wait for his neighbors to "get it" themselves before letting them in and showing them the fridge.

Once neighbors knew about Orthodox religious edicts, of course, they were a valuable resource. They understood the roundabout way of speaking as a request and could help their neighbors without the interactional ambiguities that my friend encountered. Thus, most families that I knew had one or two neighbors with whom they had cemented a Shabbos goy relationship, and to whom they could turn on the rare occasions when they needed their help. This created a specific kind of neighborly relationship, a way of interacting that seemed to puncture the boundary between Jew and non-Jew among neighbors. In fact, it propelled residents to know their neighbors probably more than they otherwise would, Orthodox or not. And I have never heard anyone speak ill about the Shabbos goys. Residents were thankful if their neighbors would help them, and in contrast to "the generalized goy," had only good things to say about them.

Yet although such interactions created ties between Orthodox residents and their non-Jewish neighbors, these relationships did not deepen much beyond the occasional exchange. As they did not usually visit their neighbors' houses, could not eat there because of kosher dietary regulations, and rarely invited them over, as far as I could tell the relationship remained superficial. It was an instance of "neighboring," the small interactions that make for good neighborly relations as well as for the creation of a (limited) sense of communal space.[18]

Indeed, the interactions between the Orthodox and their non-Jewish residents in these cases actually served to deepen their summoning as Orthodox Jews. Since the pragmatic problem they encountered was tied to religious law, the interaction was conducted under the auspices of an Orthodox self. This is not to say that nothing but an Orthodox self was evoked in these cases, or that Orthodox families never otherwise interacted with their non-Orthodox neighbors. Some, of course, did. Orthodox residents got to know their neighbors, perhaps more than did other residents of large cities. And yet such encounters were already marked, already setting the categories of Jew/non-Jew as salient markers of self.

Domestication: On Kosherizing the Goyishe World

The ways in which residents managed interaction with non-Jews could not, by themselves, make the summoning of the non-Jewish world they lived in disappear. The attempt to craft a distinct Jewish self, especially in stricter subaffiliations of Orthodoxy, included an additional challenge— that of the world of consumption and leisure. The non-Jewish world did not materialize only beyond the physical limits of the home, or only in a neatly circumscribed set of situations. Rather, Orthodox residents continually had to reconstruct and reaffirm their Orthodoxy within the private sphere, balancing ways of life that they shared with other middle-class families against a specifically "Orthodox" life.

Differences between subaffiliations were salient in this regard, and translated into different modes of balancing an "Orthodox" life and a middle-class white one. Thus, some Hasidic families did not even have internet and would not let their children play any game that smacked of the "outside" world; even playing basketball was frowned upon. On the other end of this spectrum, some strict Orthodox residents admitted to watching movies on their computers and reading world literature, while some Modern Orthodox residents struck an even more delicate balance, openly going to the movies, listening to nonreligious music, and reading literature, while trying to avoid what they saw as the extremes of American secular culture. Although the description below cannot be generalizable to "the neighborhood," in the sense that different households struck a balance in different ways, Orthodox residents did share a basic problem— that of moving between the different identification categories that they occupied as these were translated into status-group positions in the realm of consumption and leisure.

Children's leisure was one of the most explicit arenas for such precarious balancing acts. Almost all of the Orthodox residents, even those who came from the most observant backgrounds, were, by and large, raised in an era in which they read non-Jewish literature and played non-Jewish games, sometimes even with non-Jewish friends. But the strict Orthodox world has since "moved to the right" and has become more insular and wary of secular culture.[19] This became practically problematic as parents had to manage the lives of their children, to decide the kinds of games and literature to which their children were to be exposed.

This dilemma was not unique to Jewish Orthodox Los Angeles or even the Orthodox world more generally, but is a salient issue other American strict religious groups grapple with. And as in Evangelical and fundamentalist Christian circles,[20] there has emerged over the last few decades a parallel world of consumption. This market includes everything from mystery novels to computer games and board games modeled on secular American popular culture but that replace the "profanity" and nonreligious character of these products with religious counterparts. There are, for example, "Jewish" mystery novels and detective books, in which the heroes are young Orthodox kids—usually pitted against Arabs, Nazis, or some combination of the two. The goys in these books are usually the antagonists, though supporting characters such as policemen or members of the American government are often "good guys" who are grateful to the resourceful little Orthodox children for saving the world from Arab terrorists and their ilk.

Similarly, Orthodox Muppet shows could be accessed via internet (as most strict Orthodox families did not own a television set), with jokes of rogue pita sandwiches that were attempting to destroy the planet. Board and card games were also made kosher. For example, in the card game "Apples to Apples"[21] the nouns and some of the adjectives were kosherized. Nouns in the Jewish version included "sidelocks," "the Torah," "Golda Meir,"[22] "the Ten Commandments," and "the state of Israel." Thus, for example, during a game with three young girls in one family, and in response to the description "This is awesome," the game's judge had to decide which noun was more "awesome": "mothers," "Israel," or "gefilte fish" ("Israel" won by unanimous vote, as the girls giggled and could not bring themselves to pair the noun "mother" with "awesome" while not even considering "gefilte fish"). A book in another household contained a story about the pirates of evil deeds: when a shipful of pirates symbolizing religious vices see the error of their ways, the pirates reappear with yarmulkes and their evil pirate beards are transformed into the beards of pious Jews.

In this way, then, Orthodox residents could enjoy both worlds. In one sense they raised their children in a similar fashion to the way they themselves were raised—Orthodox children played familiar board games, read children's books about nice children doing good deeds, and later detective stories in which smart little kids outwitted the forces of evil. On the other hand, they replaced the content within the form. The heroes and heroines were all Jewish; instead of magicians, righteous men performed miracles with the help of God.

This construction of parallel consumption was taken one step further when parents sometimes improvised their own "kosher" topics and toys. Like parents everywhere, Orthodox residents sometimes bought their children presents they later regretted and found themselves trying in vain to claim that a pirate ship they bought was actually "a ship of explorers" so that their children would not be exposed to violence. The transformation of objects bought also gained another layer of meaning, however, when parents creatively tried to transform non-Jewish objects of consumption into "kosher" objects that their children could play with. Thus, for example, the object in figure 3 is a pencil case featuring "Snow White and the Prince" that I saw two children of a friend of mine playing with when I visited their house. The metal pencil case had different pieces of magnetic clothes that the children could use to dress the figures. However, in order to make the game palatable, their mother had added her own magnetic accouterments, cutting them out of an old religious refrigerator magnet she had. Adding these new magnets, she transformed "Snow White" into "the Eidel Princess" (the virtuous princess), and the Prince into "Ben Torah" (the man of Torah / Torah scholar). The two children, who were too young to read the names of the characters on the pencil case, were calling them by their new names. When I asked their mother why she had done this, and why she had changed the names (after all, what was wrong with the original names?), she said she did not want her children to tell others about playing with "Snow White," not because there was anything necessarily wrong with these particular toys or images, but because if they used these names, others might think that they knew who and what "Snow White and the Prince" were, thereby implying that they had seen the movie and thus transgressed into the secular world of entertainment.

Striking such a balance also required parents to constantly make fine-tuned choices regarding the secular world. Thus, some books, such as

3   "The Eidel Princess and the Ben Torah" (photo by author)

those written by Dr. Seuss, were usually deemed acceptable, while others weren't. This was a much-discussed topic. Was *Dr. Dolittle*, for example, a title that children could read? What of *Star Wars* movies (generally, no)? Or *Star Wars* Lego figurines (generally, yes)? Parents had to provide guidelines for children that were usually made in an ad hoc fashion, with every family I knew striking its own balance, often incoherently, as different situations arose. In some cases, if children went to pray at synagogue and did their (Jewish) homework, they were then allowed to read *Harry Potter* (a book that some parents first tried to ban, as it is based on the assumption of pagan-like magic), get a new skateboard, or go to Six Flags theme park on a Sunday.

A similar problem had to be managed as far as adults' leisure was concerned. Here, of course, things were often less explicit. Friends I had known for a long period of time sometimes surprised me by confessing to a perfect knowledge of movies (downloaded from the internet), by listening to "non-Jewish" music in their cars, or by turning out to be avid science fiction readers. Adults performed their own balancing acts. But these were performed away from the public eye, and they did not usually have to think about the effects of their decisions on how others might perceive them in future interactions.

One of the advantages of looking at the way that parents managed their children's leisure was that this management was made visible. Children could not be counted on to compartmentalize their lives. As the example of "Snow White/The Eidel Princess" illustrates, parents were partly reacting to the fact that they could never know what children would say, or to whom. This does not mean that they managed their children's consumption "for show." This was an existential concern and a crucial part of the way they wanted to raise their children, much like the concern of many non-Orthodox families who try to control their children's leisure. But they had to manage children's present and possible future interactions, through which they—as parents—might become implicated in raising their kids in specifically "non-Orthodox" ways.

One location that did remain visible in adult consumption of "American culture," and thus needed to be more explicitly managed, was the realm of home design: what kinds of pictures to hang on the walls, how to decorate the exterior, what brands of wine to drink and what food to eat. Although there were specifically religious objects that were posited for all to see—religious books and Judaica articles usually stored on shelves with glass doors—other decisions were less apparent. The injunction not to place images of men, and obviously not of women, in the house meant that many people framed abstract landscapes, popular throughout American homes.[23] Similarly, a couple of months after I moved into the neighborhood, I came home to see a string of blue and purple lights on the front lawn. When I saw my landlord, I said that I liked the decorations and asked if they were new. He said they were actually on most of the year but he took them down for a few months every year "so it won't look like something else"—so that passersby would not mistake them for Christmas lights.

The example that perhaps best crystallizes the kosherizing of middle-class consumption had to do with what people in the neighborhood drank. As the Sabbath meals were almost invariably accompanied by wine, there was a robust market for kosher wine.[24] Time after time, residents made fun of the common stereotype of the Manischewitz-drinking Orthodox Jew. Residents often laughed at the image, relating it to a distant, working-class immigrant past. Whereas I was never served Manischewitz, a number of better "midlevel" wines were commonly consumed. Baron Herzog, Bartenura, as well as Israeli Yarden wines, costing between twelve and thirty dollars a bottle, were the wines of choice. Although many Jews still drink Manischewitz—especially those who either cannot afford better wines or need a "kosher wine" and know that Manischewitz is a safe bet—the new selection of American, European, and Israeli kosher wines (alongside scotch, which is almost always kosher) was the hallmark of Sabbath and High Holidays meals in the Beverly–La Brea neighborhood. Much like Orthodox Jewish young-adult detective novels, board games, or abstract art, this was a way to be both strictly Orthodox and a middle-class consumer.

Boundaries and Distinctions, or, What Do Balancing Acts Balance?

Throughout this chapter, the recurring question has been how Orthodox residents manage the pulls of the non-Jewish world surrounding them—how they engage in the precarious balancing act between Orthodox and un-Orthodox selves. Taking this chapter into account along with the previous chapter, I can now say something more general about the construction of difference: how patterns of summoning can help sociologists of culture and community think about the relationship between status distinctions within the group and the boundaries between groups.

At first glance, the difference between distinctions and boundaries may seem obvious. In the case of the differences *between* Jews, there is a hierarchy (or spectrum) that operates within the "field" of Jewish life.[25] Boundaries, on the other hand, are usually conceived as binary. Rather than the visual metaphor of the field or the totem pole, boundaries are relatively sharp. You are on one side of the boundary or on the other— you either are or aren't Jewish.[26]

A closer inspection of the kind of actions described in this chapter and the previous one, however, quickly dispels such an attempt to use the metaphors' visual cues as ways to analytically distinguish them from each other. Situations are often quite binary: you are either religious from birth (an FFB) or a newly religious *ba'al tshuva* (BT), either Yeshivish or Hasidic, either Chabad or Satmar, either Jewish or not. And in the cases of both internal distinctions and the Jew/non-Jew boundary, the permeability of the boundary cannot be used as a litmus test. The boundaries between Jews and non-Jews are transcended, usually on a daily basis; the boundaries between different kinds of Jews are quite rigid in many situations.

As these actions cannot be neatly differentiated, it is tempting to move in the opposite direction and discard the notion that there is any actual difference between sustaining distinctions and boundary work. In this sense, an analysis of action reduces status hierarchies to a specific subset of boundary interactions performed within the larger categorical divide. But this view, parsimonious as it is, is misguided for both empirical and theoretical reasons. On the empirical side, such a reduction misses the different pragmatic challenges that residents faced when they located themselves socially. It misses the fact that even if these challenges had much in common, Orthodox residents were engaging in very different projects when they enacted differences between Jews and when they talked (or avoided talking) about the non-Jewish world.

From a theoretical perspective, this view misses the larger context of the situation and its intersituational pragmatics of action. By focusing on the structure of differentiation of disembedded action, we may miss its larger structure. Who is talking to whom? Where? When? How? And to what ends?[27] The difference may be located not in situated action but in the way that people were summoned *intersituationally*. Situations and practices cannot be analyzed as locked in the "here and now." Rather, the meaning of a situation is always related to the invisible situations against which it is defined. Thus, although there may be nothing inherently different between the internal differentiations discussed in chapter 5 and the external ones discussed here, the pattern of the situations in which these were embedded, as well as the pragmatic challenges that actors faced, were of a different sort.

On this pragmatic level, the problem of the "Jewish/non-Jewish" boundary was that of disentangling themselves from the webs of summoning extended by the non-Orthodox world, remaining different while at the same time partaking in the non-Jewish world in the spheres of work and of leisure; how to reconcile themselves with the fact that at least on the level of leisure and consumption—despite a life marked by religious practice and interaction—they were middle-class, white Americans who understood themselves as such. In this sense, the pragmatic problem they faced was precisely the reverse of the one that they encountered in their interaction with "other kinds of Jews." The problem with non-Jews was that intersituational difference had to be maintained even when, for all practical purposes, it was only situationally enacted; homogeneity had to be transcended. The pragmatic challenge in the case of different kinds of Jews was to know in which situations differences were relevant and in which situations they could (and indeed *should*) be transcended; to move between heterogeneous subaffiliations and biographical patterns and a homogenous category-cum-group.

The specific structure of distinctions was thus found not in the situational construction of difference but in the structure of these situations in relation to other situations. The differences between different kinds of Jews were transcended *in specific Jewish situations*, whether during prayers, at specific times of the year, or through the educational system. The pragmatics of the particular "distinction" situation had to be weighed in relation to similar situations where such distinctions were irrelevant. Similarly, everybody knew that the differences between Jews and non-Jews were transcended on a daily basis—at least for people who worked "non-Jewish" jobs. In "Jewish" situations, however, these moments had to be brushed aside, silenced, erased.

The notion of summoning thus sensitizes us to the patterned way in which identifications are evoked not only within but also *across* situations. This pattern of situations, then, is expected by actors as well as "read" by their interlocutors. Although the construction of difference may seem similar within situations, it does not seem so to actors precisely because they have learned to expect the way they move across situations, and across identifications, in their everyday life.

SEVEN

The Neighborhood as Moral Obstacle Course

Living off Melrose is a delicate affair. Although Orthodox Jews were middle-class, white residents in a middle-class, white neighborhood, they were simultaneously different both in their own eyes and in the eyes of others. Everyday life thus required Orthodox residents to navigate a space that was not "Jewish" but rather designed for non-Jews (or, at least, non-Orthodox Jews), some of whom belonged to subcultures that Orthodox residents found particularly unappealing. In this chapter, I take a look at the mundane interactions that Orthodox residents negotiated in their everyday walks in the neighborhood,[1] how Orthodox residents reconstituted their Orthodoxy as they literally bumped into the space that they inhabited; how the sights, sounds, and smells of the neighborhood continuously summoned them.

What these situations reveal is the physical and symbolic terrain that Orthodox residents expected to traverse on a regular basis. This is the realm of fleeting experiences. And though some of the interactions I describe may be quite striking, everyday life is usually not the stuff of great drama. The microdramas of everyday life, almost imperceptible, are nonetheless existentially crucial, constituting the fabric upon which larger moments play out. Although I have written about summoning mostly in the context of interactions between people, it occurs also in encountering the nonhuman world surrounding actors. Summoning emerges in the seams between actors' projects and external interactional pressures to occupy a specific identification.

And although such pressures usually come directly from people, and are always mediated through a world of human meaning, they may often emerge in moments of interaction with the nonhuman world. These moments were an important part of the texture of Orthodox commitments and patterns of summoning—the subtle situations in which they encountered their neighborhood and found themselves in interactions they did not intentionally conjure.[2]

Such moments also form a relatively silent domain. In contrast to questions such as history, organizational structures, or the grating enunciation of boundaries and distinctions, these are things that are often not deemed worthy of talking about. The data I bring out in this chapter, then, are based mostly on participant observation, not on what people usually say that they do but on offhand snippets of stories they tell, on interactions I happened to witness while living my own life in the neighborhood, and on the reactions I myself elicited as people reacted to me as "a Jew" based on markers such as the yarmulke.

Phenomenological Maps: Of Hotdog Stands and Motion Sensors

On a weekend visit to Crown Heights, Brooklyn, around the end of my ethnographic foray in Los Angeles, I took a walk around the neighborhood with my host, a relative of a friend from Los Angeles. As we were walking through the neighborhood, seemingly surrounded by a homogenous Hasidic life on the blocks around the Chabad-Lubavitcher main synagogue, he pointed out a Christian school and a church. "See this, the kind of *tum'a* [profanity] we have in *our* neighborhood," he observed, shaking his head in disapproval. Walking with him, I was struck by the fact that although I had heard Orthodox residents in Los Angeles voice their disapproval of the space they lived in, I had never heard them relate to it as "our" space, "our" neighborhood.

Indeed, as opposed to Orthodox communities in Israel and some communities on the East Coast of the United States, the Beverly–La Brea neighborhood was not considered a "Jewish space." Although Orthodox Jews were extremely visible, they were a minority, and the main transportation arteries in the neighborhood were spaces in which secular retail and subcultures thrived. Whereas in a neighborhood like Crown Heights, Orthodox Jewish residents may feel entitled to the space they live in— feeling secure enough to mobilize to reject perceived "threats,"[3] or just speaking of the neighborhood as an Orthodox space—in the Beverly–La

Brea area Orthodox Jews did not exhibit a similar entitlement. On the periphery of the Orthodox world, it was not *their* neighborhood in the same sense.

Although they usually tried to avoid the places and objects they found most sacrilegious, Orthodox resident almost never attempted to change the space they inhabited. An almost lone counterexample involved one educational institution that politely asked an advertiser to take down a condom advertisement that was placed on top of the Orthodox institution's main building. But, generally, any effort to make changes in neighborhood space was seen as a quixotic attempt. When one friend heard that a few Orthodox Jews in the neighborhood had asked a local supermarket to offer one checkout line without tabloids featuring half-naked celebrities—so they wouldn't be exposed to profanity while waiting in line—he told me he thought the idea was naïve: "And what happens when they go out of the supermarket? Will they change the ads, the streets, the city? We are living on Melrose . . . I mean, if I wanted to live in New Square [a homogeneous Hasidic-Orthodox town in New Jersey], I would move to New Square."

This mingling of Jewish and non-Jewish life in the neighborhood was especially striking since, as I noted before, Los Angeles zoning laws allowed religious organizations to inhabit only the main thoroughfares in the neighborhood—the same streets in which the transgressive shopping venues and businesses could be located. This, then, made the neighborhood an extremely dense moral space.[4] When Orthodox Jews went to synagogue or school, they inevitably encountered "profane" secular institutions—skulls and stuffed animals watched the passerby with dead bead eyes; lingerie stores paraded skimpily dressed manikins; restaurants sold and advertised nonkosher food; specialized stores sold elaborate smoking instruments to trendy teenagers; a movie theater catering to an LGBT crowd was located a block away from some of the neighborhood's main synagogues.

This overlaying of religious and secular made for a specific geography of purity and danger, a moral obstacle course where the exalted and the desecrating were literally adjacent. This, in turn, made for specific ways of mapping space, where one tried to avoid symbolic risk, calculating the shortest way to get from residential streets to a religious institution without appearing to stroll through the profanity of Melrose, Beverly, and La Brea. Furthermore, the ways in which residents avoided such threats and made sense of their surroundings transformed space into a communal place—one where Orthodox Jews could assume that other Orthodox Jews saw the invisible obstacles in similar ways, taught each other how to avoid such threats, and sometimes criticized fellow residents if they appeared to transgress the boundaries of either safety or purity of self. In all these ways, through the mediation of smells, sights, and gossip, the streets themselves summoned Orthodox residents into being.

These navigations echo those found by ethnographers studying quite different urban surroundings. Analyzing walking patterns in a black, poverty-stricken neighborhood, Elijah Anderson describes how informal patterns of neighborly interactions become existential everyday questions: how people make sense of space by avoiding "dangerous" people on the street, developing inconspicuous ways of walking, or showing off a powerful dog. The layering of racialized attitudes and the patterning of space made the residents he studied walk differently when they encountered a young black man, stopped people from crossing certain streets, and created an almost invisible, yet highly patterned, set of ways to relate and navigate the physical environment.[5] Similarly, in an ethnography of political culture in France and Finland, Eeva Luhtakallio shows how young radical activists experientially mapped their French neighborhood, avoiding the "fascist" grocery stores and pubs, and making sure they walked by, and checked out, walls upon which political slogans and information were plastered.[6]

A similar cartography helped constitute the ways Orthodox residents saw both themselves and others. Such a mapping, however, was neither completely stable nor posted on a simple totem pole of the sacred and profane. The same store that might be passed as a matter of habit became morally laden in specific situations and times; whereas the reaction to some objects connoted boundaries between all Orthodox Jews and the non-Orthodox other, others connoted differences between sub-affiliations within the Orthodox neighborhood, or even one's personal understanding of self. Moreover, this neighborhood cartography also shifted with religious time cycles such as the coming of the Sabbath and religious holidays—transformations that usually remained invisible to other residents and shoppers sharing the streets,[7] but that turned everyday navigations into a problematic endeavor.

Map 3—an actual map of a small part of the neighborhood—exemplifies some of the ways in which the neighborhood provided moral obstacles Orthodox Jews traversed. Perhaps the most mundane problem residents faced, though perhaps one of the most surprising from an outsider's perspective, was pedestrian traffic lights (see points 1a and 1b in map 3). If an Orthodox Jew had to cross a large street on the Sabbath, he or she faced an uneasy predicament. This was because the Torah decree that Jews should not perform work on the Sabbath has been interpreted

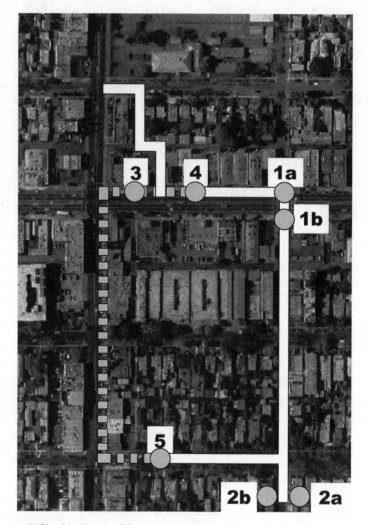

Map 3   Walking Map (source: GIS map)

broadly in the Orthodox world. Thus, manipulating electric devices is considered a forbidden form of work both because an electrical spark is considered fire (and lighting a fire is a form of work) and because it involves closing an electrical circuit (and is thus considered to be the work of finishing an unfinished object). This decree mostly concerns the organization of life at home. However, Los Angeles is a highly technological world: many crosswalks require pedestrians to press a button in order for the light to turn green.

Residents could opt for different strategies: hypothetically they could violate the laws of the Sabbath and push the button in open transgression of Torah law (which I have never seen happen or heard of); they could take their chances and cross the street on a red light, which people often did, as car traffic lights turn red periodically even when the pedestrian lights do not follow suit; they could wait for a non-Jewish pedestrian to press the button for them; or they could go out of their way to reach a crosswalk in which the lights changed automatically. This was far from an abstract theological problem, but a practical obstacle:

Ze'ev, his wife and girls, and I walk together to his place on the Sabbath. As we reach the crosswalk, we see a police car parked on the other side of La Brea. There are no other pedestrians trying to cross. Ze'ev looks at the lights and tells us we should probably continue to the next crossing. I ask why, and he says that if the police officer stops him, he will not be able to write down his details [writing is considered work, and therefore forbidden on the Sabbath], and anyway, he doesn't want a ticket. We continue walking, and I ask if he can't write a letter to the neighborhood board or something, so the pedestrian lights would turn green automatically. He says he thought about it, and talked to some people, but they never got around to actually doing it. On the next crossing, a non-Orthodox pedestrian on the other side of the street pushes the button, and we all cross.

In fact, when I asked about traffic lights at one dinner with some Orthodox neighbors, a lively discussion ensued. All four family members sitting at the table knew exactly which traffic lights were automatic and which were not, and commiserated about our living near a button-operated crosswalk. One woman recounted an episode in which she and her elderly mother had to wait for almost fifteen minutes for someone to push the button for them. Seeing a jogger running along, she inquired if he was by any chance crossing the street, in hopes that he would act as a Shabbos goy. The jogger would not, and to make things worse, laughed and said that he, too, was Jewish. The others nodded reproachfully; they had heard this story before. "He was doing it just to spite her, to make her wait," her son commented.

Crossing the streets is a simple, explicitly codified, action. All one has to do is remember *not* to touch the button. In that sense it is similar to flipping the electronic switches within the Orthodox household, which become similarly prohibited during the Sabbath. In order to avoid accidental transgressions residents sometimes plastered the electric switches with a Band-Aid on the Sabbath to prevent themselves from turning them off or on as a matter of habit. Outside the house, people simply had to be mindful.

Other elements of the environment, however, required more delicate maneuvers and a more durable cartography. Thus, for example, garages in many of the more upscale houses in the community were supplied with motion sensors, so that the garage lights automatically turned on when a car or person—including an Orthodox Jew—came close. Although this did not constitute a direct transgression of religious rules (the light was not turned on as a result of purposeful action, nor was it done in order to benefit the Orthodox Jew), Orthodox residents mapped the space to avoid this inadvertent transgression (see points 2a and 2b on map 3):

Walking back from the synagogue to Shlomo's house on Friday night, we walk along with the Rubin family. Ze'ev and his family just moved into a new house in the neighborhood, about half a block north of the Rubin family, and about five blocks east of where they lived before. While walking down the street leading to their block, Shlomo Rubin turns to Ze'ev. "We need to cross the street here, the lights turn on." Ze'ev thanks him and takes a long look at the house garage, seemingly engraving it in memory. On the other side of the street, the opposite garage has its lights on. Shlomo says, "Here too. Now it is lit, but usually you have to walk diagonally." We all walk diagonally, between the two houses, and Ze'ev thanks Shlomo. Months later, when I go to Ze'ev, he walks diagonally when he reaches this section of the street.

The work implied in this cartography is thus not a solitary endeavor. It is a collective enterprise, and creates a communal way of walking the streets. By pointing out to Ze'ev that he is in danger of transgressing a religious edict, and describing the religiously safe way to walk through the neighborhood on the Sabbath, Shlomo extends an important civility. Having known Ze'ev for a few years, Shlomo assumes that—at least ideally—they share the same religious cartography, the same experiential relationship to space. Like a neighbor pointing out a pothole or a particularly vicious dog to the new family on the block, he spares him from learning the hard way. Additionally, this action forges an understanding of a shared moral community of perception—the same areas, neutral for non-Orthodox residents, posit a moral danger for the Orthodox and should be circumnavigated. Indeed, the metaphor of navigating danger was not alien to residents. As I walked with Ze'ev to his home on a different occasion a few months later, he raised the issue himself and jokingly invoked Greek mythology, referring to the two garage motions sensors that Shlomo showed him in the last excerpt as "my Scylla and Charybdis."

Though Orthodox residents often navigated such street perils alone, these edicts and dangers afforded an opportunity for interaction. Everyday objects such as crosswalks and garage motion sensors became a resource for the production of experiential commonality.[8] Moreover, the shared navigations of space separated the perceptions and experiences of the Orthodox residents in the neighborhood from those of other groups and individuals, experientially delineating the boundary between "us" and "them" without ever having to bring this boundary into visible articulation or conflict.

So far, the interactions and areas described were shared by all the subaffiliations of Orthodoxy in the neighborhood. In this sense, the ways residents navigated these situations distinguished the boundaries between Orthodox Jews and the non-Orthodox world. However, cartographies were further differentiated in relation to subaffiliations.

One such cartographic marker was a flag—either green or red—hanging from the second floor of a synagogue on one of the main arteries of transportation in the neighborhood. What it signified was the status of the *eruv*, an area denoted by string in which it was religiously permissible to carry belongings on the Sabbath, as it had been ritually transformed from a public space into a semiprivate one. When the flag was green, the eruv string was in good condition and Sabbath life could go on in peace. If a red flag was posted, however, it signified that the string was either torn or otherwise rendered impermissible, and that the area had changed its religious status into a space where nothing could be carried on the streets.[9]

However, Orthodox residents did not unanimously agree upon the permissibility of placing an eruv as a symbolic wall in Los Angeles in the first place. Consequently, not all subaffiliations of Orthodoxy in the neighborhood "held by the eruv," and some Orthodox subaffiliations—such as most Hasidic groups—chose to treat the area as if it did not have an eruv at all. They prepared accordingly: pockets were emptied before the Sabbath; in households where children couldn't walk on their own, women stayed behind at home; special arrangements were made for the keys, which should either be placed in special locks near the house door or made "part of the garment" so that individuals would not, strictly speaking, be carrying the keys but rather "wearing" them.

The decision whether to treat the eruv as valid or not had, of course, undertones of distinction. Those who did not hold by the eruv saw themselves as more meticulous and stringent than others who relied on more lenient interpretations of religious law. Thus, for example, some residents commented on a few separate occasions that one of the important rabbis in charge of the eruv—a respected religious authority—did not actually "hold by it" himself, even though he was the one overseeing its operation and condition. Rather, his involvement with the eruv string was interpreted as an attempt to give a semipermissible way out for those "less strict" among the Orthodox.

As with button-operated crosswalks, forms of everyday navigation were directly related to codified and well-specified rules. Though there was leeway for members of different subaffiliations to interpret what constituted a moral transgression, within each group these navigations were relatively straightforward. Other forms of neighborhood navigation, however, were less practically specific. Whereas the former situations and objects were perceived unequivocally as zones of symbolic danger, walking past the nonkosher hotdog stand next to the synagogue, a marijuana dispensary, or a trendy Melrose lingerie shop was not strictly prohibited. However, most of Melrose and many areas along La Brea and Beverly were seen by many Orthodox residents as profane, as zones to be avoided whenever possible. For example, in one interview, when asked about his life in the neighborhood, the interviewee, a respected rabbi in the community, gave the following account:

It is hard. To get to synagogue, I am careful to go around . . . I do not walk through the busy streets. I go through the back streets, the quieter streets. I also go to the kollel, and I walk on [a residential street] the whole way, I don't walk on La Brea, I don't want to go there, it doesn't interest me . . . Melrose neither, when we used to go pray in our synagogue . . . we used to go on [a residential street] all these years, so we don't have to walk on Melrose.

Indeed, although Orthodox men and women had to walk at least a few blocks from their residence to synagogues and schools, many residents I knew chose to walk through residential streets, emerging into the main streets as close as possible to their destination, and walking through them quickly, almost never looking into the windows of the Melrose and Beverly shops, or—for that matter—at others walking through the street. Many Orthodox residents walked at a brisk pace, their eyes fixed on the pavement, seemingly blocking their field of perception. Of course, they were still attentive to changes in neighborhood retail. As I noted in the introduction, when a restaurant that had a large sign portraying a pig holding a knife and fork went out of business, congregation members of a nearby synagogue commented on it with relief in separate incidents;

when a gay movie theater next to it went out of business some months later, I soon heard about it from a few different residents.

The problematic nature of the neighborhood also featured in a joke that Rabbi Chelev-Chittim often made. When not enough people would come to form the ten-man minyan needed for prayer, the rabbi would patiently wait, and then, almost as a matter of course, jokingly threaten that he would "have to go and just pick somebody off Melrose." The humor in these semijokes was partly produced by the juxtaposition of the sacred status of the prayer quorum and the profanity of the sites from which he was threatening to pick the quorum—we have stooped so low, he effectively noted, that our only possible salvation is to turn to profanity.

The question of how to act toward these sites and situations, then, was not as straightforward as that of button-operated crosswalks or the eruv. Of course, if an Orthodox resident was seen standing in line or munching an unkosher "Moe's hotdog" (point 3 on map), it would indicate that he was rebelling against Orthodoxy, perhaps irreparably. But simply not eating at Moe's did not defuse its danger. The micromanagement of space—questions such as how to walk by, how to look or avoid looking, whether to ignore the long line of customers or to "look danger in the eye"—was still encountered as an existential dilemma. By developing personal styles of navigating these objects, and learning to read others' actions, residents further positioned themselves.

Indeed, when some Orthodox residents commented on specific moral dangers, others would not necessarily share their view:

After saying my goodbyes to the rabbi, Joe and I walk out of synagogue. I walk down the synagogue stairs toward the exit, as Jonathan Seifeld walks up the stairs, coming back into the synagogue from the street. He stops me and holds me by the shoulders, but also looks at Joe. "When you go out look down, there are things outside that you shouldn't be seeing," he says abruptly. His tone is serious, solemn. Joe and I walk out, our eyes fixed to the ground. I sneak a look from the corner of my eye. Outside, on the sidewalk, the clothes shop next door has put a few manikins, without clothes, in a pile of naked plastic bodies . . . As we continue going, Joe sighs, "Really . . . these are manikins."

Whereas Seifeld saw the manikins as a moral danger, representing human nudity and thus transgressing the edicts and practices of modesty (tsni'yes), Joe took a stance of bemused detachment. To him, the manikins were pieces of plastic, a far cry from a contaminating influence to be avoided. Poking a little fun at Seifeld's presentation of self as a carefully pious Jew, he constituted himself as more sophisticated in his practice, perhaps more "modern." This, of course, did not mean that he was oblivious to the "contamination" of what he saw as transgressive secular spots. On another occasion, walking to a synagogue nearby, Joe would not walk near a cinema that showed "gay movies" and asked me if we could cross the street. In yet other situations, he was vocally critical of the sexualized "secular culture of Melrose" and said he tried to avoid the street when he could. Faced with less fixed questions of morality and danger, different residents constructed different strategies of action, navigating neighborhood space differently. Doing so, they thus developed personal stratifications of moral danger and presentations of self that were not precisely the same across residents.

To continue with the example of walking by Moe's—the hotdog stand next to the synagogue—people acted differently vis-à-vis what most of them saw as impure. Most residents I knew simply ignored Moe's, appearing to treat it as if it did not exist at all. They averted their eyes and looked at the opposite side of the street, concentrated on the pavement, or looked to a distant point on the horizon. Some of them even made it a point to walk through a parking lot between buildings so they wouldn't need to go by it on their way to synagogue (see solid line between points 3 and 4 on map 3).

But not everyone who could avoid it did so. The rabbi in the small synagogue noted on the map by point 4 always walked from his house through the main thoroughfares (see broken line connecting points 4 and 5 on map 3), sometimes even stopping to have a quick glance at the newspaper stand by Moe's and catch the headlines of current events. Since he headed the congregation and was a well-respected Torah scholar, no one in the congregation ever hinted that stopping by Moe's pointed to any impurities of self.[10] It was, rather, a way of holding oneself, a balance he struck between being an urbanite who liked the hustle and bustle of the streets and still noting what he saw as their spiritual poverty. His wife, on the other hand, usually chose to walk a longer route from the synagogue to her house (see solid line connecting points 4 and 5 on map 3), calling it "the pretty way" and sometimes, facetiously, "the shortcut." And while part of the difference between the ways they navigated between home and synagogue had to do with the enactment of gender—men were more likely in general to be slightly more "daring" than women—it wasn't the only reason. The rabbi and his wife also had different ways of enacting Orthodoxy, and while they were both deeply religious, her stance was more critical of and distanced from the secular world.

Moreover, the symbolic erasure of Moe's was not the only strategy residents could creatively construct, not the only "correct" thing to do. Some Orthodox men actually made sure they smiled at the people standing at Moe's. One resident made it a point to greet the people standing in line with "Good Shabbos" every Sabbath day after prayer. "You don't know if there is a Jew standing in the line," he told me one day. After all, if there was a Jew in line his greeting would perhaps influence him or her, awakening an immanent spark of holiness and showing a way out of secular darkness.

In other words, as a specific course of action was not prescribed or codified, there was always more than one way to act "correctly." Moreover, some residents could also flirt with danger: play with the definitions of membership precisely through the summoning of these morally laden objects.[11] In the following excerpt, two brothers use the provocations of the neighborhood environment to play with different definitions of self:

Arriving at the bus station on La Brea and Wilshire I see two young Hasidic guys sitting and waiting—one teenager and one who looks in his early twenties. The younger one is dressed in yeshiva student garb, black suit and hat. The other, though with a beard and sidelocks, is wearing jeans, fashionable shades, and a beret-style hat. I join them and we begin talking. It turns out that the younger of the two goes to yeshiva. The older one, wearing the beret, is his elder brother and tells me he wants to be a movie maker of religious films. In the station, a large poster shows a fashionable Henry VIII holding a very skimpily clad Anne Boleyn, who is standing with a large ornamented cross on her breasts. It is titled "King Takes Queen." Jokingly, the elder brother says to his younger sibling, "This is beautiful, did you see this poster?" His brother, not looking in the direction of the poster, just nods his head. His elder brother then gets up and props himself beside the poster, "C'mon, what do you think?" His brother, looking neither at his brother nor at the poster, says, "I don't like the thing she is wearing . . ." "You mean the cross?" his brother taunts him. The younger brother nods his head again, exasperated. His brother laughs and rejoins us on the bench.

Reacting to the sexually provocative and Christian imagery, the brothers enact different definitions of self. The younger brother refuses even to look at the poster (though, mysteriously, he knows exactly what Boleyn is wearing). His elder brother, on the other hand, flirts with danger and, in a gesture connoting a devil-may-care attitude, physically props himself against the poster. Again, what makes the poster into a moral provocation that summons an Orthodox self was thus not the specific action that residents took towards it. On the contrary—the moral provocation of this poster could be either flirted with or studiously ignored. What made it into a moment of summoning was that whatever they did, or failed to do, defined what kind of Orthodox Jews they were.

In a series of articles, Margarethe Kusenbach argues that by following people along their daily routines, one can glean a realm of experience that is usually invisible.[12] By seeing how people walk through space—what areas they avoid, what reminds them of their past and what of their future—sociologists can access the existential terrain they understand themselves through. Over time, we develop a relationship to residential space—we "see" the high school that is gone, a favorite restaurant that was converted into a laundromat, or the house we hoped we would live in but now realize we can never afford.

But there is more to daily navigations than our encounters with our pasts and futures. Orthodox residents in the Beverly–La Brea neighborhood were summoned by an invisible moral obstacle course. The streets were peppered with pragmatic and moral problems that most other residents simply did not experience. The encounter with the streets, including shops, posters, and hotdog stands, provoked Orthodox residents to locate themselves symbolically. The moral density of space was a constant summoning that posited and reposited the question "What kind of person am I?" and more specifically "What kind of Orthodox Jew?"

The Summons of Strangers: On Disattended Signs

The neighborhood café in which I used to write fieldnotes—a hip establishment, brimming with script writers and young professionals staring intently at their laptop screens—often posted photography taken by its habitués. The photos were usually nature shots or sensitive portraits. At one point, however, one of the regulars posted photos he had taken in the neighborhood. One of these, a black and white picture taken during a rare Los Angeles winter day, showed Orthodox men walking in the rain. Their faces blurred in the mist, they seemed like apparitions in black. The picture, as the photographer told me, captured the mystery and allure that Orthodox residents held for him, alien-looking men walking through the streets, almost ethereal. Of course, the picture tells us more about the photographer's mystification of Orthodoxy than about Orthodox neighborhood residents. But for all that, such a photograph reminds us of an important point, though not quite the one the artist was making, a reminder of just how *visible* Orthodox men are.

Being an Orthodox Jew is to be born into, or later to enter, a world of visible signs. Even those considered less observant post signs of belonging on their bodies, on their doorstep, in their houses. Some of these signs seem welded to the Orthodox body: the black overcoat and hat, beard, sidelocks, yarmulke.[13] Like other uniforms, Orthodox attire provides a clear sign of belonging.[14]

For Orthodox residents there were many forms of dress and attire, signifying varying degrees of observance or subaffiliation—a round hat meant something different than a flat Borsalino, a shaggy beard was different from a well-trimmed one. And yet, beyond this dizzying array of gradations and differentiations known to insiders, simply wearing the yarmulke, the most minimal sign of belonging, made Orthodox residents widely recognized and categorized as Jewish and somewhat observant.[15]

Although it has specific meanings known to the wearers, the yarmulke, like other parts of religious attire, is usually worn as a matter of course, without thinking of its symbolic meanings. In fact, Hasidic men usually sleep with their yarmulkes on, taking them off only when they go into the shower. When I asked a few friends if they thought about their dress and yarmulke or attended to their signification on an everyday basis, most told me that although they were acutely aware of them on certain occasions and in specific situations, they were usually worn nonreflexively, as a matter of habit.[16]

Yet wearing the yarmulke produces an effect. Without initiating interaction, or even being thematically aware of it, the yarmulke provides an affordance for interaction in its automatic denotation of Jewishness for a general audience. Thus, when I started fieldwork, one poignant moment of transformation for me as an ethnographer was my donning the yarmulke for the first time, and the ways in which I subsequently became both visible and invisible. As I walked on the main streets, non-Jewish women would take special care to "not look" at me, extending civil inattention to its utmost. On the other hand, Orthodox residents are visible in ways that they would otherwise not be. People at bus stops approached me every now and then to ask me "if it is true that Jews believe that . . ." Bearded Orthodox Jews wearing their sidelocks and black hats suddenly noticed my existence, sometimes nodding, returning nods that they had previously ignored.

The yarmulke was an interactional hook marking the wearer. With the yarmulke, residents became Jews whether they sought out interaction or tried to avoid it, whether actually "doing-being Jewish" or engaging in other activities in which Jewishness is far from the relevant facet of self. Whether or not they meant it, the attire allowed strangers to summon Orthodox residents, to remind them, again and again, that they were in fact Orthodox Jews. If the interactions with street life I described above were one set of obstacles Orthodox residents needed to traverse, the summons of strangers was another. Being recognized as a certain kind of person evoked this self in ways that residents could never precisely predict, yet that were common enough to be partially predictable.

Some interactions, which usually occurred within the neighborhood, were initiated by other Jews. Most often, these interactions were barely visible—a nod on the street and at the bus stop from other Orthodox Jews, or the words "Good Shabbos" uttered quietly on a Saturday. But sometimes these interactions were more elaborate, spelling out the assumptions underlying more fleeting interactions:

As I am walking outside Ralph's [a local supermarket] on a Friday afternoon, I am stopped by a woman in her fifties or so, wearing a *sheitl* [wig worn by married Orthodox women] and a long black skirt. "Excuse me, when is candle lighting today?" she asks, referring to the time in which Sabbath candles are lighted, eighteen minutes before sundown on Friday. I am not sure, but say I think it is 6:55. The woman looks at her watch and cracks a smile. "Thirteen minutes to get home, eh?" I say we should probably start walking fast, and she laughs.

Because she could categorize me as a "religious Jew," I instantaneously became a pragmatic resource. Wearing a yarmulke denoted not only that I was a "Jew" in the abstract, but that I should possess a specialized body of knowledge. With candle-lighting times changing every week, I was assumed to be up to date, summoned as part of the same moral community that holds similar things to be worth knowing. And as I responded to her overture, the interaction elicited a community *in situ*. Providing the correct candle-lighting time, or even a weak approximation of it, served to solidify not only the assumption of a general "Jewishness," but the commonality of a shared project, a "we" that was not explicitly worked out prior to interaction.

The ways in which the yarmulke allows some to practically summon anonymous others in the process of achieving particular pragmatic ends can also be observed in the very different case below:

I walk down the street in Westwood when a homeless man asks me for money. I ignore him and continue walking, barely noticing his call. He calls after me, loudly, "*Tzedakah*" (Hebrew for "alms/charity"). I stop and look back, realizing that I am still wearing my yarmulke on my way to the university. He starts talking to me, he went to a synagogue early in the morning and people wouldn't give him money, "I am wax poor, I told them . . . wax poor," but still, they wouldn't budge. "Some people just become rabbis for the money, they aren't good Jews," he tells me. I say I am sorry. In my synagogue people usually give alms. He perks up, "Really? Where is it?" I realize I might have just brought a new schnorrer to shul and try to weasel my way out of it. "We start really early . . ."

When he did not elicit the kind of reaction he had hoped for by approaching me as an anonymous passerby, the panhandler shifted his own frame of reference and used the Hebrew word *tzedakah*. By actualizing this shift, he signaled three interrelated things: first, that he knew exactly "what" I was; second, that he himself was a fellow Jew. But most effectively, from an initially diffused form of begging, in which I was another person walking down the street who was morally entitled to ignore his call, the request was shifted to a personalized, moral summons. Implicit in his shouting of tzedakah was an imperative, as *tzedakah* is not only the Hebrew translation of the word "charity" or "alms," but a mitzvah, a religiously prescribed act of charity. This personalized demand lifted the "Jew" from the status of an anonymous person on the street to that of a member of the same group that he himself belonged to—someone who would not only give him money but might also listen to him and sympathize with his complaints about different synagogues or other clubs where "our" members meet.

This form of summoning, though used here as a way in which commonality is assumed, reconstituted, and manipulated, could also position the wearer of the yarmulke as a moral superior in interaction. In certain situations, it was not only a commonality that was called forth, but also an accompanying stratification of membership. Thus, in the next excerpt, I was walking by Moe's, the nonkosher hotdog venue, smoking a cigarette, when a young man who was waiting in line approached me:

"Do you have a cigarette?" he asks me in Hebrew. I say I do, and hand him one. "I don't eat here, really, I don't. I am here with a friend. I wouldn't eat here," he says. Surprised, I try to laugh it off, saying that I think the owner of the place is himself Jewish. He doesn't respond to the joke. "No, really, I don't eat here." He points to another young man with a ponytail, standing in line, who is watching us and smiling. "He eats here. I wouldn't. Really."

Wanting a cigarette, and noticing my yarmulke (and maybe my body language), the man took his chances. But when he began the interaction, he used the yarmulke to constitute me not only as a Jew, but also as a moral entity. His interlocutor was not only Jewish, but religious, and thus someone who might frown upon his standing in line for nonko-sher meat. In initiating interaction, he thus entered into an unsolicited series of self-justifications. The yarmulke afforded him with a means not only to constitute the other as a Jew, but also—in initiating interaction, and perhaps in the very act of perception—to constitute *himself* as a fellow Jew, albeit a morally dubious one.

This summoning of the yarmulke wearer as Jewish in the eyes of others was not limited to fellow Jews. Since residents shared space with a host of non-Jewish others, in many interactions non-Jews asked them questions pertaining to Judaism, or simply used the category "Jew" as a relevant membership category. Thus, for example, within the space of two days I had the following (friendly) non-Jewish reminders of identification:

Monday: Boarding the bus, there is a drunk man who seems to be in his forties, sitting in the front of the bus, taking swigs from a bottle of cherry wine. "Are you Jewish?" he asks as I stand next to him. I nod. "I knew you were Jewish," he astutely observes. Tuesday: Again, as I wait for the bus, a woman standing next to me smiles, "Are you Jewish?"

These were both friendly encounters. The comments were made not to offend but to strike up a conversation, to enter a space of sociability. And yet in both of these encounters, I was reminded that I was, first and foremost, a Jew. The yarmulke was a perceptual resource that could be used to achieve different ends—from civility rituals to attempts to obtain money. Yet each overture used a distinctive grammar, that of summoning the subject as interactionally Jewish.

The situational demands placed on Orthodox Jews at such moments of summoning could also conflict with their position in the hierarchy of the Orthodox social world. The next excerpt is the account of a resident who became religious not long ago, a newly minted BT, who had relatively little knowledge of religious law and practice. Within his own social circle, other synagogue members knew this and would sometimes remind him of his novice position. However, in his interactions with non-Jews, he was often constituted as a religious authority. When I asked him if non-Jews interacted with him as a Jew, he gave the following account:

"It happens a lot, mainly when I go shopping." He had two such incidents last week, in the large department store he shops in. In one incident, someone in the shop asked him what kind of vegetables to put in a kosher sandwich. He was happy he could answer them. On the other occasion, however, somebody asked him if an oven was or wasn't kosher. He looked, and it didn't say anything about being kosher, so he couldn't really tell. "They always call me rabbi and ask questions. But I am not a rabbi, not close. Maybe my sons will be, if they want. They can be anything they want to be, but not me. I still try to answer them, but a lot of times I can't."

Thus, there could be an extra layer within moments of summoning, in which the interactants in the situation presume a self that cannot be interactionally delivered. In this instance, though the resident tried to interact as expected of him, he was also reminded of his own position in the group. Especially in a social world in which knowledge of religious law is highly regarded, there was a gap between what the stranger expected of him and what he felt were his own capabilities. In this sense, the interaction has a transcendent facet, hidden in interaction, in which the "Orthodox Jew" who is summoned must come to terms with his insecurities in the very group he has been constituted into.

Additionally, although residents did not usually attend to the possibility that non-Jews would use the yarmulke or garments as membership categorization devices, when either their "Jewishness" or other aspects of their performance as religious people were scrutinized, they sometimes paid special attention to these markers. This was the case even when it was actually questionable whether others were paying attention to the yarmulke and other such signs:

As I sit at dinner at Jonathan's, he tells me and his family of an interrogation he had at work. There was a case of fraud somewhere in the finance firm he works in, and as he occupies a central managerial position, he was asked to answer some questions posed by investigators from the central headquarters of the company. As he is telling of the long interrogation he just went through, he says, "Though there was nothing I did wrong, I wasn't even in the firm at the time, I kept feeling like I had to look good, being a Jew, and looking like I do."

What is telling about this narrative is the way in which the interrogation was transformed within the account. The theme of the interrogation had nothing to do with Jewishness, and the same man had told me on another occasion that at work he very rarely felt "Jewish," being too preoccupied with his work. When he was interrogated, however, signs of Jewishness suddenly took on a central meaning. The scrutiny of his conduct and person became, in his experience, or at least in its narration, the interrogation of a "Jew," who must perform as best he can since any suspicion of his person becomes a suspicion of "Jews." In a sense, even without being explicit, the summoning is actualized, becoming a relevant aspect of experience and interaction, even though Jonathan was probably the only one who was aware of it in the room.

Last, the summoning of strangers is not always as friendly as described above. In some rare instances, the moral obstacle course turns invidious as the constitution of residents as "Jews" takes the shape of anti-Semitic remarks and episodes:

I walk down Melrose with Joe. We just got some tea at a kosher café and are walking back. As we are walking down the street, a guy peeks out of one of the cars going east, lifts the black Halloween mask he is wearing, shouts "Jews," and gives us the finger as the car zooms off. I am completely shocked. "Did he say 'you'?" I ask Joe. He laughs, "Jews." Joe sees my expression, and remarks, "What, were you never called a kike before? It happens . . . usually on holidays, when people drink and lose their inhibitions." I ask him if it happens a lot. "Not a lot, a few times a year, on the main streets. La Brea, Melrose. They never stop. Cowards . . . you just ignore them."

As we were walking down Melrose, neither of us was thematically performing a Jewish identification; although wearing "Jewish" attire, we were not attending to it as meaningful in the interaction between us. We just had coffee in the local kosher Starbucks and were arguing about gun control, which I was all for and he was vehemently opposed to. But when the passenger shouted "Jews!" I was violently summoned from one performative identification to another, instantaneously becoming "a Jew" whether I liked it or not.

More telling than my own reaction, however, was Joe's nonchalant acceptance of the incident. Before the slur, Jewishness was far from the theme of his performance—if anything, he was doing-being a libertarian-leaning Republican. And yet, Jewishness was still available enough to allow him to effortlessly appraise the situation. In this sense, on the crowded streets shared with non-Jews in the neighborhood, Jewishness was constantly on the margins of embodied consciousness,[17] forming a facet of everyday strolls down the street even when it was not attended to. Even when they didn't think of it explicitly or attend to their Jewishness, residents tacitly expected to be summoned and knew how to reorient themselves to the situation.

These incidents were also a place where a folk sociology of the non-Jewish other could be formulated. In an attempt to come to terms with these incidents, Joe produced a double sociology of motives: "It happens, usually on holidays, when people drink and lose their inhibitions." First, the anti-Semitic incidents are coherently put on a calendar—these things happen at certain times of the year, periods in which one should perhaps be more careful. Second, in this folk-sociological formulation, the non-Jewish other is inherently perceived as an anti-Semite. These episodes occur on holidays not because there are different people driving down Melrose in their cars, but because the same people, once drunk, "lose their inhibitions." The Gentile is always an anti-Semite; alcohol unfetters and makes visible his true face.

When I asked other residents if such episodes occurred to them, I was assured that they did, though some members told me that it happened often and others less so. Across the board, however, my interlocutors said that they were not surprised when these incidents occurred. They were sometimes frightened, as a friend of mine was when approached by a group of young men who screamed "Heil Hitler" at him; residents were often angry, some of them hollering slurs back at the anti-Semites; one person I knew told me he once stopped and tried to educate a group of young men who shouted a slur at him. But no one was surprised.

The tacit expectation of such incidents means not only that Orthodox residents reorient effortlessly when they encounter such instances, but also that vague incidents are interpreted as anti-Semitic, that people react as if they are summoned into being even when they are not. Thus, either when it was unclear what aspect of self was being stigmatized, or when a passerby offered a vague perceptual cue, residents sometimes interpreted the instance as anti-Semitic:

Jonathan, Dov-Ber, and I are walking back from synagogue. They are both wearing black Orthodox garb. I am wearing a black jacket and yarmulke. As we cross one of the quiet residential streets, taking our time and talking about Jonathan's trip abroad, a car goes by, honks, and the driver shouts at us, "This is jaywalking!" Dov-Ber turns to Jonathan. "Did he say 'Jews-walking'?" Jonathan, shakes his head, " 'Jaywalkers,' we *were* walking in the middle of the road . . ." Dov-Ber laughs. "Oh, jaywalkers."

Unsure what the driver had actually said, Dov-Ber reached for the ready-at-hand interpretation of the incident. The situation in which a passerby shouts at three people crossing the street was automatically translated into an anti-Semitic incident directed against three "Jews." Similarly, when I was talking with one resident about anti-Semitic incidents in the neighborhood, his wife, sitting on the sofa on the other side of the room, added her own account of anti-Semitism:

"It happened to me only once, a few years ago, at Ralph's [a local supermarket]." I ask her what happened. She was walking with her children when a man came up to her. "You only know how to reproduce, don't you?" he muttered. Telling it even now, years later, she gets visibly upset, slightly reddening, eyebrows furrowed. "They weren't even misbehaving. Not that it matters, and he just came and said it . . . the way he said it, it was really nasty. But I let him have it, my husband heard me shout at the guy all the way from the other side of the store. He didn't expect it, started to mumble that he is sorry."

Although she describes it as an anti-Semitic incident, one can raise questions as to whether the incident really was directed at her "Jewishness." The man's remark was surely sexist, disparaging, and anti-Orthodox, but was not necessarily anti-Semitic. Though it is possible that the man was targeting her as a Jew, there are plausible alternatives—he could have been, for example, an antireligious Jew targeting her as *Orthodox*.[18] In her narrative she nonetheless constructed the incident as anti-Semitic, adding that though the content of the remark might have been ambiguous, its tone was not. Not used to these incidents, she still tried, in her narrative account, to dispel the "reason" for the slur. The children "weren't even misbehaving"—the slur was uncalled for, anti-Semitic.

In fact, the only incident I witnessed in which anti-Semitism produced shock was an incident in which Jewishness was supposedly invisible:

I stand near the bus stop at La Brea and Wilshire. An elderly man, dressed in a black jacket, slacks, a cap, and a cane, stands at the stop. As I walk around, I hear shouts from the stop. I come closer and see an apparently homeless woman, dressed in rags, shouting at the old man. "You are all going to hell . . . I was celibate for 27 years . . . You think you are so good, you Jews, but you will all go to hell." I come closer. The woman continues to shout at the man. He shrinks back. Now and then he says, "But what do you want from me?" I stand by the man, and the woman retreats, shouting a few more incoherent remarks. I ask the man what it was about, and he says, "I don't know what she wanted." He seems distraught, keeps asking me, "Why did she come and shout at me? Something must have happened to her . . . How did she know I am a Jew?!" I stand next to him as the woman returns and shouts, "I will put his picture on the wall, his naked picture . . . *Shiksas* [Yiddish, derogatory term for non-Jewish women] are good enough to have sex with, but aren't good enough to marry . . . You think you know Torah, you don't know Torah, you Jews." Luckily, the bus comes, and we board it. The man looks at me, "Maybe she had some kind of affair with a rabbi, and she is all mad? She is crazy, sick . . . But how did she know I am Jewish?" He is a Holocaust survivor, he tells me on our bus ride, a death camp survivor from Poland.

Somewhat similar to Joe's reaction in the episode above, the man's reaction, as he found himself the target of an anti-Semitic rant while standing at the bus stop, was to create a folk psychology of the incident. The incident was not constructed as denoting any general anti-Semitic undercurrent in non-Jewish society, but rather called for psychological analysis. Yet what is striking is the reiteration of the question: "How did she know I am Jewish?" Without the visible perceptual clue of the yarmulke, the other was not supposed to be able to construct him as Jewish. The question he repeated was how he was "recognized"; he was shaken by the possibility (which became all the more chilling given his biography) that his Judaism was somehow bodily inscribed.

On Street Summoning

Orthodox residents were constantly reminded of "who they were," summoned as Orthodox Jews. Whenever they walked through the streets, the non-Orthodox character of the neighborhood they lived in constantly provided challenges and provocations that members needed to traverse, a moral obstacle course.

These everyday navigations summoned residents in two complementary ways. On the one hand, people had to reorient themselves toward purity and danger in their everyday lives. The streets they walked through constantly threw pragmatic-moral challenges at them: how to cross a street, how to bypass a pile of naked manikins, how to walk to synagogue. These obstacles reminded pedestrians of their Orthodoxy by pushing them to attend to their surroundings in particular ways—to modify their actions, to change their course in mid-flight. And as the rhythms of religious life were overlaid upon the rhythms of street life, Orthodox residents had to constantly be alert. Failing in their navigations had repercussions that transcended the situation—they constantly needed to be on their guard, to manage the *provocations of self* that the streets put in their way.[19]

If these moral navigations were responses to the non-Orthodox environment, the second set of processes show how anonymous others within the environment situate and reconstitute Orthodox residents. It was not only through residents' own effort that their identification as Orthodox Jews was constructed, but also in the way they effectively relegated their identification to others. Orthodox residents were reconstituted through the interactional pressure to be a certain kind of person, a summoning that materialized simply when passersby approached them with the assumption that they would interact back in a specific kind of way. Like the school or the synagogue rabbi, strangers both nudged Orthodox residents to *be* Orthodox and afforded them with the opportunity to play out their identification.

As with every form of summoning, these moments not only were the result of residents' intentional projects, but were also brought into being by others. People were provoked and invoked through smells, sights, and mundane interactions with strangers. And yet, for such interactions to work effortlessly, people needed to somehow expect their summoning across situations, to keep it within the margins of possibility even when they enacted other facets of themselves. They needed to know both how to act and what the stakes of such action were for their definition of selfhood.

EIGHT

The Density of Worlds

In their specificity, the snippets of life presented in this book add up to a moving picture of a dense, overdetermined social world. The Orthodox residents of the Beverly–La Brea neighborhood were inundated with moments of action and interaction that constituted and reconstituted them as specific kinds of people. From the inanimate world of street signs, crosswalks, and whiffs of nonkosher smells to their morning prayers, from their organizational entanglements to strangers passing by, they were identified, located, summoned. Time and time again.

At first blush, there is something unsurprising about the dense fabric of summoning that emerges through the different chapters. After all, these are people who live a life that explicitly sets them at odds with the world that surrounds them, while deepening ties with fellow travelers on the Orthodox road. As with modern-day Evangelical Christians, part of the seduction of being Orthodox is precisely its embattled existence.[1] Living through a moral obstacle course is not only religiously required, but often personally exhilarating. And, then again, there are deep currents of meaning and emotion that come from the relationships with other Orthodox Jews, the relationship with Scriptures through learning and recitation, as well as moments of deep religious experience.[2]

Yet such a "project-based" vision of their world, taken on its own, is not only incomplete but misleading. While being an Orthodox Jew requires action, this work is shared. It is both distributed among other Orthodox Jews and— usually unwittingly—relegated to non-Jews. Summoning, then, first highlights that any social self emerges and congeals in action and interaction. When, for example, congregants were asked to pray for the health of an ill student who was hovering between life and death, they were asked both to *do* something and also to *be* someone. When a non-Jewish panhandler angrily muttered "no problem, I'll just go to the church" when he was ignored, my friend had to "become" a Jew.

Like interaction itself, summoning is both an effect and the active accomplishment of a project. The most "active" moments of summoning I describe congealed in action and interaction. Even as I was inculcated into Orthodox life by friends, my willingness to see them as religious authorities constituted their understanding of themselves; when an Orthodox engineer actively sought to distance himself from the non-Jewish world in which he worked, his attempt was reaffirmed through the way others reacted to it and allowed him to construct the complex choreography of belonging and detachment.

Similarly, even in the most "passive" of moments—when an Israeli meshulach knocked on their doors asking for money, or when they were called and asked to participate in a multitude of religious causes—people had to work to sustain interaction.[3] They not only had to set themselves up for the interaction (e.g., by placing the mezuzah on their door, or by giving their email or address to an organization) but also had to know how to play along with the interaction, how to occupy the identification into which they were summoned, even anticipate it. The most jarring moments of summoning, such as when internal hierarchies became apparent or when anti-Semitic incidents occurred, required preparation, if only in learning how to tacitly expect and make sense of what had happened.

That any moment of summoning is both an active accomplishment and the outcome of external pressures does not mean that identification is equally distributed in an undifferentiated haze of call and response. Residents in the neighborhood initiated such situations in different ways in different situations, and to different effects. The processes described here thus had a predictable situational and personal nexus. Organizational forms of summoning were formed by specific residents and visitors; synagogue life was organized in patterned ways and propelled by a set of characters (the rabbi, for example); even forms of distinction and boundary-making were more or less predictably distributed.

And in such a distribution, there were different possibilities open to different people. How people walked through the streets, for example, was important for all Orthodox residents. But for some the possibilities of navigation were more constrained than for others: although there may have been no precisely "right" way to traverse the neighborhood, there were different degrees of freedom actors had to define their selves. The synagogue rabbi could ignore his surroundings in ways that novices couldn't; men, it seemed, were able to publicly occupy risky selves that women I saw did not. Seen through the lens of a sociology of summoning, the possible space of identification was closely related to what sociologists often talk of as power.

Still, this distribution was not set in stone, nor did it easily translate into an ability to make others do thy will. As in any social world, what people learned was "a sense of the game" rather than a rigid set of expectations.[4] A homeless alcoholic could, in certain situations, silence his middle-class (and more learned) co-congregants by telling them that their topic of conversation "was not Sabbath-appropriate [*shabbosdik*]"; a previously secular Jew could go so far as to doubt whether the kitchen of the rabbi who initially helped him learn religious law was good enough for his new religious standards. Although there were patterns and expectations, such patterns did not form straightforward rules of interaction but sculpted the domain of the possible.

Moreover, although all the different forms of summoning described in this book were related to each other in that they co-constituted a fabric of situations and in that they were part of the same general moral project, they were not identical. It was not only the "Jewishness" of the giver that was summoned by a schnorrer in synagogue, but also his status as a middle-class neighborhood resident; when schools made demands on students' families, they were summoning not only "a good Jew" but also a good parent; when synagogue congregants called to nudge the tenth man on a weekday, they summoned not only a religious identification but also a "comrade in arms" who had been in the same situation many times before and could thus sympathize with their plight. There was a family resemblance between moments, not an identity. It was the overlaying of different moments, and slightly different selves, that made the social world what it was. Seen from the point of view of summoning, then, the relationship between identification and social worlds becomes clearer. A social world is precisely the choreography of moments, relations, and selves, along with their patterned rhythms, pragmatic challenges, and anticipations.

As developed here, then, summoning is a sensitizing concept used to focus on the construction of identifications and social worlds at the intersection of actors' ongoing projects and their invocations by others within a patterned set of situations.[5] At its most general, summoning is thus the shadow of identification in action and interaction. Actors are constantly summoned into different worlds in different ways. No act is ever innocent of overtones of identification, as people always posit themselves and are elicited as specific kinds of subjects. As the horizons of thought and action are socially formed, and as even the most unreflexive of moments defines selfhood, summoning seems to be a general feature of social life.

But if there is an aspect of "summoning" in any ongoing action and interaction, the metaphor loses its analytic power. In such a wide use the term ceases to be of much analytic use. Instead of opening up new questions, it provides a general reminder.

An alternative use is more focused. Summoning is a useful sensitizing concept when the researcher attends to the relationship between identification and the construction of social worlds across situations. When we limit the concept's extension in this way, there are indeed situations in which actors are *not* summoned in any meaningful way. For Orthodox residents, once again, a walk through the secular streets was experienced as meaningful; for many other people sharing the same neighbourhood space it was not. This is not to say that those "others" do not walk through the streets in socialized ways, or that "anything goes" (how long can a man stare at lingerie-clad manikins before unease settles in?). What it does mean is that there is no specific social world—"a universe of regularized mutual response"—that the actor is summoned into in this situation. Although walking "normally" as a non-Orthodox person makes sense only within the bounds of a socialized "normal," such action and interaction are not connected to a specific social world.[6]

Thinking Intersituationally: Action and Its Potentials

As summoning highlights the interplay between actors' projects and the emergence of their identifications in interaction, it also cuts through the false choice between fixed renditions of identity and the notion that identifications are purely situationally emergent. It is through the incorporation of temporality and its rhythmic structure—the *intersituational* texture of social life—that such a view is possible.

As I have argued throughout the book, summoning not only occurs in but emerges through concrete situations. As interactionists and ethnomethodologists have long argued, situations matter.[7] They matter because the ordered fabric of social life emerges in their enactment and because meanings are both reaffirmed and creatively played with in concrete situations—giving social life its inherently open, frequently exciting, sometimes daunting character.

And yet as theorists of situations have looked deeper and deeper into the ongoing structuring of meaning, they have often lost sight of the ways in which situations are related to each other. The problem with the way such theorists describe interactional achievements is that they seem to assume that identifications are made anew in each situation. The temporality of identification in these renditions of social action has become identical to the temporality of the situation. When people's lives are seen through these lenses, it becomes quite confusing how they sustain a modicum of order, how they end up recreating situations that look and feel familiar both to them and to the ethnographer.

To solve this obvious problem, a stream of research emphasized how ongoing institutional pressures end up structuring situations in predictable ways—a mode of analysis that I have drawn upon throughout the book.[8] Seen from this angle, the recurring structure of interaction arises primarily through an interactional form. To take an example of my own work here: the attempt to meet the requirement of ten men for a minyan in a small synagogue gives rise to a predictable "team spirit"; the institutionalized visibility of Orthodox men makes them a predictable target for anonymous interaction on the street. Patterns emerge, then, because a general social form shapes interaction in recurrent ways, not because of the specific texture of meaning of actors' lives.

But though important, this is only a partial solution. It is partial since such an approach accounts for the structure of situations rather than for the structure of anticipations, knowhow, and expectations that actors use to navigate them. Situations seem far more complex than the actors who find themselves in them—actors are usually depicted as problem-solving subjects who act upon straightforward pragmatic exigencies rather than upon complex worlds of meaning. More problematic still, such an approach fails to account for the fact that people act not only in relation to the specific situation that they find themselves in, but by locating it in relation to other situations.

To understand the problem of situational accounts of identification and action, it is useful to move to a different language—that of potentiality and actualization. In a situational account, the active force of potentiality inheres in the situation itself. The situation exerts the pressures that shape interactional outcomes. To the extent that actors shape situations, they do it as relatively simple problem solvers, as molded matter.[9]

Partly as an attempt to rethink the location of potentiality and overcome the limitations of situated achievements without reverting to a norm-driven theory of action,[10] the past two decades saw the increasing popularity of notions of disposition, developed primarily in the work of sociologist Pierre Bourdieu. According to such a reading of social life, people internalize not values and rules of conduct but a set of dispositions and tastes that they carry around as propensities for experience and action (what Bourdieu termed the *habitus*).[11] Situations, then, are the specific arenas in which these active potentials become finally actualized.[12]

This notion of self and action solves some of the problems of rule-driven renditions of social action and connects different moments of action through the dispositional structure of the subjects going through them. And yet the emphasis on a unified structure of tastes and dispositions exposes this notion to many of the same criticisms that situational accounts originally leveled against norm-based theories of action. Much like earlier conceptions of identity, the dispositional version of the relationship among social worlds, identifications, and action assumes a relatively fixed core, even if this core provides a "feel for the game" rather than fixed courses of action. And by doing so, it downplays the importance of what happens—and what is expected to happen—in specific situations.

To switch metaphors, we can begin to think about the relationship between situation and self in terms of a topographical map—a metaphor first offered by social philosopher Alfred Schutz to describe the distribution and structure of knowledge in everyday life.[13] Rather than thinking about knowledge as a unified and well-organized whole, Schutz suggested we think about it as we think about navigational maps. For some areas we have high-resolution detailed maps. But other places are far less well-mapped. There are areas in the map that are hazy and that we know only well enough to get by, other areas we simply know nothing of. Knowledge, as he argued, is essentially patchy and contradictory. We inhabit a social world not by knowing everything there is to know about it, but rather by ignoring its incoherences and contradictions—by knowing specific things well, having vague "recipe knowledge" about others, and knowing that other things can be safely and totally ignored.

Schutz's metaphor provides a useful way to think not only about knowledge, but also about identification. Entering interaction, we usually have a "feel" for how we should go about it. We know more or less what to do, what selves our actions embody. As Bourdieu argues, it isn't primarily that we know specific rules of action—although, especially in the case of Orthodox Judaism, actors must also know codified law. Instead, we have a feel for the situation, a sense of the game. Beyond this surface similarity, however, the theory suggested by Schutz's image radically departs from Bourdieu's. For, as a Schutzian approach would point out, there is no reason to assume a priori that there is a *unified* geography of self underlying the situations we know so well. It is not that a unified set of dispositions is impossible to imagine. Rather, the assumption of a stable set of dispositions forecloses inquiry precisely where it should be opened up.

As situations unfold, actors position themselves by connecting them to the embodied past of similar situations and to different situations that they have learned relate to them both in the past and in an anticipated future. Some situations (e.g., non-Jewish work situations and Orthodox narratives of superiority) remain predictably unconnected—and when actors happen to connect them, they quickly learn that making such a connection is the wrong move in this moment in the social game. Other situations, however, are interwoven so that the meaning of one situation is crystallized precisely through the way it fits in with other anticipated situations. In place of a unified set of dispositions, the temporal structure of situations along with their connections and disconnections serves as the key to understand how people act and understand their position in a social world. It is both in the etching of situations over time and by implicitly learning their rhythms, syncopations, and interconnections that predictable forms of identification emerge.

Moreover, what becomes relevant within a certain situation, and what other situations it is connected to, are determined by a *collective* act. As I argued above, summoning points to the interplay of actors' projects and the way that their identifications are evoked in interaction. The answer to the question "What situations would be connected to which, and which will remain unconnected?" resides in patterns of summoning that are temporally organized and anticipated.

Tracing the rhythms, syncopations, expectations, and tacit anticipations of summoning thus leads us back to the structure of identification through a different—and more promising—route. It stresses both that there is no reason to assume that actors enter situations with a stable set of dispositions in order to explain patterns of action and sense making, and that what happens within and across situations is a collective project that is congealed through their patterning in time. Thus, interactions are patterned in ways that become etched in everyday routinized action and shape the outlines of creativity.[14]

To return to the case of the Orthodox Jews in this study, the etching of identification occurred in different ways. On one level, it happened through the repetition of situations, of modes of summoning and the rhythmic logic that defined the situation. Going to morning prayers was not an isolated incident. Although any actual instance was specific, what gave the experience its particular feel was precisely that it was expected to recur every morning. The experience of prayer would be very different if this repetition weren't already assumed. In a different register, being "hit" by an organization for a donation of money or time did not come out of the blue. Residents had a sense of organizational rhythms and a vague notion (some more so, some less) of the pragmatic challenges that made these interactions possible. Residents also set themselves up in a variety of ways for the moments of summoning. They did so physically, when they did things as mundane as setting their alarms for the Sabbath; they did so when they gave their phone number to the synagogue rabbi, or their email for a class. And even when rhythms of interaction were less precisely predictable, as in the cases of anonymous interactions on the streets or the meshulach at the door, a background of embodied anticipations was already inculcated. To inhabit a social world was precisely to implicitly anticipate the kind of situations that *could* emerge.

Similarly, and much harder to see, the erasure of the non-Jewish work world was something that residents could expect. It was precisely by *never* being asked about it, and by having to repair their own interaction when they did, that residents learned how to cut off parts of their lives in religious settings. Although the erasure (or at the very least, the minimization) of the goyishe world was an explicit project for many strict Orthodox residents, it was also something that happened in and through social interaction.[15]

As a sensitizing concept, summoning thus recasts the relation between situational patterns, embodied knowhow, and identification. As social worlds extend in time, actors who inhabit them learn what to expect within situations and how to tie different situations to each other. They do so not by realizing a disposition but by connecting their embodied anticipations of situations to the way in which they are invoked by others in the situation. Anticipation then is both inscribed in bodies and engraved into material resources that are regularly accessed. It is not only that actualization "happens again and again." In their temporal extension, patterns congeal (though never hermetically) into a life.

How situations are related, how they are temporally patterned, how they constitute actor's identification, and to what degree such identifications are stable are all questions that cannot be answered a priori. These are essentially empirical questions. Different social worlds will have different patterns of connections among situations and will keep different situations, and selves, clearly separated from each other. Summoning, then, is not a way to recast familiar observations through the use of a different metaphor, but a position that provides new questions and suggests new comparisons.

Beyond the Orthodox Neighborhood

In addition to its possible payoff as a theory of action, summoning provides a methodological provocation. Pulling one thread of the theoretical skein, there is potential use value in thinking about the "density" and patterning of moments of identification—the location, salience, and sheer number of actions and interactions in which people are reconstituted as certain kinds of people. The density of summoning thus appears as a spectrum. At one end would be an imaginary world in which *all* action and interaction summons people into a single identification and social world; on the other, a postmodern protean utopia in which identifications freely shift between situations, where people are endlessly malleable and decentered.

Conceived in this way, the density of summoning is not primarily a religious phenomenon. While religious social worlds may be useful examples, and while "summoning" is a religious metaphor, not all religious worlds are particularly dense; not all dense social worlds are particularly religious.

Perhaps the most radical cases of dense social worlds are what sociologist Erving Goffman called "total institutions"—places like army barracks, asylums, or prisons where people are practically locked into a specific identity (soldiers, madmen, sailors, etc.).[16] Such total institutions, with their totalitarian edge, depend on their practical isolation from the world. Thus, in those cases in which people aren't forced into a total institution (such as some communes), new recruits are expected to forgo their previous ties, effectively enclosing them in a world where both the symbolic universe they construct and the social structures that sustain them are "universally" accepted.[17]

Whereas such total institutions are perhaps the most extreme example of hermetically dense social worlds, the presumption of isolation forecloses much of the social "action." For Goffman's inmates there are precious few enclaves in which it is even possible for different identifications to emerge. There is the possibility of "role distance," in which a prisoner or mental patient attempts to be something more; there may be situations, or even regular enclaves, within the ship or the barracks in which people are allowed to be something different from soldiers (lovers, perhaps?). But these moments or interactions are rare: the social world is, indeed, total. Since actors are already physically encased in their social world, it almost makes no sense to ask how their identifications are reconstituted. After all, in a total institution, it's the only game in town.

Most social worlds we live in are not so hermetic. Social worlds may vie with each other for the construction of specific identifications, but they rarely have an absolute monopoly. It is this situation that makes the density of summoning an achievement, rather than a "given," and allows us to appreciate the choreography of interactional and experiential patterns of identification in everyday life. In other words, if we want to think about how a set of actions and interactions crystallize specific identifications over time, it is not all that useful to think of prisons or ships. It is better to think about social worlds that are closer to most of us. These are worlds in which other identifications are always available, yet where people are socially pulled by their own projects, by the interactions they encounter, and by those that they expect to encounter in the course of their daily routines.

Religious lives are indeed telling in this regard. As sociologists of religion have long argued, in order to sustain a religious self, a compatible social network needs to be in place—a set of others who share the journey and who help sustain a religious commitment through ongoing interaction.[18] Like Orthodox Jews, members of new religious movements, strict Evangelicals, or devout Muslims in the United States live in a world that does not share their commitments. Much like Orthodox Jews, they need to sustain institutionalized forms of commitment, to foster specific seductions of belonging, and to erect and uphold symbolic boundaries between themselves and the profane world in which they live.

But religious groups are only the tip of a vast social iceberg. Once we think in terms of density, these worlds can be found on all sides of the social—from the worlds of the early modern aristocracy, to the urban underclass, from worlds organized around a political project to those organized by class positions. These social worlds can be evidenced in the work of social scientists but are often more vividly described in works of literature.

Thomas Mann's novel *Buddenbrooks* describes the slow downfall of a family of the nineteenth-century German bourgeoisie. In one of the early episodes of the saga, before the bourgeois world crumbles around and through them, the family's daughter attempts to resist a merchant's

match—what seems to be a perfectly "good, advantageous, match, worthy of her family."[19] But her entire social world—her family, friends,
even the sermons at church—constantly pulls her back, reminding her
that she was born to advance the family's fortunes through marriage.
Trapped in a web of summoning, she goes on a summer vacation and,
without the constant pull of her social world, almost immediately falls
in love with a young man of little means, an impossible match that she
desperately clings to. But, as she realizes even as she is driven in her car-
riage back home, her social world encloses her:

> Tony looked at the gray gabled buildings, the oil lamps strung across the streets. The
> Holy Ghost Hospital—the lindens out front had lost most of their leaves already. Good
> Lord, it was all just as it had been before. It had stood here, immutable and venerable,
> and all the while she had thought of it as an old, easily forgotten dream . . . At that
> moment—the carriage was rattling along Breite Strasse—Mathiesen the grain hauler
> passed them and doffed his homely top hat with a deep sweep of his hand, and his
> gruff face was so full of respect it seemed to say "I swear I'm at the bottom of the
> ladder."[20]

Coming home, she surrenders to her fate and thrusts herself into a
match she loathes. Her family, friends, pastor—but also the streets themselves and the momentary interaction with the grain hauler who knows
just "who she is"—close upon her.

Although it is set in northern Germany of the nineteenth century,
there is something familiar about the social world *Buddenbrooks* describes. As with Orthodox Jews in the Beverly–La Brea neighborhood,
"being a Buddenbrook" was a moral project. Being part of the successful merchant class was not only something one did but also what one
was. And much as in the case of the Orthodox, being summoned as
a Buddenbrook was something that happened around them but also
something that the protagonists actively cultivated. Indeed, when they
stop doing so, the family slowly descends into madness and bankruptcy.

Such literary depictions of dense social worlds, along with their moral
seductions as well as their oppressive suffocation, are quite common.
Thus, to take a well-known example, the women in Jane Austen's *Pride
and Prejudice* live surrounded by their identifications as small landed
gentry. The men may go around the world, occupying colonies and different selves. Yet the lives of the women Austen describes are circumscribed by their class, the balls they go to, the neighbors who come to
visit, or the vacations that they all seem to take simultaneously.

The cases above are worlds that provide identifications that protagonists usually strive for. Mann's Tony is proud of her identification, even while it destroys her chances for happiness. And like Mann's Buddenbrooks and Austen's Bennets, the people I described in this book inhabited identifications that they usually talked about—in their deliberative moments—as moral.

But a deeper look at both the works of fiction and the ethnographic materials I have presented shows the dense interactional moments to be ambivalent. While coming to classes and to morning prayers was sometimes deeply meaningful, and usually routine, people sometimes felt exasperated by their constant summoning. The density of summoning was experienced as supportive, even exhilarating, by some; but at the same time, and often for the same set of characters at different moments, it could become suffocating. Thus, thinking about the relationship between the density of summoning and the constitution of selfhood tempers some of sociology's optimism regarding the imagined premodern community, the *Gemeinschaft* of personalized, noncontractual relationships. Precisely because summoning is both something that actors do and something that is also done to them, they may sometimes find themselves wishing that the world would let them be.

Noting this ambivalence of summoning allows us to see more clearly the relationship between these social worlds and those that inhabitants may morally devalue, or even try to explicitly disavow; worlds where the identifications into which actors are constantly summoned are not necessarily those they strive for. A particularly telling set of cases of dense worlds is the corpus of studies of the urban and suburban poor.

As generations of sociologists in the United States have told the tale, ghettos are not only marked by poverty and structural racism. They are also defined by a host of mutual obligations to other residents living there, by the everyday ways in which police officers put residents under surveillance, by the unease that middle-class residents—and especially middle-class whites—exhibit when "ghetto people" cross their neighborhood boundaries. Extreme poverty thus marks the poor in ways that spill over to their interactions in ways that most middle-class people would not even recognize.[21]

A telling example is a recent ethnography of suburban poverty conducted by Alexandra Murphy.[22] One of the striking moments Murphy lingers on is a seemingly inconsequential puzzle. The people she spoke to asserted, both in interviews and as they went about their lives, that "they stayed to themselves"—that they did not actively take part in their poor suburban environment, that they lived in that world but were not of it. Talking about one of her friends' lives, one of Murphy's interlocutors stressed that:

"My aunt on my dad's side of the family, they were just real people who lived in society's rules. They went to work, they had jobs, police officers, kids in college . . . So I was kind of experienced to that. And they always would tell me, 'When you move somewhere, you don't condone with your neighbors. You had a neighborly respect but you don't let your neighbors all in your house and all in your business, you stay to yourself.' And that's kind of how I am, I stay to myself."[23]

And yet everything that Murphy saw belied the claim that people in the neighborhood "stayed to themselves." The neighborhood was buzzing with people going in and out of each other's houses, trading favors, watching each other's children, and becoming romantically involved. Instead of an imagined white middle-class morality in which residents were ensconced in their private realms, the suburban blocks Murphy studied were a vibrant social world, in which people were constantly summoned into interaction and into being.

The claim "I stay to myself," then, was partly a way to make a moral claim about an idealized life—what their lives "should have been." When they reflected on their condition, or when they got into arguments and altercations with neighbors, the image of a world in which they were not, in fact, constantly summoned into suburban poverty was a compelling one.

The density of poor ghetto residents' social worlds is a central issue for sociologists of poverty. In what has become one of the key explanations of structural poverty in the African American ghetto, William Julius Wilson noted that the situation is so dire precisely because once previously "white neighborhoods" were opened up to African Americans, those who could leave took flight, leaving the poorest, most vulnerable populations to fend for themselves. This disintegration of community makes sense if we attend to the density of summoning in ethnographies of the ghetto. As ethnographers have noted, poverty is defined by multiple networks of obligation and support. People are constantly "in" each other's lives, constructing semilegal economic networks, lending each other money, socializing in the streets, and so on.[24] But far from an idealized story about communal upward mobility, this means that once someone gets ahead—whether by securing a job, avoiding a criminal record, or simply getting money—he or she is under immense pressure to distribute the goods or perform favors for family and acquaintances.[25] In order to extricate themselves from these obligations, those who left severed many of their social ties, and those who stayed thus ended up in an even worse condition since all the ties they had were to people who shared their predicament.

Perhaps the most extreme example of the way poverty is translated into dense webs of summoning is that of the social world of the homeless. Thus, in an ethnography of homeless street vendors in New York, Mitchell Duneier describes life on the sidewalk as an incredibly dense world.[26] A few of the people he spoke to could leave the streets to embody different selves, like a homeless man who could sometimes go and visit his grandson—a toddler who did not yet "know" that his grandparent was a homeless street vendor—or one man who became an unofficial mentor for another young black man, elevating himself to the status of wise older man. But the opportunities to escape the world of homelessness seem few and far between. In their everyday lives, the men Duneier describes were constantly "reminded" that they were homeless, not simply as a pragmatic state, but as an identification. They encountered these identifications when they interacted with each other, when middle-class women ignored them, or when they were kicked off the streets if they tried to keep their vending spot overnight. But they also encountered their identifications in much more mundane situations—for example, when they needed to come up with strategies in order to urinate, whether building relationships with workers at stores that had bathrooms or pissing into a cup. Like garage motion sensors and button-operated crosswalks, the streets themselves seemed to summon the homeless men into their identifications.

These cases of poverty thus allow us to think about situations in which, when asked, people reject the dense world of summoning they partake in. Rather than celebrating their world, they discursively reject it. But for all the symbolic work, the social world they live in is as dense as, if not denser than, that of the Beverly–La Brea Orthodox neighborhood. Whereas many Orthodox Jewish residents moved between Orthodox lives and non-Orthodox worlds of work, the homeless people Duneier traced could not afford situational transcendence. Both materially and symbolically, they were locked into their identification. And much like the spectrum of density of summoning, the different balances between moral project and interactional evocation allow us to think about variation among cases. In some situations and social worlds, actors routinely set themselves up to be summoned in action and interaction; in other worlds actors may attempt to escape identification, only to be summoned by others.

This spectrum between project and unwanted interaction allows me to return, one last time, to the Orthodox neighborhood. Although this book was about the moments in which people are summoned *into* social life, and thus often dwelled upon the seductions of belonging, some residents left both Orthodoxy and the neighborhood. Four teenagers and two adults I knew in the neighborhood became non-Orthodox while I was there. They did so for complex reasons: the teenagers became disillusioned with Orthodox Judaism on intellectual grounds, rebelled against the density of summoning that surrounded them (and perhaps their parents), or had personal travails that convinced them that the Orthodox world did not live up to its promise; the adults I knew gave different reasons—some religious, some having to do with their marital relationships.[27]

Whatever reasons they gave, however, it was difficult for them to continue living in the neighborhood. Although the teenagers I knew did continue to live in their parents' house, they usually felt beleaguered as their parents tried to nudge them back into Orthodoxy.[28] Much like neighborhood residents in the African American ghetto described by Wilson, the adults I knew left not only Orthodoxy but also the neighborhood. And while this was also due to the dynamics of divorce, it was also the case that when they tried to live as non-Orthodox *with* their families, they found it extremely difficult—both because they still needed to keep religious law (e.g., they had to keep kosher in the house, as they could render the entire kitchen unkosher if they cooked nonkosher food in it), and because they were still pulled to occupy the category they tried to distance themselves from. By remaining in place they were still subject to the situational pressures from schools, meshulachim, and rabbis who tried to talk to them about their predicament. There was a geography of summoning that they needed to depart from in order to live a non-Orthodox life.

Last, then, one more comparison suggests itself. Although neighborhood geography was crucial in most cases above, social worlds need not be place-based, something that becomes clear in another case of dense summoning, that of celebrity status. As people attain celebrity, they become the center of a social world in which they are continuously summoned to enact their image—from paparazzi taking their pictures and making news of their love lives or nail polish, through simple moments of recognition on the streets in which strangers ask for their autographs or offer unsolicited advice about their lives and roles.[29] Since they are the locus of the social world, this structure of summoning shadows them almost wherever they may be. This personalized density of summoning is often enticing. But like other forms of density, it may become predictably overbearing. As a well-known actor put it when he was asked what he would dream of doing but couldn't do because of his celebrity status: "I'd go in every ride and I'd walk through Disneyland with my kids and let them experience all the things most kids do. They don't get to with daddy. When daddy walks through Disneyland with them, things get weird."[30]

That celebrities cannot simply walk the streets with their families and that their attempts to occupy different selves may be routinely jeopardized are the fare of any celebrity magazine. More interesting is that they are not only interfered with but forced to occupy the self they are known for. Thus, a minor health and bodybuilding celebrity, talking about how her life has changed, complained that "the minus part of it that I don't like is when you just want to go out and have a cheeseburger and French fries and there is someone at the next table who recognizes you. It seems that because I'm a well known trainer I'm not supposed to be eating those foods."[31] Structurally equivalent to the Orthodox Jew who is supposed to already know what is or isn't kosher based on his attire, the celebrity becomes a personal locus for people to summon her identification.

And like the Orthodox Jews who begin to expect their identification in situations where it is unclear if such an identification is being evoked in interaction, celebrities find themselves second-guessing the world around them not only when they are actively summoned by others but also through their own anticipations of interaction. As one celebrity lamented, such anticipations taint even interactions in which their celebrity status is supposedly not the center of attention: "Why? Why do they want me? Why are they interested in me? Are they laughing at my jokes because they think I am funny or because it is me saying them? And you start double guessing yourself."[32]

The example of celebrity status—even more than that of poverty—seems worlds apart from the Orthodox neighborhood. After all, the Orthodox saw themselves precisely at odds with the Hollywood celebrity culture they lived so close to. And yet a theory of summoning provides a useful provocation. To be constituted as an Orthodox Jew is more than a matter of inhabiting a membership category. It is tied to the moments in which one is recognized, needed, and made valuable both in interaction and in a wider cultural imagery. Although Orthodoxy and celebrity evoke different connotations—a religious landscape of redemption on the one hand, and that of tabloids, bikinis, and television shows on the other—they occupy social worlds in which their identification is constantly invoked and made meaningful.

The case of the Orthodox Jewish neighborhood is a strategic one. It provides a methodological exemplar that allows researchers to think about other cases. And although, like all social worlds, the Orthodox neighborhood is distinct, the dynamics of identification, of seduction and exasperation, are a general feature of social worlds. Tracing the relationship among situations, and the ways in which anticipations are both inscribed and invoked, provides a research agenda. How are people summoned, and in which situations? What are the "mute" areas in which their identification subsides? What is the relationship between summoning and the projects of self that actors profess? What degree of freedom do actors have to enact different permutations of self? Finally, then, summoning provides a way to think about the relationship between people's projects and the interactions they live through and anticipate—how situations are patterned in social worlds, and how social worlds then become etched into patterns not only of interaction but also of self.

Appendix: *Summoned* and *Abductive Analysis*

While I was researching and writing this book, Stefan Timmermans and I were writing another one—*Abductive Analysis: Theorizing Qualitative Research*.[1] In it, we proposed a pragmatist-inspired way to think about the relationship among methods, observations, and theorizing in qualitative research. And although *Summoned* is meant to be read on its own, the two projects are intertwined. If *Abductive Analysis* is a treatise in the theory of method, *Summoned* is partly my attempt (Stefan was engaged in a different empirical project)[2] to flesh out its implications in my own research. In this appendix, I thus want to lay out some key aspects of abductive analysis and say something about how it informed my work here.

Abductive analysis is an attempt to break through deductive and inductive approaches to theorizing in qualitative research by returning to the work of the architect of American pragmatism, Charles S. Peirce. One of Peirce's most important insights was that the logic of inference that people use when they creatively puzzle out their world cannot be neatly captured by either induction (where we generalize from empirical repetition) or deduction (where we come already armed with a theory that we then test against the empirical). Rather, he suggested the notion of abduction and gave it the following form:

The surprising fact C is observed,
But if A were true, C would be a matter of course
Hence there is reason to suspect that A is true[3]

In other words, we begin with a surprise and work our way to a conjecture about the world that would "normalize" the surprise. Then, as Peirce notes, we go back to the world and check our hunches against further observations, moving iteratively through abduction, deduction, and induction.

Our second key move in *Abductive Analysis* was to note that the level of analysis that serves as our "bottoming out" processual level is that of the semiotic chains through which people make meaning. Again, we draw on Peirce to note that semiotics must be thought of as an active process rather than a frozen set of relations among signs. The effect of any sign-object in conjunction with actors' habits of thought and action (an effect that Peirce called an "interpretant") is constitutive of meaning-making.

Relying on these two pragmatist moves, we then developed an approach to theorizing qualitative research, and to the place of method in such a process. Doing so allowed us to discard notions such as the divisions of "the context of discovery" and "the context of justification," helped us develop a processual theory of mechanisms in social research, as well as think about the difference between everyday abduction, which all actors are constantly engaged in, and the kinds of abductive analyses that systematic qualitative research demands.

In the limited space of an appendix, I would like to make two points: first, that the theorization of summoning emerged through different forms of "surprises" in the fieldwork; second, that each such iteration—even when the analysis was at its most organizational—relied on careful attention to ongoing chains of meaning-making (whether implicit or explicit) in action.

Perhaps the key move in abduction as a mode of inference is focusing on surprises. And yet what surprises are and how they emerge is not as clear. As we develop the idea in *Abductive Analysis*, surprises always emerge at the intersection of observations and actors' expectations—whether theoretical or prototheoretical. Without expectations there can be no surprises. Still, there are different modes of surprise in the fieldwork. It is one thing to be surprised when a prototheoretical expectation is not met in the field and quite another to be surprised by observations in relation to the expectations set up by our disciplinary field. Different kinds of surprises also presume different forms of generalizations, different modes of extension and intension.

As a way to begin thinking about these differences, I would like to outline three modes of surprise that structured this work in the different phases of the research. I will term them "focused empirical puzzles," a "general empirical puzzle," and a "general theoretical puzzle."

I began the work with only a vague notion of why the Orthodox neighborhood was interesting. Enamored with grounded theory at the time, I tried to avoid early theorization. Instead, the early phases of the work focused on specific interactional surprises that emerged in the field and that still provide most of the empirical backbone of the work: How could I explain the reactions of the people I knew in the neighborhood to the *meshulach* phenomenon, in which international panhandlers found it economically viable to travel from Israel to the United States? How could I explain Joe's blasé reaction to an anti-Semitic incident that left me shaken? How could I explain the intricate ways in which prayers structured interaction in the synagogue? These were focused empirical puzzles. Although part of what made these surprises compelling was the interactional and phenomenological literature that was all too ready-to-hand, they were based more on failed prototheoretical expectations than on full-blown theory. Moreover, at this stage I didn't try to link each puzzle to other puzzles in the field either empirically or theoretically. Each puzzle was informed by a somewhat different set of theoretical resources that I found useful.

Starting in this way was useful both intellectually and practically. It was easier to write research articles based on focused puzzles than it was to wait patiently for a grander narrative to emerge. But as the fieldwork progressed I found that separating the puzzles missed something about how these processes interact in a way that sustains a certain texture of life. Instead of looking at each process on its own, I moved to look at the way these processes intersected. On this level, I found what seemed in retrospect to be an obvious puzzle: how an Orthodox neighborhood thrives in the midst of secular space. Feeling for the first time that the different processes congealed into a research project, I posited the research as answering the question *how urban spaces sustain ways of life that the modern city was supposed to erode and extinguish*. Here was a puzzle that, I felt, spoke to the sociology of religion as well as to urban sociology, and could bring together the different processes into a coherent whole.

This second phase of surprise-finding in the field was additive: I turned the different puzzles I already found in the fieldwork into elements in a newly constructed set. The "trick of the trade" was to turn smaller questions into cogs in a more general one, where the explanation of each of the processes serves as part of a solution to a larger puzzle.[4]

But this phase still left something to be desired. The more I read my fieldnotes, the less the existing approaches to interaction and identity seemed to capture the processes described. And as I tried to think about the relationship among situations, these approaches became even less satisfactory. How could I do justice to the ways in which situations were related? How did people come to anticipate the rhythms of situations and the way they were overlaid or kept apart? The third puzzle thus emerged as a theoretical puzzle. It is not a puzzle easily communicable to people who are not enmeshed in a specific community of inquiry of social researchers interested in the theory of action. It emerges—even more than the first two puzzles—through the juxtaposition of familiarity with multiple theoretical accounts and reading through notes and transcripts.

These different modes of abduction, however, do not simply move into larger and larger circles of extension. When we move between focused puzzles of interaction and a general empirical puzzle, the scope of extension is not easily definable. On the one hand the focus is on the wider neighborhood and communal life as a whole, yet on the other hand interactional processes are more easily generalizable beyond the specific case. Similarly, in the move between the second and the third form of abduction, the extension widens in the move to a theory of action, but it occurs at the expense of some of the attention to the empirical extension of the first two phases.

Despite the idiosyncrasies of the research project, it may be useful to think about these three modes of puzzlement as methodological provocations. In each moment, surprise motivates theorization; in each moment there are different stakes in abductive analysis. Qualitative researchers do not need to put themselves on hold indefinitely until they realize what their work is a case of (although neither do they need to move through all three modes). At every stage of the research there are useful puzzles to be explored and useful engagements to be had with the wider community of inquiry the researcher is enmeshed in.

Moving from abduction to semiotics, I would like to make a second point here: although there are different modes of surprise being mined through the research project, each of these needs to be grounded in the ways in which actors enact meaning over time. Meaning-making, to follow Peirce, does not necessarily entail explicit negotiations of symbols. It could be an implicit, embodied affair. The key is to show how meaning makes a difference over time—how signs, objects, and habits of thought and action (including expectations about possible futures) affect actors' ongoing navigation of the social world.

This methodological guideline means that the researcher needs to be attentive to action on the ground, even when the analysis seems most detached from these lived realities. To take one example, it pushed me to think, as I was assembling the organizational network in chapter 3, how being enmeshed in such a network affected people's lives—what were the different ways in which I could *show* that dense organizational networks mattered in everyday action and interaction? It also allowed me to see what I could not possibly capture with a network map (for example, that the self summoned was moralized in such a way that other actors could make demands that would not be possible if the same ties evoked a different kind of self). Similarly, it meant that I needed to ask in what specific ways was the neighborhood's history relevant to the ways meaning-making occurred. Instead of simply setting the scene, this approach pushed me to show how, for example, immigration history set up certain organizations and relations in persistent ways.

And, wherever possible, it meant that the analysis needed to trace a process as completely as possible. As Timmermans and I have argued, attending to semiotic chains in action provides a useful specification of what "mechanisms" in the social sciences may mean.[5] As a relational "bottoming out" level it avoids the methodological individualism inherent in too many approaches to mechanisms. But to think in such processual terms, the analysis needed to follow meaning-making over time. Thus, thinking through abductive analysis pushed me to ask what I think of as one of the key ethnographic questions: *and what happens then?*

Last, the approach to meaning-making in action outlined in *Abductive Analysis* is not theoretically innocent. While such pragmatism can be read in different ways (after all, for example, the notion of "habits of thought and action" is almost a floating signifier that can be filled in myriad ways, through many different theoretical sensibilities), it does point to a certain view of social life. Although I did not make extensive use of Peirce's terminology, the theory of action he hints at informs this work. It pushes the researcher to perceive the social world as a patterned arrangement, a choreography of semiotic chains. And by pushing the researcher in this direction, it moves the intersection of actors' projects and their invocations, as well as the intersituational patterns through which social worlds are constructed and sustained, to the center of sociological theorizing.

Notes

1. The metaphor of social density was used by Durkheim (1997 [1893]) to discuss the volume of interactions that people have to sustain. While I borrow this metaphor, I am interested in the density of particular kinds of interaction—those that, as I will argue, identify the person as a particular *kind* of subject.
2. See Calvino (1974).
3. Emirbayer and Goodwin (1994); Grannis (2010). This is also not a "fixable" aspect of network analysis, but the circumscription of its usefulness. Although some of the most interesting theorists of networks tried to go beyond these limitations and construct a space where meanings and relationships intersect (see, especially Harrison White's work: White 1992; Mische and White 1998), these attempts have so far not yielded their promised fruits. Network analysis is important, and I will draw upon some of its insights below (and especially in chapter 3), but as a root metaphor it says too little.
4. In more precise terms, for Althusser (1971) it is the process whereby an ideology addresses the pre-ideological individual, forcing him into both subjectivity and subjection within the ideological matrix of domination. This notion includes both important insights and crucial omissions. It makes the crucial point that interactionists have made: that it is (inter)action that produces subjectivity. But, as with many Marxist structuralists, his view of ideology is too overdetermined and, in the last instance (whether or not it arrives), economic.

5. In this regard the differences between interactionists, ethnomethodologists, and conversation analysts, who are otherwise at odds about the construction of social life, aren't as great. As the founder of pragmatism, C. S. Peirce (e.g., 1992–99; see also Short 2007) noted over a century ago, meaning making is completed only in its *effects* (what he called its "interpretant"). For turn taking in conversation analysis, see Sacks, Schegloff, and Jefferson (1974). The examples of stickups and street violence are taken from Katz (1988) and Jackson-Jacobs (2013), respectively.

6. For the notion of "family resemblance," see Wittgenstein (1953).

7. See, for example, Katz (1999).

8. Csordas (1996: 5). For a summary of the problem of "identity" and the suggestion to use the term "identification" instead, see Brubaker and Cooper (2000).

9. Sacks (1979).

10. The concept of the "social world" is borrowed from Tamotsu Shibutani (1955), Anselm Strauss (1978), and Howard Becker (1982). For Shibutani, who first explicitly defined the concept, a social world relates to "a universe of regularized mutual response" (566).

11. Pierre Bourdieu had something similar in mind when he attacked ethnomethodologists and other interactionists as suffering from what he called "the occasionalist illusion" (1977: 81). For Bourdieu, however, the *habitus* (a learnt structure of perception, appreciation, and embodied temporality) mediates social structure and action. Instead of positing a deeply socialized *habitus*, this book proceeds to show how things cohere within patterned situations. In that sense, the notion of summoning has more affinities to Butler's (e.g., 1990) idea of the performativity of selfhood.

12. For a theorization of temporality in interaction, see Tavory and Eliasoph (2013).

13. One could call this aspect of self-identification the *moral* aspect of self-identification. As I will show below, this does not mean that people have set norms they adhere to, thus returning to a value-norm analysis of social life. Instead, what this means is that certain actions, decisions, or turns-of-talk are loaded with meaning to the self, so that these actions are experienced, or at least expected to be seen, as consequential. For similar approaches in social psychology, see Hughes (1945), who came up with the term "master status"; Stryker (1968); Stryker and Burke (2000). For an attempt to construct a theory of moral action along these lines, see Tavory (2011).

14. This is both in reaction to the growing influence of the Hasidic movement in Orthodoxy, which stressed the experiential ever since its birth in the eighteenth century, and in reaction to American Protestantism, which lent it an emphasis on man's personal relationship with God.

15. See, e.g., Mahmood (2005); Winchester (2008).

16. Coser (1974).

17. For some of the work on the area done before, and while, I was conducting my work, see Margarethe Kusenbach's dissertation (Kusenbach 2003a) and Katz, Ibarra, and Kusenbach (2014).
18. This aspect of Chabad made them a popular study subject. For ethnographic and neojournalistic accounts of Chabad, see Davidman (1991); Harris (1985); Fishkoff (2005).
19. In keeping with ethnographic and IRB traditions, all names of people and organizations are changed to preserve anonymity. And, of course, אשביעך מחלב חטים.
20. Although the bulk of the data used in this work are notes from participant observation, and I use observations wherever possible, I conducted forty-five interviews to supplement the ethnographic data. Interviews were especially important in reconstructing the neighborhood's history and where organizational structures and histories were concerned. As I didn't record conversations (though I did record interviews), all fieldnotes quotes are necessarily imprecise. I therefore do not make arguments based on specific sentence construction and mention specific word use only when I am sure this specific word was used. For the historical section, I also spent a few weeks in the archives at USC and UCLA, looking at Jewish journals from the end of the nineteenth century and into the 1950s. Like any ethnographer, I used whatever data I could put my hands on, and include synagogue plays, posters, emails I received, donation request letters, etc.
21. I published three articles that made use of observations that I also use in the book (Tavory 2010a, 2010b, 2013). I thank the journals *Theory and Society*, *Qualitative Sociology*, and *Ethnography* for allowing me to make use of these previously published observations and insights in this work.

CHAPTER TWO

1. On neighborhood "branding," see Katz (2010); Sheth (2010). This organizational logic is reminiscent of Ratcliff's (1935) argument in marketing theory, showing why it makes sense for retail to cluster in the same area despite competition. As an area becomes known for a specific good, different retailers come to feed off the efforts of other retailers (in a restaurant district, for example, the overflow of people from one restaurant end up in another, etc.). In that way, over time, a certain kind of retail may come to dominate a given space. That being said, the Beverly–La Brea neighborhood is, at best, a small, exotic island.
2. See Vorspan and Gartner (1970: 256–62).
3. On a theoretical level, this chapter has an additional aim, shadowing the historical narrative. The neighborhood formation narrative I present challenges assumptions posited by rational choice sociology of religion, according to which the key to thriving religiosities lies in the relationship between religious pluralism—or, in economic terms, an "open

market"—and religious competition, i.e., the attempt of different groups to enlist members for their denominations (see, for example, Stark and Finke 2000; Warner 1993). In such a scenario, religious groups' "supply" of spiritual goods will generate "demand" for their services either as they cater to the spiritual needs of the laity, or as they offer the kinds of transcendent "utilities," such as salvation, that people find attractive. The history of the Beverly–La Brea neighborhood seems to fit this description. Thus, the neighborhood contained ethnically Jewish but weakly affiliated Jews; into this "niche" entered a plethora of religious organizations, with some measure of friendly competition between them. The neighborhood then changed into a blossoming religious center—precisely the kind of transformation expected under those conditions (Stark and Finke 2000; see also Sherkat and Ellison 1999: 384–86). A look at the histories of different institution clusters and congregants in this chapter, however, shows the limitations of such economic models. I argue that these narratives are much more amenable to analyses offered by urban sociologists studying place entrepreneurship (see Light and Bonacich 1988; Logan and Molotch 1987), who stress the role of "urban pioneers" and the dissemination of public image (Godfrey 1988; Katz 2010; Sheth 2010). These sociologists, like supply-side rational choice sociologists, hold that neighborhoods are constructed through the actions of a specific set of actors rather than growing organically from residents' needs. But instead of assuming that "suppliers" cater to the demand of local residents, such urban sociologists present an explanation of neighborhood emergence that takes into account the ways in which the construction of a neighborhood brings in people from beyond its circumscribed space. Such a view changes the question from that of generating demand to that of constructing a public image and an organizational presence that attract residents while at the same time transforming the characteristics of a neighborhood. As I show, the neighborhood did not become Orthodox through the operations of a rational choice market. Rather, the success of the neighborhood was dependent on the relationship between supply, the far-reaching Orthodox social geography, and the social networks through which this institutional geography was disseminated.

4.   I mainly use two kinds of data in this chapter. For the second section, relating to the early Jewish settlement in Los Angeles and the formation of the neighborhood as an ethnic enclave, I rely both on secondary sources and on archives of the *B'nai B'rith Messenger* and *Los Angeles Times*, memoirs of Jews who lived in Boyle Heights from UCLA's archive, the records of urban revitalization programs, and other official documents. I was also aided by Rebbetzin Miriam Adler-Huttler, a local persona and historian, who generously allowed me to use a historical manuscript about the early days of Orthodoxy in Los Angeles and the neighborhood (Adler-Huttler 2008). For the third section, regarding the entry of Orthodox institutions from

the East Coast, I relied primarily on interviews. At each of the institutions I mention, I spoke to the rabbi or to other knowledgeable congregation members. I have conducted thirty-four formal organizational interviews, in addition to many more informal conversations and interviews with congregation members. In the formal interviews, I asked interviewees to tell me about the history of the institution, how it arrived in the neighborhood, the specific choice of locations, movements of the institution within the neighborhood, and its ties to other institutions (with respect to both cooperation and competition). Interviews were conducted in English and Hebrew and lasted between thirty minutes and four hours.

5. Of course, there will always be people who end up living some distance away, either because they were born there or because the rents are lower. These people have to walk a mile to go to synagogue, but they themselves consider themselves to be outside of the neighborhood, or at least at its edges.

6. Based on 2008 data.

7. These numbers were extrapolated from a few observational strategies. First, I used the 2000 US census. As the census does not ask directly about religion, percentages were gauged by looking at the percentage of white households with five or more people. This is a rough approximation, based on the large family size of Orthodox Jews. Families where children had already left the household were offset by the fact that at least some of the families captured by this measure were non-Orthodox. Second, I went to all the synagogues in the neighborhood on different Saturdays and major holy days and counted the adult men in each. Third, I asked the woman in charge of the *mikveh*, the ritual bath, for an approximation of the number of premenopausal married women.

8. See Katz, Ibarra, and Kusenbach (2014); Kusenbach (2003a).

9. Jayanti (1995).

10. See, for instance, Klein (2006).

11. Vorspan and Gartner (1970: 287).

12. Young (1928: 241).

13. Dash Moore (1994); Adler-Huttler (2008).

14. Dash Moore (1994: 95).

15. Vorspan and Gartner (1970: 212).

16. See, for what remains the most insightful study of Jewish neighborhoods, Louis Wirth's (1938) *The Ghetto*.

17. On the mobility of Jews in Los Angeles, see Gelfand (1981).

18. McWilliams (1946: 322).

19. As a careful look at map 2 shows, the actual area between La Brea and Fairfax—today the center of the neighborhood—was still not heavily populated by Jews in 1930. This is because the area was still undeveloped until the mid- to late-1930s—in 1930 it was still oilfields. I thank Jack Katz for this insight. As the area became developed, Jews moved in.

20. Home Owners Loan Corporation (1939).
21. See Phillips (1986).
22. Young Israel Community Development Corporation (1982).
23. Vorspan and Gartner (1970: 287).
24. Where no references are given, data are derived from interviews or other primary resources.
25. On the rates of Jews marrying non-Jews, see, e.g., Cohen (1988).
26. For place entrepreneurship, see Logan and Molotch (1987). In both the cases below, I focus on educational institutions. The reason for this focus (rather than, for example, a focus on synagogues) is that congregants, and often the rabbis running them, came to the neighborhood as a result of the emerging educational institutions.
27. See Heilman and Friedman (2010) for a controversial history of Chabad's last rebbe and the Chabad movement in the twentieth century.
28. See Fishkoff (2003).
29. The Chabad Telethon was begun in 1980, after a fire destroyed Cunin's Chabad House in Westwood, Los Angeles.
30. The founder, Simcha Wasserman (1900–1992), was in fact an important figure in Los Angeles Jewish history, instrumental in educational efforts both at the Yeshiva Ohr Elchonon (named after his father, Elchonon Wasserman) and even beforehand, brought over by one of Boyle Heights's most important religious figures, Rabbi Osher Zilberstein (see Adler-Huttler 2008). Throughout this chapter, I only skim the history of the minor pioneers of strict Orthodoxy in Los Angeles—those who opened small synagogues, ritual baths, and so on. However, a fuller urban history and sociology would need to pay careful attention to the role of minor pioneers. In all the stories of success I outline, these pioneers served as "organizational hooks" for later and more successful pioneers. However, the development of an urban sociology of organizational hooks is beyond the scope of this study.
31. As an extra boon, the yeshiva could operate in the quiet tertiary streets of the neighborhood, away from the hustle and bustle of the main arteries of transportation. In a city known for its strict zoning laws, this was unusual, but since the lot used to be a home for the elderly, it could be "grandfathered in" as an educational institution.
32. Today, headed by Kotler's grandson, it is also one of the largest in the United States, with an enrollment of 6,500 students in 2012. See Helmreich (1982) for the Lakewood yeshiva's early years.
33. According to the kollel's founder, Rabbi Fasman, the Los Angeles Kollel was the third of these kollels, after those opened in Toronto and Detroit. The term "community kollel" was, according to Fasman, first used in Los Angeles.
34. The kollel's founder did look into other "Jewish" neighborhoods such as Beverly Hills and Pico-Robertson. However, he said he found people in

other neighborhoods more resistant. In the Beverly–La Brea area he found not only Jews but also a number of "organizational hooks"—religious organizations that would provide him with space, and some support, in the early days.

35. Data about kollel alumni are taken chiefly from an interview with the kollel principal, in which he outlined where his alumni ended up. I also triangulated some of the specific information with other interviews.

36. For a fuller depiction of the varieties and meanings of different forms of Orthodoxy, see chapter 5.

37. One of the effects of the success of the Orthodox neighborhood since the 1980s is that, at the writing of this book, subaffiliations shared fewer and fewer organizations. However, there were still important organizations many of them shared, including the girls high school, one of the primary schools, the main ritual bath, and some welfare organizations. See also chapter 3.

38. Herman (1998).

39. The numbers of students in Jewish schools changed from 1,862 children in 1979 (most of them in pretty lax schools that had a religious program complementing a strong secular program), to 4,911 in 1998 (in far stricter, religious-centered schools). See Abrahamson (1998).

40. Fischer (2000).

41. See Loveman and Muniz (2007) for a similar case of the movement of categories rather than people.

42. Kronzek (1990: 24).

43. Indeed, in the long run, these newcomers may end up "taking over" the synagogue—changing its prayer structure and affiliation. This transformation, in fact, led to legal battles in another neighborhood in Los Angeles and was a real threat to at least one of the congregation rabbis, who explicitly spoke about it in an interview.

44. For the more general Orthodox "slide to the right," see Heilman (2006).

45. More fully, the number of organizations is affected by: (a) the construction of parallel organizations by subaffiliations; (b) the attempt of trained rabbis to find their own "niche," as in the case of the kollel; (c) the laissez-faire environment of organizational entrepreneurship and the neighborhood's reputation, and (d) the fact that the upkeep of a religious organization is relatively cheap, since they pay no property taxes.

46. See also chapter 5.

CHAPTER THREE

1. For a useful discussion of the ways institutions pull people into social networks and participation, see also Mario Small's (2009) *Unanticipated Gains*.

2. A *minyan* is a quorum of ten adult men, needed for daily prayers; a *shul* is Yiddish for synagogue. See also next chapter and glossary.

3. For a sustained evaluation and critique of the meaning of network ties, see Emirbayer and Goodwin (1994); Grannis (2010). The thrust of these evaluations, as I also note in the introduction, is that in the absence of a qualitative description of what ties *mean*, limited information can be gleaned from network structure.

4. The network map I present in figure 1 is based on coding of five years of fieldnotes and transcripts. That being said, I did *not* conduct a systematic survey, and the data are thus incomplete—it is an impressionist's network map. Although fieldnotes probably capture some relationships that would have been obscured by a survey, relying on qualitative work results in an underestimation of the number of network ties. In organizations where I knew more people intimately, I was made aware of more ties over time. Additionally, network analysts usually attempt to keep both the kinds of actors and the kinds of ties constant in their analyses (see, e.g., Scott 1991). In figure 1 I deviate from both these heuristics. I would like to thank Fabien Accominotti for his generous assistance in constructing this network map, and for his insights regarding its possibilities and limitations.

5. See Brubaker et al. (2006), as well as Small (2004), for a similar point in a Latino housing project. The theorization of "institutional completeness," crucial for both Brubaker and Small, is derived from the work of Breton (1964).

6. I expand on the ways residents navigate work and Orthodox neighborhood life in chapter 6.

7. This remark appears in Ann Swidler's note on her recollections of Goffman. See Swidler (2010).

8. In the language of network analysis, these were "multiplex ties." The term is derived from an insight of the founder of the "Manchester school" of anthropology, Max Gluckman (1955).

9. For a definition and discussion of centrality in network analysis, see, e.g., Scott (1991).

10. This mapping also shows some relative distances and proximities among affiliations, a subject I will return to in chapter 5. As an interim note, the "strict" Orthodox residents—Hasidic and Yeshivish alike—were tightly clustered; similarly, the "traditional" and the Sephardic residents were tightly connected since a number of Sephardic minyans rented space in "traditional" synagogues. Chabad tended to occupy an intermediate position, related to both, but had some degree of institutional completeness (Breton 1964). Some organizations seem like "islands" in other affiliations. One, a small Yeshivish organization, catered to newly religious residents and was thus tightly connected to Chabad (an affiliation that also caters to this constituency); another was a small Chabad organization whose founder was close to the non-Chabad Hasidic residents.

11. Shibutani (1955: 566).

12. Another question, which I can only touch lightly upon here, is what accounts for the friendly tenor of relationships among affiliations. In comparison with some neighborhoods on the East Coast or in Israel (see, e.g.,
Goldschmidt 2006; Heilman 1992; J. Mintz 1992), there were relatively few
tensions among Orthodox affiliations that seemed to be at each other's
throats elsewhere. As one resident in the neighborhood once told me, it all
seemed "very California." Among the reasons for this was the fact that Los
Angeles was at the periphery of the Orthodox world—there were no major
Orthodox power structures in the city, and thus there was little "at stake."
More to the point, the neighborhood emerged out of the few institutional
entrants outlined in the previous chapter. Historically, then, members
of different affiliation had to use the same organizations, thus fostering what may be thought of as an "idioculture" (Fine 1979) of friendly
relations. That being said, I am far from convinced that friendly relations
among affiliations are as rare as they appear in the literature describing
the Orthodox world. The tendency to present Orthodox worlds as purely
consisting of one affiliation stems, in my view, from researchers' tendency
to focus on homogenous neighborhoods or towns and to overplay an
affiliation-based insularity that may be more the exception than the rule.
Differences and tensions indeed exist, but they are very often bridged (see
also discussion in chapter 5).

13. It is important to note that although network analysts tend to analyze flows
of information rather than of identity, network theorists recognize the larger
questions at stake. As John Mohr and Harrison White (2008: 486) put it, "an
institution links together different orders and realms of social life, notably
the agentic with the structural, the symbolic with the material, and the mi-
cro with the meso and the macro structures of social organization." Although
Mohr and White refer to any institutionalized activity rather than to organizational belonging, their observation is only heightened in the case of the
links I describe. An organization, after all, is a codified and materially located
set of institutions. Moreover, the discussion of "netdom" and "catnet" as well
as the very title and assumptions behind Harrison White's (1992) *Identity and
Control* provides ways to talk simultaneously about flows of information and
of identity (see also Ann Mische's 2008 study of political activism in Brazil,
where ties confer identity; see also Mische and White 1998).

14. Coser (1974: 4).

15. The reference to the web of group affiliations is Georg Simmel's (1964),
which Coser explicitly invokes (1974: 2). Focusing on symbolic demands
rather than the extreme cases of physical separation assumed by E. Goffman
(1961) makes "greedy institutions" a much more generative theoretical
concept than its far-better-known cousin, the "total institution."

16. For a sociology of rhythm, see Henri LeFebvre's (2004) "rhythmanalysis
(see also Snyder 2012). Rhythm, here, means "a patterned movement of

presences and absences" (Snyder 2012: 16). Although I am inspired by Snyder and LeFebvre's analyses in the use of rhythm, the categories that LeFebvre develops for defining rhythmic action—isorhythmia (when rhythms are identical), eurhythmia (when they intertwine), and arrhythmia (when they clash)—miss the syncopations of action that I describe below.

17. Schools, whether Orthodox or otherwise, *always* pull both children and parents into patterns of interaction and commitment—children tend to make friends, and parents meet each other in parent meetings and committees, school plays, or graduation ceremonies. And yet, they do so to differing degrees (see Small 2009 for an extremely useful analysis of childcare organizations).

18. A 2000–2001 survey of Jewish households in the United States found that the birth rate for married Orthodox women ages 40–49 is 4.4 children, as compared with a combined average of 1.45 children for Reform, Conservative, and nonaffiliated Jews (Jewish Federations of North America 2001).

19. For a family with seven children, each of them studying for twelve years for an average of $11,000 per year, paying half a million dollars actually means they received more than 40 percent tuition reduction.

20. For an informative ethnography of Bobover Hasidic girls and schools in Brooklyn, see Fader (2009).

21. For a more nuanced depiction of summoning in the synagogue, see next chapter.

22. In his excellent ethnography of a Modern Orthodox synagogue, Samuel Heilman (1976) presents "the schnorrer" as one of the social types that inhabit the synagogue. As far as I am aware there is no academic study of the meshulachim.

CHAPTER FOUR

1. The translations in brackets, here and throughout, are the author's.
2. See figure 1 in chapter 3.
3. See Hayden White (1987).
4. To borrow Victor Turner's (1974) framework, this incident can be seen as a social drama. Much as in the dramas Turner analyzes, the illness is a breach in the social, which produces a crisis. This crisis then requires some kind of "redressive action" (39–41), a way for the community to work through the crisis (see also Myerhoff 1979).
5. For a mechanism-based approach to ethnographic work, see Tavory and Timmermans (2013).
6. The notion of "inhabiting" is adapted from Heidegger (1971). See Mucahit Bilici's (2012) ethnography of American Muslims for an excellent use and working-through of the term. I have termed the synagogue a "place," echoing Yi-Fu Tuan's (1977) distinction between "space" and place.

7. Heilman (1976).

8. Or, as interactionists may put it, a synagogue is where a local idioculture (Fine 1979) is bound to emerge, as well as where group styles take shape (Eliasoph and Lichterman 2003).

9. For street corners see, e.g., the work of Whyte (1943); Liebow (1967); for bars see, for instance, May (2001); for mushroom collectors see Fine (1998).

10. For the definition of Ortho*doxy* as Ortho*praxy*, see Sharot (1991).

11. See Parry's (1986) work extending Mauss's (1990 [1923–24]) *The Gift*, where he describes how religious formations refract the ways in which gifts structure relationships. See also the current literature on organ and egg-and-sperm donation (e.g., Almeling 2011; Healy 2006) for ways in which the logic of the gift shifts in heavily moralized situations.

12. A small number of synagogues in the neighborhood started the morning-prayer session precisely at sunrise throughout the year. Although they were generally revered, few synagogues in the neighborhood attempted to emulate them and ask congregants to arrive, during the summer months, at 5:15 a.m. if not earlier.

13. Although this was not the case of this particular synagogue, "outreach" synagogues that see it as their mission to bring nonaffiliated (or non-Orthodox) Jews into the fold of Orthodoxy seem to sometimes use the minyan challenge as a powerful inclusionary practice. The minyan becomes a way to generate commitment from new members, by signaling that they are, in a very practical sense, "needed." This may also be the case in dwindling religious communities (see Kugelmass 1986).

14. There is a confusing difference between family names and the religious "Cohen" designation. Though people with surnames such as "Cohen," "Kahn," or "Katz" are usually Cohens in the religious sense, this is not always the case. It is thus part of a family tradition that congregants have to attest to.

15. Patterns of sociality and community formation thus should not to be equated with warm and harmonious feelings of belonging. Exasperation, as this case points to, is also a predictable outcome.

16. Barthes (1975); Ginzburg (1999); Perry and Sternberg (1986).

17. This list of characteristics is adapted from Perry and Sternberg (1986).

18. In other words, the "necessity" arises from a combination of the civility rituals of everyday life (E. Goffman 1967) and the highly specialized structure of liturgy. It is tempting, here, to assume that over time, prayers were structured in this way precisely to produce this "latent function" (Merton 1968). This is a seductive, if highly speculative, possibility.

19. Durkheim ([1912] 1965). For work on "emotional energy" and a development of Durkheim's work to provide an overarching theory of emotion and interaction, see Collins (2004).

20. A partial genealogy of this position would include Durkheim's ([1897] 1979) *Suicide*, and pass through Berger's (1967) *Sacred Canopy* and Geertz's (1973) "webs of meaning." See also Yamane (2000) for the centrality of narrative in understanding religious experience.

21. The increased specificity of meaning in the study of religion also percolated into studies that take interaction more seriously than did early meaning-centered analyses. Thus, for example, such studies have shown how the organizational structure of new Catholics afforded them a way to influence Vatican decisions (Wilde 2004); how poor Evangelicals can mobilize their faith to avoid violence (Smilde 2007); how black neighborhood residents transpose church-style patterns of interaction into the political arena (Pattillo-McCoy 1998); or how Boston spiritualists cement relationships by recourse to the narratives afforded by the idea of "past lives" (Bender 2010). Additionally, recent studies regarding the intersections of religious involvement and social activism have emphasized the importance of situated interaction (e.g., Lichterman 2005, 2012; Wood 2002) in developing group styles (Eliasoph and Lichterman 2003). In such studies, interaction is seen as important for understanding the ways religiosity is lived in everyday life (see also Ammerman 1997; Hall 1997), as well as in sites and situations that may not be seen prima facie as religious (see, e.g., Bender 2003). For an early precursor of such attention to interaction in the sociology of religion, and a particularly relevant one, see Heilman (1976).

22. See Collins (2004). For a perspective that focuses on time consciousness in ritual experience, see the incorporation of Alfred Schutz's and of Mihalyi Csikszentmihalyi's work on time consciousness by Neitz and Spickard (1990); Spickard (1991).

23. See Reed (2011).

24. Thus, for example, although my study was conducted in one neighborhood, comparing my findings with other studies of Orthodox Jewish life shows striking similarities. Thus, to take the example of the minyan, in his study of a Modern Orthodox synagogue in Philadelphia in the 1970s Samuel Heilman (1976) describes an almost identical minyan dynamic. Of course, people were called on the telephone rather than on their cellular phones, and text-messaging was not a part of the interactional detail. However, the congregation rabbi constantly had to know where his minyan-men were, and people called their friends in the mornings when they didn't wake up and developed a similar team spirit. In Kugelmass's (1986) ethnographic study of a synagogue in the Bronx, to take another example, one of the ways that the lay rabbi got the few remaining Jewish men and women to participate was through the constant threat of not having a minyan, framing their participation as crucial not only for themselves but for the entire congregation.

25. The notion of "institutional fingerprint" was developed in conversation analytic studies of institutional settings. See Drew and Heritage (1992).

CHAPTER FIVE

1. For the classic semiotic definition of meaning, see Saussure (1986 [1916]).
2. The notion of distinction in sociology is currently dominated by the work of Pierre Bourdieu (see, e.g., Bourdieu 1984). For Bourdieu, distinctions are hierarchical, based on the ability of actors to define the good (in both the ethical and the libidinal sense) in a given field. While this notion may be useful, I find it doesn't capture the situational nature of distinctions, nor is it able—without common consecration mechanisms—to account for multiple centers. I am also indebted to the work of Barth (1969; see also Lamont and Molnár 2002; Pachuki, Pendergrass, and Lamont 2007) for the semiotics of boundaries in everyday life, and to that of Brubaker et al. (2006) and Small (2004) for thinking through the organizationally located aspects of distinctions.
3. Klein (2006).
4. Although playing an instrument on the Sabbath is not prohibited per se, the Talmud warns against it, as people would be tempted to fix or tune their instruments, which would be directly prohibited by Torah law.
5. See E. Goffman (1959) for an analysis of tact.
6. See also Heilman (2006) for the stratification of Orthodox subaffiliations.
7. See also Poll (1962).
8. Snyder (2012), following LeFebvre (2004), depicts such symmetry as a form of "eurhythmia"—the congruous matching of social rhythms.
9. See Adam (1990); Tavory and Eliasoph (2013); Zerubavel (2003).
10. See also Wieder (1974).
11. For the difference between character trait and moral attributions, see Tavory (2011).
12. *Misnagdic* is a Hasidic term, as it is the Hebrew for "naysayer," or "opposer." The Yeshivish are called "naysayers" by Hasids, as they were opposed to Hasidism in the late eighteenth and nineteenth centuries. The term *Litvisch* arises from the fact that the center of resistance to Hasidism was in Lithuania.
13. Again, a partial exception is the case of the Messianic branch of Chabad—those within the Chabad-Lubavitcher Hasidic movement who believe the late Rebbe Menachem Mendel Schneerson was potentially, or still is, the Messiah. Both within the nonmessianic branch of Chabad, and in other affiliations, some saw this as bordering on idolatry.
14. Tavory (2010b).
15. A stricture that defines kosher dairy products as only those dairy products that were supervised from the time of milking, whereas regular "kosher dairy" usually means that the products were supervised only in the factory itself.
16. Like other Orthodox jokes, it also has another referent, the paradoxes of meticulous observance.

17. The general term for nonreligious Jews in strict Orthodox circles, in this context, is *tinok she'nishba*, "a captured infant." The assumption is that the Jewish "infant" was captured by a world devoid of Torah and cannot be held responsible for his transgressions.

18. See Boyarin (2011: 17).

19. In the terms of the sociology of religion, whereas the FFB experienced Orthodoxy as a "church"—a taken-for-granted and encompassing structure they grew into—the BT's trajectory was sect-like, a chosen way of life. And despite the churchlike aspect of Judaism, Orthodox rabbis and authorities across generations had an ambivalent appreciation for the choice made by BTs and converts. See Weber (1978) and Troeltsch (1931) for an analysis of this aspect of religious life.

20. See Davidman (1991); Fishkoff (2005); Harris (1985); Heilman (1992).

21. Note that the category of convert comes at the end, after the ascending order of religious prestige. Although I do not touch on this aspect, this location is telling, effectively outside the categorization of Jews.

22. Additionally, Modern Orthodox were less prone to be averse to marrying a BT.

23. Aviad (1983); Davidman (1991); Harris (1985).

24. See Aviad (1983).

25. See Bourdieu (1984). Moreover, the *nouveau riche* attitude seems even more pronounced, as the symbolic inability to understand is translated into a literal inability to understand the texts. But rather than viewing the incident cynically, as tends to happen with the failed attempts of the nouveau riche, it is more productive to view the books in this household as a provocation of self. When he sees the books, the owner sees not only his present condition, but also a hopeful future for himself (and for his children). Thus the books remind him not only of his present incompetence but of a future potential.

26. For the notion of tacit knowledge, see Polanyi (1966).

27. In phenomenological terms, this is a specific, and hierarchically organized, form of "apperception" (Husserl 1960)—the fusion of perceptual affordances and preconceived ideas about the object, constructed through past experiences. In Alfred Schutz's (1967) terms, the BT is typified, in perception, as a specific "kind" of person about whom certain characteristics are already known.

28. See figure 1 in chapter 3. For the ways religious trajectories emerge and are reproduced in Orthodox schools, see also Fader (2009); Heilman (1992, 2006); J. Mintz (1992); Shaffir (1974).

29. See chapter 2.

30. In this chapter, I did not attend to the Ashkenazi (European origin)/Sephardic (Middle Eastern/North African) distinction. This is because the neighborhood is, by and large, composed of Ashkenazi Jews.

31. In relatively rare cases, strict Orthodox families would not marry their children to a son or daughter of a newly religious person, ostensibly because of the risk that at some point their secular forefathers had divorced and remarried through secular law—thus technically making the children bastards. But these cases appeared to be relatively rare. Although people spoke of them, it seemed to be a lurking suspicion rather than an open reason for rejecting a match.

32. To a certain extent, this resembles a pattern of intergenerational interaction seen in immigrant families where children speak the language of the land better than their parents do, and as a result take on responsibilities that are usually the prerogative of the parent generation. See Portes and Rumbaut (2001). Also, if less dramatically, a similar intergenerational movement occurred in the case of the traditional Orthodox who sent their children to an Orthodox school, only to find their children moving to a different Orthodoxy.

CHAPTER SIX

1. There is a small cottage industry of such studies, vying for ways to depict this "postmodern" self—*The Saturated Self* (Gergen 1991), *The Protean Self* (Lifton 1993), *Liquid Life* (Bauman 2005), and so on. For all extents and purposes, however, it is enough to note with Simmel's (1964) initial, and brilliant, formulation that we are increasingly caught in a diverse web of overlapping affiliations and entanglements and therefore possible selves.

2. To use Hughes's (1945) terms, being an Orthodox Jew was supposed to be a *master status*, a definition of self that was considered as more salient than others—and one that needed to be intersituationally so (see Tavory 2011).

3. The mobilization of the Holocaust to refer to unborn children and other social issues is also used by pro-life activists (see Beisel and Lipton-Lubet 2003), Palestinians regarding the Israeli occupation, Israelis regarding Palestinian terrorist attacks, and many more.

4. Statistics seemed to back this claim: the percentage of intermarriage of Orthodox Jews who went through K–12 Orthodox schools was 3 percent, as compared with 47 percent for the entire Jewish population in the United States (see the NJPS 2000–2001 survey). Of course, it is hard to know whether this is an effect of schooling or if it simply reflects the kinds of families that send their children to Orthodox schools.

5. The explicitness of the poster is also due to the fact that the school in question is not one of the more stringent schools in the neighborhood. For the demographic targeted by the ad—Israelis who moved to the United States—it is necessary to make an implicit threat into an explicit articulation, as the intrinsic value of a religious school cannot be taken for granted.

6. See Brodkin (1998).
7. See, e.g., Cohen (1988); Della Pergola (1996).
8. See Gordon and Horowitz (2006).
9. For the differentiation between symbolic and social boundaries, see Lamont and Molnár (2002). As Sherman (2005, 2007) points out, the potential problem with a wholesale reliance on the notion of boundaries is that it neglects the situational aspect of boundary-making and distinction.
10. I use "speech genres" as defined by Bakhtin (1986: 60–103): patterned ways of speaking that include grammatical structures; the use of specific words and figures of speech; a particular way of speaking; circumscription to a specific situation.
11. For an analysis of bisociation between worlds of meaning as the primary vehicle for humor, see Koestler (1964); Tavory (2014).
12. This was, to a certain extent, dependent on residents' biographies. People born into Orthodox families (FFBs) tended more often to work in "Jewish jobs" in the neighborhood and beyond it, jobs in which non-Jews were still relegated to the position of an "other." Thus even a kosher supervisor who worked with non-Jews on a daily basis at every restaurant that he supervised viewed these non-Jews as others whom he was working, in a certain regard, "against."
13. This was not only because of a deliberate erasure of non-Jews. In addition to such erasure, the Sabbath and religious holidays, the times when a lot of my interactions with community members took place, were precisely the situations in which talking in detail about work would be frowned upon. The association of non-Jews with the realm of the profane excluded them as topics of discussion and made most interactions between members "goy-free."
14. This section is indebted to Eliasoph and Lichterman's (2003) note about the relation among boundaries, ties, and speech norms. Although I do not treat speech norms as analytically separable from the boundaries and the ties they sustain, the emphasis on speech, and silence, is illuminating.
15. For the notion of repair in conversation analysis, see Schegloff, Jefferson, and Sacks (1977).
16. This is exacerbated by the fact that the conversation took place between Chabad members. Unlike other strict Orthodox strands, Chabad has a staunch pro-Israel bent that translates into quite virulent anti-Arab sentiment. Being an Arab, then, is much worse than simply being a Gentile.
17. Most families used a *Shabbos zeiger* [Sabbath clock] in order to handle these issues—a timer that made sure that lights and necessary appliances would go on and off at preset times without necessitating religiously proscribed actions. However, as people sometimes forgot to set their Sabbath clock, they still found themselves in the predicament I describe.
18. See Keller (1968, 2003).
19. See Heilman (2006).

20. See Hendershot (2004); Rossman (2009).
21. A game in which cards containing different nouns are given to all players, who then have to choose one of them to fit an adjective. The player who comes up with the funniest or most creative fit—as decided by a judge appointed for each round—wins the round.
22. Golda Meir (1898–1978) was Israel's female prime minister between 1969 and 1974.
23. And across social classes (see Halle 1994).
24. The *kiddush* blessing before the meal could have been done on grape juice, but this was rarely the case. And since a bottle of wine was already opened for the blessings, it usually ended up being consumed.
25. See, e.g., Bourdieu (1984).
26. See Lamont (2000); Lamont and Molnár (2002); Pachuki, Pendergrass, and Lamont (2007). Note that another literature concerning the metaphor of the boundary considers it to be a domain that different actors actually *share*. This use of the metaphor gave rise to the notion of "boundary-object" (Star and Griesemer 1989). And yet, in the study of demarcation of groups, it is the first form of the metaphor—as a dividing line—that has held sway.
27. See Burke (1945).

CHAPTER SEVEN

1. I have been inspired, throughout the chapter, by Margarette Kusenbach's excellent work on the ethnography of walking (Kusenbach 2003b, 2012; see also Katz, Ibarra, and Kusenbach 2014). Both philosophers and phenomenological geographers have long been attentive to the importance of local mappings, developing a language of space and place that I use throughout (see Heidegger 1971; Casey 1993; Relph 1976; Tuan 1977). I note, however, that whereas the analyses of emplacement in the phenomenology of space and place often stress the way in which people make space "their own," the analysis here points to a different case, where people emplace their surroundings precisely by making them *predictably challenging*.
2. Throughout the chapter I assume that the physical environment is not simply a passive canvas Orthodox Jews paint, but an active element that they have to contend with. In that, I am influenced by actor-network theorists (ANT), who have emphasized what they call the "interobjectivity" of the social world, including both human and nonhuman actants (see, e.g., Callon 1986; Latour 1996, 2005). However, with critics of ANT, I note that there is a difference between *action* and *agency*. Although the streets may act upon Orthodox Jews, agency is not symmetrically distributed. As I show, the possibilities of self-definition depend on the way Orthodox residents wish to understand and portray themselves—a form of agency that posters, for examples, simply don't have (see also Jerolmack and Tavory 2014; Ingold 2011).

3. See, for example, Levy (1988) regarding the cases of the Orthodox populations in Jerusalem and Bnei Brak in Israel. See also the heated debates on bicycle lanes going through the Orthodox section of Williamsburg, Brooklyn (Moynihan 2009; Olshan and Schram 2009), and Goldschmidt's (2006) work on the Chabad neighborhood in Crown Heights.

4. For a more sustained analysis of morality and "moral density," see Tavory (2011).

5. See Anderson (1990).

6. Luhtakallio (2012).

7. For other groups sharing the streets, of course, the neighborhood space changed in accordance with other time cycles, such as the shopping seasons or the passage of day and night. See, for instance, Melbin (1978).

8. See, for instance, Wuthnow (1987).

9. More specifically, the string eruv is an adaptation of the rules of *eruv chazeirot*. Those edicts pertain to ways to make permissible the moving of objects between different domains (i.e., the public and private domain, though later religious interpretation recognizes four such domains including the "exempt domain" and the intermediate *Karmelit*), as well as the act of carrying in public space. Whereas Orthodox Jews are not allowed to change the location of objects from one domain to another on the Sabbath or carry objects in public space, as this is considered work, a walled area is exempt from this prohibition, if it is ritually turned into a shared household by placing a shared food item in a house in the neighborhood. The eruv string—a string tied to poles surrounding the designated space—makes the area within it legally considered a walled enclosure, a symbolic common household where carrying and moving objects are allowed. The question of what is regarded a "permissible" eruv is subject to much religious controversy within the Orthodox world. See also Rabbi Adam Mintz's (2011) dissertation, an excellent account of eruv laws and history in America. In this sense, the eruv is the paradigmatic territorial marker. There are well-documented contestations regarding its construction, and the tensions between Orthodox and non-Orthodox, Jews and non-Jews that surface when it is erected. For some detailed descriptions of controversies surrounding the eruv, see Cooper (1996); Diamond (2000); Valins (2000).

10. Which they did, in other contexts; see chapter 5.

11. In moral psychology (e.g., Haidt 2001), sociology (Hitlin 2003, 2008; Vaisey 2009), and philosophy (see, e.g., Stevenson 1944), a prominent theoretical perspective sees the moral as a realm of gut-reaction, emotive reactions. In the evocative metaphor used by Jon Haidt, there is a cognitive rider on top of an emotive elephant. The rider may believe he is steering the elephant, but it is actually the elephant dictating the direction. As I argue here, although this is an important insight, it risks making an untenable distinction between cognitive and emotive, between elephant and rider (see also

Tavory 2011; MacIntyre 1984). What emotivists miss is precisely the way that emotions and cognitive stances are intertwined through multiple schemata of action. In this sense, emotive stances operate more like resources than like elephants (for arguments along these lines, see Giddens 1984; Sewell 1992; Swidler 2001; Tavory and Swidler 2009).

12. See Kusenbach (2003b; 2012).

13. I focus on men, rather than women, because the signs of belonging coded in dress are more visible for this category. While there is a dress code for women—long skirts, long-sleeved shirts, and a head cover or wig for married women—it is harder to immediately recognize. The black silk coat and fur hat of some Hasidic men are not religiously prescribed but remnants of eighteenth-century non-Jewish Polish aristocratic fashion. Chabad's wide-brimmed Borsalino hat was worn by the seventh rebbe of Chabad, Menachem Mendel Schneerson (Heilman and Friedman 2010). The yarmulke itself is not a Torah edict but a custom dating back to the early Middle Ages, and only lightly adumbrated by Talmudic law as a sign of extra piety (Kidushin 31a; Shabbos 156b).

14. See, for example, Davis (1992) and Joseph (1986) for a discussion of the role of uniforms in solidifying identity.

15. The yarmulke, as a sign, thus mediates between signs "given" and those "given off"—between the signs that are intentionally posited and those that are read without ever having been intended to be legible. See E. Goffman (1959) for the distinction between signs "given" and those "given off." The notion of "interactional hook" that I use below is also derived from this work.

16. Those residents who said that they were usually aware of the yarmulke were those who had only recently donned these signs for the first time, or ba'alei tshuva (BTs). As another interlocutor told me about donning the yarmulke: "In the beginning, I was feeling for it and thinking about it all the time, but after a while . . . you just go on autopilot." The relation between habit and creative action was cogently captured by pragmatist philosophers (see Dewey 2002 [1922]; James 1950 [1890]; see also Joas 1996; Gross 2009).

17. The notion of the "margins of consciousness" was developed by phenomenologist Aron Gurwitsch (1985). The notion pertains to those aspects of perception that are neither in the conscious foreground nor in the background, but rather remain on the "sidelines" of experience (Gurwitsch 1964, 1985). These margins of consciousness are precisely "a field of potentiality in that it founds the possibility of the subject dropping one theme and picking up another" (Embree 1985: xviii).

18. For the importance of plausible alternatives in constructing causal claims, see Tavory and Timmermans (2013, 2014).

19. The notion of "provocations of self" was suggested, though never written up, by Jack Katz.

CHAPTER EIGHT

1. For a depiction of Evangelical life as "embattled and thriving," see Smith (1998).
2. Although I have not discussed religious experience in this work, see Tavory and Winchester (2012) for some of the elations and the existential challenges that such experiences entail over a religious career.
3. For the ongoing construction of order, see Garfinkel (1967, 2002).
4. For the notion of learning "the sense of the game," see, e.g., Bourdieu (1977, 2000). These games, it should be stressed, are not frivolous. They are, as Sherry Ortner (2006) puts it, "serious games."
5. See Blumer (1954).
6. In other words, the less the researcher is attentive to the relationship between identification and social worlds, the more the notion of summoning turns into a truism—that identifications are etched in and among concrete situations.
7. E.g., Blumer (1969); Garfinkel (1967).
8. This attempt to rework situations into a pattern of social life emerged in different contexts. For interactionism, it emerged through the work of "the second Chicago school"—see, e.g., Becker et al. (1961); Davis (1961). In reaction to ethnomethodology, and especially conversation analysis, "institutional talk-in-interaction" took a similar approach (see, e.g., Drew and Heritage 1992). See also Brubaker et al. (2006).
9. The discussion of active and passive potentiality is based on Aristotle's *Physics* (1996). See also Arruzza's (2011) work on the notions of actualization and potentiality in the work of Aristotle and Plotinus. I note that the notion of an interactional form's power to shape action is akin to that of Aristotle's "formal cause."
10. See Parsons (1951).
11. See, e.g., Bourdieu (1977).
12. To use Aristotelian terms, they move from "possession" (a transitional category between pure potentiality and pure actualization, "first energeia"), to "use" (completed actualization, Aristotle's "second energeia"). See Aristotle (1996).
13. Both the map metaphor and the criticism of Bourdieu's understanding of disposition in these terms are based on a reading of the work of Alfred Schutz. See, especially, Schutz (1964); Schutz and Luckmann (1973: 178–82).
14. The crucial relationship between habit and creativity was best captured in American pragmatism. See James (1950 [1890]); Dewey (2002 [1922]); Joas (1996).
15. See also Eliasoph (1998).
16. E. Goffman (1961).
17. Moss Kanter (1972).
18. See, for a perspective interested primarily in the sociology of knowledge,

Berger and Luckmann's (1967; also Berger 1967) notion of "plausibility structures"—the set of institutions and interactions that make a certain form of knowledge plausible.

19. Mann (1994 [1901]: 102).
20. Mann (1994 [1901]: 153).
21. See, e.g., Liebow (1967); Suttles (1968); Anderson (1978); Wilson (1987).
22. See Murphy (2010, 2012)
23. Murphy (2010: 18).
24. In addition to the work referenced earlier, see also Stack (1974) and Venkatesh (2006) for networks of gift giving and exchange.
25. Wilson (1987); A. Goffman (2014).
26. Duneier (1999).
27. Since I have only six cases of people I know who left Orthodoxy—two men and four teenagers—I hesitate to make too much of limited observations, especially since I was mostly privy to post hoc vocabularies of motive (Mills 1940) rather than situated actions. Additionally, as the unit of analysis in the book is not individuals but the patterning of interactions, the specific characteristics of those who distanced themselves from Orthodoxy are less crucial.
28. For the distancing of young men and women from Orthodoxy in New York, see Winston (2005). In Winston's cases, teenagers and young adults needed to leave their families, often being ostracized. I note that in Los Angeles *none* of the teenagers I knew were shunned by their families. This was partly due to the fact that Los Angeles was still less dense than some New York neighborhoods, but may also be due to sampling decisions made by Winston. A current study of strict Orthodox young adults who left Orthodox Judaism in New York found that even in the strictest affiliations and the densest locations, these men and women were not completely ostracized by their families (see Newfield 2015).
29. This is, of course, commonplace in the sociological and psychological literature about celebrity. See, e.g., Adler and Adler (1989); Rockwell and Giles (2009).
30. Dittman (2009).
31. Gethin (2008).
32. Rockwell and Giles (2009: 187).

APPENDIX

1. Tavory and Timmermans (2014); Timmermans and Tavory (2012).
2. See Timmermans and Buchbinder (2013).
3. Hartshorne, Weiss, and Burks (1931–58): 5.117.
4. For the notion of theoretical and methodological "tricks of the trade," see Becker (1998).
5. See also Tavory and Timmermans (2013).

Glossary

Throughout the book, terms are explained as they are brought up in context. But, for good measure, this glossary is meant to help readers explicate terms they might find confusing. This is not meant to be a definitive glossary of Jewish terms, as definitions here are highly simplified. For the purpose of this book, however, these explanations are accurate enough to help readers find their bearings. The spelling follows the Ashkenazi pronunciation. As the Talmudic sage put it, ואידך זיל גמור (if you want to know more, go and learn).

Ashkenazi: Jews of European ancestry (not including Southern Europe). Originally denoted Jews from the area of modern Germany (*Ashkenaz*, in medieval use, referred to areas in western and northern Germany).

Ba'al tshuva (BT): Someone who was raised in a non-Orthodox home and becomes Orthodox later in life. Literally "master of return," but practically a dubious status marker in the Orthodox world.

Chabad: Alternatively called Chabad-Lubavitch. A Hasidic group that hails from Belarus, with their current headquarters in Crown Heights, Brooklyn. Since this is one of the world's larger Hasidic groups, and especially as they vocally attempt to bring Jews "back to the fold," they are extremely visible in the Orthodox landscape. The last rebbe of Chabad, Menachem Mendel Schneerson, died in 1994 and is believed by some Chabadniks to have potentially been (or to be, in some cases) the Messiah.

Eruv string: String surrounding a designated area, part of a religious transformation of the enclosure into a communally shared space. The eruv solves the practical problem caused by the religious proscription on carrying items in public on the Sabbath, as it becomes admissible to carry and move objects within its boundaries. Rules regarding where and how it is admissible to construct an eruv—and thus the admissibility of particular eruv strings, such as the one enclosing the Beverly–La Brea neighborhood—are hotly debated within the Orthodox world. See also chapter 7, note 9.

Frum: Yiddish, literally "devout." Used to denote either an Orthodox person as opposed to non-Orthodox, or degrees of strictness within Orthodoxy.

Frum from birth (FFB): Someone born to an Orthodox family (and thus, for example, a product of the Orthodox education system).

Goy (pl. *Goyim*): Literally "nation" but used to denote Gentiles.

Goyishe: Adjective form of *goy*. Used to denote things that are "of the Gentiles," usually with a connotation of profanity.

Hasidism; Hasid: Movement within European Judaism that emerged in the late eighteenth century and emphasizes piety and experience over more academic learning. Organized around the figure of the rebbe, usually a charismatic leader, and his lineage (with the exceptions of Chabad and Breslov Hasidic groups that survive even without an acting rebbe). The movement was strongly resisted in its early years by the Orthodox establishment. A Hasid is a member of a Hasidic group.

Kabbalistic: Refers to a mystical tradition in Judaism, crystallized in the Middle Ages. Studied throughout the Orthodox world, but stressed most prominently in Hasidic and Sephardic circles.

Kaddish Yatom: The mourner's supplication. A section of the three main daily prayers that needs to be said by men who have lost one of their parents in the previous year, as well as when commemorating the parent's yahrzeit.

Kashrus laws; kosher: Laws of what can, and can't, be ingested. Well-known laws include the proscription on eating pork, on mixing dairy and meat, and on eating shellfish. Food and drink that are religiously admissible are kosher. Also used metaphorically to denote whether something is done right or is suspect (e.g., "this glossary doesn't seem kosher"). Also used as a verb, to kosherize (to make kosher).

Kiddush: Light meal Orthodox men and women eat after the morning prayers on the Sabbath. Usually consists of some food, a small drink, a blessing over the food and wine, some words of Torah and much chatting. Often sponsored by a member who is celebrating a special event or commemorating a yahrzeit.

Kollel: Institute for religious learning designed for married men. In the United States, kollels are attended only by a relatively small portion of Orthodox men. The Orthodox Jewish version of graduate school.

Meshulach (pl. *meshulachim*): Literally, "emissary." Poor Orthodox Jews from Israel who travel to Orthodox communities in Europe or North America, asking for support either for Israeli religious organizations (in which case, they still keep around half of the money they raise in addition to expenses), or explicitly for their own need. Organizations checking their credentials, that they are who they say they are and actually have the organizational ties they claim, have emerged in the United States. The roots of the meshulach phenomenon lie in the late Middle Ages, when paid emissaries would travel to collect money to help support Jewish settlements and Torah study in Israel.

Mezuzah: Encased piece of parchment, located at the upper right side of the door-post of Jewish homes. The parchment contains the prayer "Shema Israel" (Hear, Oh Israel). In Orthodox households, there is a mezuzah on the door-post of all rooms, with the exception of the bathroom. When entering or leaving the house, people often symbolically kiss the mezuzah.

Minyan: Prayer quorum. Ten or more Jewish men, over the age of thirteen, who come together for prayer. It is inadmissible to recite parts of the major prayers if a minyan is not available. Not a problem in large synagogues, a daily preoc-cupation in small ones.

Mitzvah (pl. *mitzvos*): Religious precepts proscribing or prescribing specific courses of action. Also used metaphorically to denote a good deed as such.

Modern Orthodox: Strand of Orthodoxy that attempts to balance secular culture and learning with strict adherence to religious law. As such, Modern Or-thodoxy usually adheres to a more minimalist interpretation of religious law than other strict Orthodox affiliations, though following the letter of the law. Modern Orthodoxy is theologically closer to Ashkenazi Yeshivish Orthodoxy than to any other strand. In the Beverly–La Brea neighborhood, Modern Orthodox shuls are quite strict, falling on the "strict" side of a Mod-ern Orthodox spectrum.

Parshah: Portion of the Torah read every week across the Jewish world. Over the course of a year, the parshahs (especially in Orthodox synagogues, though also in many Conservative and Reform synagogues as well) cover the entire text of the Pentateuch. As students learn the weekly parshah at school, they are given parshah questions that their parents are supposed to quiz them on over the Sabbath.

Purimshpil: Comic play performed on the holiday of Purim (a holiday that cel-ebrates the Jews' narrow escape from annihilation by Persian emperor Xerxes). Usually makes light fun of aspects of Jewish life, often with a moral twist.

Rebbe: Leader of a Hasidic group. In Chabad, the rebbe (when it is not specified which one) refers to the late Menachem Mendel Schneerson (1902–94).

Satmar: Hasidic group, originally from Hungary. Current centers of the move-ment are in New York (in Williamsburg and Kiryas Joel). Considered one of the stricter Hasidic groups; anti-Zionist on religious grounds.

Schnorrer: Yiddish, literally a beggar, freeloader. Specifically used for people asking for money in synagogue. Since people get to know them, since they some-times join the minyan, and since there is an obligation to give tzedakah, their moral standing is more ambivalent than that of their non-Orthodox counterparts.

Seminary: Learning institute for young Orthodox women after high school age.

Sephardic: Jews of North African and the Middle Eastern ancestry (as well as some southern European communities). Literally, "Spanish," originally denoting the Jews of Spain, expelled in 1492.

Shabbos: Ashkenazi pronunciation of *Shabbat*, the Sabbath. The time between sundown on Friday and an hour after sundown on Saturday, when work (understood broadly, in religious terms) is proscribed. Among the forms of work disallowed on Shabbos: driving; manipulating electricity; carrying items into the public domain (unless an eruv exists); dealing with money; writing; playing a musical instrument.

Shabbos goy: Non-Jew who is asked (or sometimes paid in advance) to help Orthodox Jews with forms of work they are not allowed to do on Shabbos. Arrangement is possible since non-Jews are not obligated (indeed, religiously not allowed) to keep the Sabbath.

Shabbos shul: Shul people go to on the Sabbath (for Friday evening and Sabbath day services). Marks the primary synagogue affiliation of Ashkenazi Orthodox Jews. This is the shul that people would usually pay membership fees to and feel most strongly about. Also, almost inevitably, the synagogue tied to members' specific Orthodox subaffiliation.

Shabbos zeiger: Timer set for electricity, allowing Orthodox Jews to control the lights in the house without manipulating them directly on Shabbos (e.g., automatically shutting lights around bedtime, lighting them up in the morning).

Shtreimel: Large fur hat worn by married men in many Hasidic groups (although not in Chabad). Usually worn on special occasions—on Shabbos, the High Holidays, and special events.

Shul: Yiddish for synagogue, literally "school." Used to denote an Ashkenazi Orthodox synagogue.

Siddur: The common prayerbook, used daily. There are different versions (*nusachim*) of the siddur, partly depending on subaffiliation.

Talmud: Central text of religious exegesis codified 200–500 CE (this refers to the Babylonian Talmud). Considered the most important text elucidating the proscriptions and prescriptions found in the Torah. Studied heavily in all strands of Orthodoxy. Also studied in many congregations on a daily basis, where one page is learned every day (the *daf yomi*), a tradition that dates to 1923 and has rapidly spread in post-Holocaust Orthodoxy.

Torah: In its most narrow denotation, the five books of the Pentateuch; in a wider denotation, the entire Old Testament, with the Talmudic commentary; in the widest denotation, any form of Orthodox learning.

Traditional Orthodoxy: In this book, refers to European immigrant Orthodoxy. Usually marked by relatively lax observance in comparison to current strict Orthodoxy: no partition between men and women in synagogue; most men shaved, and women without head cover; synagogue members coming mostly on the Sabbath and High Holidays; children going to secular schools, with perhaps some Jewish additions on Sunday or afternoon. In current terms, closest in observance to lax versions of the Modern Orthodox. All but extinct.

Tzedakah: Literally, "justice/righteousness" (Hebrew) but used to denote the practice of charity, of giving to the poor. Considered a mitzvah.

Yahrzeit: Commemoration of the day that an Orthodox person's father or mother passed away. The son is obligated to say Kaddish on the yahrzeit, and would often sponsor a kiddush in shul.

Yeshiva: Strict Orthodox counterpart to boys' middle and high school (usually ages 13–19). Strictly speaking, the word yeshiva denotes boys' schooling more generally, with *yeshiva ktana* used for middle school, and *yeshiva gedolah* for high school. Usually, however, *yeshiva* is used for middle and high school.

Yeshivish (synonyms: *Litvish*, *Misnaged*): Main branch of Ashkenazi Orthodox Judaism that resisted the rise of Hasidism in the late eighteenth century. Sometimes called *Litvish* because the center of learning and criticism of the Hasidic movement was Vilnius, Lithuania. Nicknamed *Misnagdim* (naysayers) by Hasids. The moniker *Yeshivish* comes from the word *yeshiva* and denotes the stress on the yeshiva system rather than on the charismatic leaders and lineages that mark Hasidism.

References

Abrahamson, Alan. 1998. "Debate Rises over Jewish Census." *Los Angeles Times*, July 25.

Adam, Barbara. 1990. *Time and Social Theory*. Cambridge, UK: Polity Press.

Adler, Patricia A., and Peter Adler. 1989. "The Glorified Self: The Aggrandizement and the Constriction of Self." *Social Psychology Quarterly* 52 (4): 299–310.

Adler-Huttler, Miriam. 2008. *A Mini-Biography of Grand Rabbi Eliezer Adler, Zviller Rebbe, and a Mini-History of Chassidism in Los Angeles*. Los Angeles, CA: Self-publication.

Almeling, Rene. 2011. *Sex Cells: The Medical Market for Eggs and Sperm*. Berkeley: University of California Press.

Althusser, Louis. 1971. *Lenin and Philosophy and Other Essays*. New York: Monthly Review.

Ammerman, Nancy T. 1997. *Congregation and Community*. New Brunswick, NJ: Rutgers University Press.

Anderson, Elijah. 1978. *A Place on the Corner*. Chicago: University of Chicago Press.

———. 1990. *Streetwise: Race, Class, and Change in an Urban Neighborhood*. Chicago: University of Chicago Press.

Aristotle. 1996. *Physics*. Oxford: Oxford University Press.

Arruzza, Cinzia. 2011. "Passive Potentiality in the Physical Realm: Plotinus' Critique of Aristotle in Enneads II 5 [25]." *Archiv für Geschichte der Philosophie* 93 (1): 24–57.

Aviad, Janet. 1983. *Return to Judaism: Religious Renewal in Israel*. Chicago: University of Chicago Press.

Bakhtin, Mikhail M. 1986. *Speech Genres and Other Late Essays*. Austin: University of Texas Press.

Barth, Fredrik. 1969. *Ethnic Groups and Boundaries: The Social Organization of Cultural Difference*. Oslo: Universitetsforlaget.

Barthes, Roland. 1975. *The Pleasure of the Text*. New York: Farrar, Straus and Giroux.

Bauman, Zygmunt. 2005. *Liquid Life*. Cambridge, UK: Polity Press.

Becker, Howard S. 1982. *Art Worlds*. Berkeley: University of California Press.

———. 1998. *Tricks of the Trade: How to Think about Your Research While You're Doing It*. Chicago: University of Chicago Press.

Becker, Howard S., Blanche Geer, Everett C. Hughes, and Anselm L. Strauss. 1961. *Boys in White: Student Culture in Medical School*. Chicago: University of Chicago Press.

Beisel, Nicola, and Sarah Lipton-Lubet. 2003. "Appropriating Auschwitz: The Holocaust as Metaphor and Provocation in the Pro-Life Movement, 1970–1988." Paper Presented at the Annual Meeting of the American Sociological Association, Atlanta, GA.

Bender, Courtney. 2003. *Heaven's Kitchen: Living Religion at God's Love We Deliver*. Chicago: University of Chicago Press.

———. 2010. *The New Metaphysics: Spirituality and the American Religious Imagination*. Chicago: University of Chicago Press.

Berger, Peter L. 1967. *The Sacred Canopy: Elements of a Sociological Theory of Religion*. New York: Doubleday.

Berger, Peter L., and Thomas Luckmann. 1967. *The Social Construction of Reality: A Treatise in the Sociology of Knowledge*. New York: Anchor Books.

Bilici, Mucahit. 2012. *Finding Mecca in America: How Islam Is Becoming an American Religion*. Chicago: University of Chicago Press.

Blumer, Herbert. 1954. "What Is Wrong with Social Theory?" *American Sociological Review* 10 (1): 3–10.

———. 1969. *Symbolic Interactionism: Perspective and Method*. Englewood Cliffs, NJ: Prentice Hall.

Bourdieu, Pierre. 1977. *Outline of a Theory of Practice*. Cambridge, UK: Cambridge University Press.

———. 1984. *Distinction: A Social Critique of the Judgment of Taste*. Cambridge, MA: Harvard University Press.

———. 2000. *Pascalian Meditations*. Stanford, CA: Stanford University Press.

Boyarin, Jonathan. 2011. *Mornings at the Stanton Street Shul: A Summer on the Lower East Side*. New York: Fordham University Press.

Breton, Raymond. 1964. "Institutional Completeness of Ethnic Communities and the Personal Relations of Immigrants." *American Journal of Sociology* 70 (2): 193–205.

Brodkin, Karen. 1998. *How Jews Became White Folk and What That Says about Race in America*. New Brunswick, NJ: Rutgers University Press.

Brubaker, Rogers, and Frederick Cooper. 2000. "Beyond 'Identity.'" *Theory and Society* 29: 1–47.

Brubaker, Rogers, Margit Feischmidt, Jon Fox, and Liana Grancea. 2006. *Nationalist Politics and Everyday Ethnicity in a Transylvanian Town*. Princeton: Princeton University Press.

Burke, Kenneth. 1945. *A Grammar of Motives*. London: Prentice Hall.

Butler, Judith. 1990. *Gender Trouble*. New York: Routledge.

Callon, Michel. 1986. "Some Elements of a Sociology of Translation: Domestication of the Scallops and the Fishermen of St Brieuc Bay." In *Power, Action and Belief: A New Sociology of Knowledge*, ed. J. Law, 196–233. London, UK: Routledge & Kegan Paul.

Calvino, Italo. 1974. *Invisible Cities*. Orlando, FL: Harcourt.

Casey, Edward S. 1993. *Getting Back into Place: Toward a Renewed Understanding of the Place-World*. Bloomington: Indiana University Press.

Cohen, Steven M. 1988. *American Assimilation or Jewish Revival?* Bloomington: Indiana University Press.

Collins, Randal. 2004. *Interaction Ritual Chains*. Princeton: Princeton University Press.

Cooper, Davina. 1996. "Talmudic Territory? Space, Law and Modernist Discourse." *Journal of Law and Society* 23 (4): 529–48.

Coser, Lewis A. 1974. *Greedy Institutions: Patterns of Undivided Commitment*. New York: Free Press.

Csordas, Thomas J. 1996. *The Sacred Self: A Cultural Phenomenology of Charismatic Healing*. Berkeley: University of California Press.

Dash Moore, Deborah. 1994. *To the Golden Cities: Pursuing the Jewish American Dream in Miami and L.A.* Cambridge, MA: Harvard University Press.

Davidman, Lynn. 1991. *Tradition in a Rootless World: Women Turn to Orthodox Judaism*. Berkeley: University of California Press.

Davis, Fred. 1961. "Deviance Disavowal: The Management of Strained Interaction by the Visibly Handicapped." *Social Problems* 9 (2): 120–32.

———. 1992. *Fashion, Culture, and Identity*. Chicago: University of Chicago Press.

Della Pergola, Sergio. 1996. "Jewish Intermarriage in America: Some Thoughts of a Non-American." *Gesher, Journal of Jewish Affairs* 42 (133): 7–24 (in Hebrew).

Dewey, John. 2002 [1922]. *Human Nature and Conduct*. New York: Dover.

Diamond, Etan. 2000. *And I Will Dwell in Their Midst: Orthodox Jews in Suburbia*. Chapel Hill: University of North Carolina Press.

Dittman, Earl. 2009. "The Johnny Depp Interview: On Dillinger, Mad Hatter & Capt Jack." *Digital Journal*, available at: http://www.digitaljournal.com/article/275336

Drew, Paul, and John Heritage. 1992. "Analyzing Talk at Work: An Introduction." In *Talk at Work: Interaction in Institutional Settings*, ed. Paul Drew and John Heritage, 3–66. Cambridge, UK: Cambridge University Press.

Duneier, Mitchell. 1999. *Sidewalk*. New York: Farrar, Straus, and Giroux.

Durkheim, Emile. 1965 [1912]. *The Elementary Forms of Religious Life*. New York: Free Press.

———. 1979 [1897]. *Suicide: A Study in Sociology*. New York: Free Press.

———. 1997 [1893]. *The Division of Labor in Society*. New York: Free Press.

Eliasoph, Nina. 1998. *Avoiding Politics: How Americans Produce Apathy in Everyday Life*. Cambridge, UK: Cambridge University Press.

Eliasoph, Nina, and Paul Lichterman. 2003. "Culture in Interaction." *American Journal of Sociology* 108 (4): 735–94.

Embree, Lester. 1985. "Editor's Introduction: Gurwitsch's Phenomenology of the Margin, Body and Being." In Aron Gurwitsch, *Marginal Consciousness*, xii–xli. Athens: Ohio University Press.

Emirbayer, Mustafa, and Jeff Goodwin. 1994. "Network Analysis, Culture and the Problem of Agency." *American Journal of Sociology* 99 (6): 1411–54.

Fader, Ayala. 2009. *Mitzvah Girls: Bringing Up the Next Generation of Hasidic Jews in Brooklyn*. Princeton: Princeton University Press.

Fine, Gary A. 1979. "Small Groups and Culture Creation: The Idioculture of Little League Baseball Teams." *American Sociological Review* 44: 733–45.

———. 1998. *Morel Tales: The Culture of Mushrooming*. Cambridge, MA: Harvard University Press.

Fischer, Dov. 2000. *American Jews: How the 2000 Los Angeles Jewish Federation Census Was Calculated to Undercount Torah-Observant Jews*. Available at http://rabbidov.com/American%20Jews/howjewishfederationundercounted.htm

Fishkoff, Sue. 2003. *The Rebbe's Army: Inside Chabad-Lubavitcher*. New York: Schocken.

Garfinkel, Harold. 1967. *Studies in Ethnomethodology*. Englewood Cliffs, NJ: Prentice Hall.

———. 2002. *Ethnomethodology's Program: Working Out Durkheim's Aphorism*. New York: Rowman and Littlefield.

Geertz, Clifford. 1973. *The Interpretation of Cultures*. New York: Basic Books.

Gelfand, Mitchell B. 1981. "Chutzpah in El Dorado: Social Mobility of Jews in Los Angeles, 1900–1920." PhD diss., University of California, Los Angeles.

Gergen, Kenneth. 1991. *The Saturated Self: Dilemmas of Identity in Contemporary Life*. New York: Basic Books.

Gethin Kris. 2008. "Kim Lyons: Celebrity Interview of the Month." Available at http://www.bodybuilding.com/fun/krisgethin47.htm

Giddens, Anthony. 1984. *The Constitution of Society: Outline of the Theory of Structuration*. Cambridge, UK: Polity Press.

Ginzburg, Carlo. 1999. *History, Rhetoric and Proof: The Menachem Stern Jerusalem Lectures*. Hanover, NH: University Press of New England.

Gluckman Max. 1955. *The Judicial Process among the Barotse of Northern Rhodesia*. New York: Free Press.

Godfrey, Brian J. 1988. *Neighborhoods in Transition: The Making of San Francisco's Ethnic and Nonconformist Communities*. Berkeley: University of California Press.

Goffman, Alice. 2014. *On the Run: Fugitive Life in an American City*. Chicago: University of Chicago Press.

Goffman, Erving. 1959. *The Presentation of Self in Everyday Life*. New York: Doubleday.

———. 1961. *Asylums: Essays on the Social Situations of Mental Patients and Other Inmates*. New York: Doubleday.

———. 1967. *Interaction Ritual: Essays on Face-to-Face Behavior.* Garden City, NJ: Anchor.

Goldschmidt, Henry. 2006. *Race and Religion: Among the Chosen People of Crown Heights.* New Brunswick, NJ: Rutgers University Press.

Gordon, Antony, and Richard M. Horowitz. 2006. "Will Your Grandchildren be Jewish?" Paper presented at "The Future of American Jewry" symposium, Boston. Available at http://www.aish.com/jw/s/48910307.html

Grannis, Rick. 2010. "Six Degrees of 'Who Cares?'" *American Journal of Sociology* 115 (4): 991–1017.

Gross, Neil. 2009. "A Pragmatist Theory of Social Mechanisms." *American Sociological Review* 74 (3): 358–79.

Gurwitsch, Aron. 1964. *The Field of Consciousness.* Pittsburgh: Duquesne University Press.

———. 1985. *Marginal Consciousness.* Athens: Ohio University Press.

Haidt, Jonathan. 2001. "The Emotional Dog and Its Rational Tail: A Social Intuitionist Approach to Moral Judgment." *Psychological Review* 108: 814–34.

Hall, David D., ed. 1997. *Lived Religion in America: Toward a History of Practice.* Princeton: Princeton University Press.

Halle, David. 1994. *Inside Culture: Art and Class in the American Home.* Chicago: University of Chicago Press.

Harris, Lis. 1985. *Holy Days: The World of a Hassidic Family.* New York: Simon and Schuster.

Hartshorne, Charles, Paul Weiss, and Arthur Burks. 1931–58. *Collected Papers of Charles Sanders Peirce.* 8 vols. Cambridge, MA: Harvard University Press.

Healy, Kieran. 2006. *Last Best Gifts: Altruism and the Market for Human Blood and Organs.* Chicago: University of Chicago Press.

Heidegger, Martin. 1971. *Poetry, Language, Thought.* New York: Harper and Row.

Heilman, Samuel C. 1976. *Synagogue Life: A Study in Symbolic Interaction.* Chicago: University of Chicago Press.

———. 1992. *Defenders of the Faith.* Berkeley: University of California Press.

———. 2006. *Sliding to the Right: The Contest for the Future of American Jewish Orthodoxy.* Berkeley: University of California Press.

Heilman, Samuel C., and Menachem Friedman. 2010. *The Rebbe: The Life and Afterlife of Menachem Mendel Schneerson.* Princeton: Princeton University Press.

Helmreich, William B. 1982. *The World of the Yeshiva: An Intimate Portrait of Orthodox Jewry.* Hoboken, NJ: Ktav.

Hendershot, Heather. 2004. *Shaking the World for Jesus: Media and Evangelical Culture.* Chicago: University of Chicago Press.

Herman, Pini. 1998. *Los Angeles Jewish Population Survey, '97.* Los Angeles: Greater Los Angeles Jewish Federation.

Hitlin, Steven. 2003. "Values as the Core of Personal Identity: Drawing Links between Two Theories of the Self." *Social Psychology Quarterly* 66: 118–37.

———. 2008. *Moral Selves, Evil Selves: The Social Psychology of Conscience.* New York: Palgrave Macmillan.

Home Owners Loan Corporation (HOLC). 1939. *Area Description: Beverly–Fuller District*. Los Angeles, CA: Home Owners' Loan Corporation Publications.

Hughes, Everett C. 1945. "Dilemmas and Contradictions of Status." *American Journal of Sociology* 50: 353–59.

Husserl, Edmund. 1960. *Cartesian Meditations: An Introduction to Phenomenology*. Trans. Dorion Cairns. The Hague: Martinus Nijhoff.

Ingold, Tim. 2011. *Being Alive: Essays on Movement, Knowledge and Description*. London: Routledge.

Jackson-Jacobs, Curtis. 2013. "Constructing Physical Fights: An Interactionist Analysis of Violence among Affluent, Suburban Youth." *Qualitative Sociology* 36 (1): 23–52.

James, William. 1950 [1890]. *Principles of Psychology*. New York: Dover.

Jayanti, Vimala. 1995. "From Russia to Fairfax Avenue: The Integration of Soviet Jewish Immigrants in Los Angeles." PhD diss., University of California, Los Angeles.

Jerolmack, Colin, and Iddo Tavory. 2014. "Molds and Totems: Nonhumans and the Constitution of the Social Self." *Sociological Theory* 32 (1): 64–77.

Jewish Federations of North America. 2001. *National Jewish Population Survey (NJPS), 2000–2001*. Available at http://www.jewishfederations.org/local_includes/downloads/3905.pdf

Joas, Hans. 1996. *The Creativity of Action*. Chicago: University of Chicago Press.

Joseph, Nathan. 1986. *Uniforms and Nonuniforms: Communication through Clothing*. New York: Greenwood.

Katz, Jack. 1988. *Seductions of Crime: Moral and Sensual Attractions of Doing Evil*. New York: Basic Books.

———. 1999. *How Emotions Work*. Chicago: University of Chicago Press.

———. 2010. "Time for New Urban Ethnographies." *Ethnography* 11 (1): 25–44.

Katz, Jack, Peter Ibarra, and Margarethe Kusenbach. 2014. *Six Hollywoods Ethnographic Project*. Unpublished manuscript.

Keller, Suzanne. 1968. *The Urban Neighborhood: A Sociological Perspective*. New York: Random House.

———. 2003. *Community: Pursuing the Dream, Living the Reality*. Princeton: Princeton University Press.

Klein, Amy. 2006. "Two Neighborhoods Reveal Orthodox Community's Fault Lines: Pico-Robertson vs. Hancock Park." *Jewish Journal*, November 10. Available at http://www.jewishjournal.com/community_briefs/article/two_neighborhoods_reveal_orthodox_communitys_fault_lines_20061110

Koestler, Arthur. 1964. *The Act of Creation*. London: Hutchinson.

Kronzek, Lynn C. 1990. "Fairfax: A Home, a Community, a Way of Life." *Legacy: Journal of the Jewish Historical Society of Southern California* 1 (4): 1–112.

Kugelmass, Jack. 1986. *The Miracle of Intervale Avenue: The Story of a Jewish Congregation in the South Bronx*. New York: Columbia University Press.

Kusenbach, Margarethe. 2003a. "Neighboring: An Ethnographic Study of Community in Urban Hollywood." PhD diss., University of California, Los Angeles.

———. 2003b. "Street-Phenomenology: The Go-Along as Ethnographic Research Tool." *Ethnography* 4 (3): 449–79.

———. 2012. "Mobile Methods." In *Handbook of Qualitative Research in Education*, ed. Sara Delamont, 252–64. Cheltenham, UK: Edward Elgar.

Lamont, Michèle. 2000. *The Dignity of Working Men: Morality and the Boundaries of Race, Class, and Immigration*. Cambridge, MA: Harvard University Press.

Lamont, Michèle, and Virag Molnár. 2002. "The Study of Boundaries in the Social Sciences." *Annual Review of Sociology* 28: 167–95.

Latour, Bruno. 1996. "On Interobjectivity." *Mind, Culture, and Activity* 3: 228–45.

———. 2005. *Reassembling the Social*. Oxford: Oxford University Press.

LeFebvre, Henri. 2004. *Rhythmanalysis: Space, Time and Everyday Life*. New York: Continuum.

Levy, Amnon. 1988. *Ha'haredim*. Tel Aviv: Keter (in Hebrew).

Lichterman, Paul. 2005. *Elusive Togetherness: Church Groups Trying to Bridge America's Divisions*. Princeton: Princeton University Press.

———. 2012. "Religion in Public Action: From Actors to Settings." *Sociological Theory* 30 (1): 15–36.

Liebow, Elliot. 1967. *Tally's Corner*. Boston, MA: Little, Brown.

Lifton, Robert J. 1993. *The Protean Self: Human Resilience in an Age of Fragmentation*. Chicago: University of Chicago Press.

Light, Ivan H., and Edna Bonacich. 1988. *Immigrant Entrepreneurs: Koreans in Los Angeles, 1965–1982*. Berkeley: University of California Press.

Logan, John R., and Harvey L. Molotch. 1987. *Urban Fortunes: The Political Economy of Place*. Berkeley: University of California Press.

Loveman, Mara, and Jeronimo O. Muniz. 2007. "How Puerto Rico Became White: Boundary Dynamics and Inter-Census Racial Reclassification." *American Sociological Review* 72 (6): 915–39.

Luhtakallio, Eeva. 2012. *Practicing Democracy: Local Activism and Politics in France and Finland*. London: Palgrave Macmillan.

MacIntyre, Alasdair. 1984. *After Virtue*. South Bend, IN: Notre Dame University Press.

Mahmood, Saba. 2005. *Politics of Piety: The Islamic Revival and the Feminist Subject*. Princeton: Princeton University Press.

Mann, Thomas. 1994 [1901]. *Buddenbrooks: The Decline of a Family*. New York: Vintage Books.

Mauss, Marcel. 1990 [1923–24]. *The Gift: The Form and Reason for Exchange in Archaic Societies*. London: Routledge.

May, Reuben A. B. 2001. *Talking at Trenna's: Everyday Conversations at an African American Tavern*. New York: NYU Press.

McRoberts, Omar M. 2003. *Streets of Glory: Church and Community in a Black Urban Neighborhood*. Chicago: University of Chicago Press.

McWilliams, Carey. 1946. *Southern California: An Island on the Land*. Layton, UT: Gibbs Smith.

Melbin, Murray. 1978. "Night as Frontier." *American Sociological Review* 43 (1): 3–22.

Merton, Robert K. 1968. *Social Theory and Social Structure*. New York: Free Press.

Mills, C. Wright. 1940. "Situated Actions and Vocabularies of Motive." *American Sociological Review* 5 (6): 904–13.

Mintz, Adam. 2011. *Halakhah in America: The History of City Eruvin, 1894–1962*. PhD diss., New York University.

Mintz, Jerome. 1992. *Hasidic People: A Place in the New World*. Cambridge, MA: Harvard University Press.

Mische, Ann. 2008. *Partisan Publics: Communication and Contention across Brazilian Youth Activists Networks*. Princeton: Princeton University Press.

Mische, Ann, and Harrison C. White. 1998. "Between Conversation and Situation: Public Switching Dynamics across Network-Domains." *Social Research* 65: 295–324.

Mohr, John W., and Harrison C. White. 2008. "How to Model an Institution." *Theory and Society* 37: 485–512.

Moss Kanter, Rosabeth. 1972. *Community and Commitment: Communes and Utopias in Sociological Perspective*. Cambridge, MA: Harvard University Press.

Moynihan, Colin. 2009. "New Bike Lanes Touch Off Row in Brooklyn." *New York Times*, January 3. Available at http://www.nytimes.com/2009/01/04/nyregion/04lanes.html?pagewanted=all

Murphy, Alexandra K. 2010. "'I Stay to Myself': What People Say versus What They Do in a Poor Black Neighborhood." Paper presented at *The Craft of Ethnography* conference, New York.

———. 2012. "The Social Organization of Black Suburban Poverty: An Ethnographic Community Study." PhD diss., Princeton University.

Myerhoff, Barbara. 1979. *Number Our Days: Culture and Community among Elderly Jews in an American Ghetto*. New York: Meridian.

Neitz, Mary Jo, and James V. Spickard. 1990. "Steps toward a Sociology of Religious Experience: The Theories of Mihaly Csikszentmihalyi and Alfred Schutz." *Sociological Analysis* 51 (1): 15–33.

Newfield, Zalman-Schneur. 2015. *Degrees of Separation: Patterns of Personal Identity Formation beyond the Boundaries of Ultra-Orthodox Judaism*. PhD diss., New York University.

Olshan, Jeremy, and Jamie Schram. 2009. "Hipsters Repaint Bike Lanes in Brush Off to Hasids." *New York Post*, December 8. Available at http://www.nypost.com/p/news/local/brooklyn/bike_war_paint_g7EizkFEZktV3IlNUJosQM

Ortner, Sherry. 2006. *Anthropology and Social Theory: Culture, Power, and the Acting Subject*. Durham, NC: Duke University Press.

Pachuki, Mark A., Sabrina Pendergrass, and Michèle Lamont. 2007. "Boundary Processes: Recent Developments and New Contributions." *Poetics* 35: 331–51.

Parry, Jonathan. 1986. "The Gift, the Indian Gift, and 'the Indian Gift.'" *Man* 21 (3): 453–73.

Parsons, Talcott. 1951. *The Social System*. Glencoe, IL: Free Press.

Pattillo-McCoy, Mary. 1998. "Church Culture as a Strategy of Action in the Black Community." *American Sociological Review* 63 (6): 767–84.

Peirce, Charles S. 1992–99. *The Essential Peirce.* 2 vols. Bloomington: Indiana University Press.

Perry, Menahem, and Meir Sternberg. 1986. "The King through Ironic Eyes: Biblical Narrative and the Literary Reading Process in Theory of Character." *Poetics Today* 7 (2): 275–322.

Phillips, Bruce. 1986. "Los Angeles Jewry: A Demographic Portrait." *American Jewish Yearbook.*

Polanyi, Michael. 1966. *The Tacit Dimension.* New York: Doubleday.

Poll, Solomon. 1962. *The Hasidic Community of Williamsburg: A Study in the Sociology of Religion.* New York: Free Press.

Portes, Alejandro, and Ruben G. Rumbaut. 2001. *Legacies: The Stories of the Immigrant Second Generation.* Berkeley: University of California Press.

Ratcliff, Richard U. 1935. "Some Principles of Site Selection in Outlying Retail Subcenters." *National Marketing Review* 1 (2): 106–19.

Reed, Isaac. 2011. *Interpretation and Social Knowledge: On the Use of Theory in the Human Sciences.* Chicago: University of Chicago Press.

Relph, Edward. 1976. *Place and Placelessness.* London: Pion.

Rockwell, Donna, and David C. Giles. 2009. "Being a Celebrity: A Phenomenology of Fame." *Journal of Phenomenological Psychology* 40: 178–210.

Rossman, Gabriel. 2009. "Hollywood and Jerusalem: Christian Conservatives and the Media." In Steven Brint and Jean Reith Schroedel, eds., *Evangelicals and Democracy in America,* vol. 1: *Religion and Society.* New York: Russell Sage.

Sacks, Harvey. 1979. "Hotrodder: A Revolutionary New Category." In *Everyday Language: Studies in Ethnomethodology,* ed. George Psathas, 7–14. New York: Irvington.

Sacks, Harvey, Emanuel A. Schegloff, and Gail Jefferson. 1974. "A Simplest Systematics for the Organisation of Turn-Taking for Conversation." *Language* 50: 696–735.

Saussure, Ferdinand de. 1986 [1916]. *Course in General Linguistics.* New York: Open Court.

Schegloff, Emanuel A., Gail Jefferson, and Harvey Sacks. 1977. "The Preference for Self-Correction in the Organization of Repair in Conversation." *Language* 53 (2): 361–82.

Schutz, Alfred. 1964. *Collected Papers II: Studies in Social Theory.* The Hague: Martinus Nijhoff.

———. 1967. *The Phenomenology of the Social World.* Evanston, IL: Northwestern University Press.

Schutz, Alfred, and Thomas Luckmann. 1973. *The Structures of the Life-World.* Evanston: Northwestern University Press.

Scott, John P. 1991. *Social Network Analysis: A Handbook.* Thousand Oaks, CA: Sage.

Sewell, William H., Jr. 1992. "A Theory of Structure: Duality, Agency, and Transformation." *American Journal of Sociology* 98 (1):1–29.

Shaffir, William. 1974. *Life in a Religious Community: The Lubavitcher Chassidim in Montreal.* Toronto: Holt, Reinhart and Winston.

Sharot, Stephen. 1991. "Judaism and the Secularization Debate." *Sociological Analysis* 52 (3): 255–75.

Sherkat, Darren E., and Christopher G. Ellison. 1999. "Recent Developments and Current Controversies in the Sociology of Religion." *Annual Review of Sociology* 25: 363–94.

Sherman, Rachel. 2005. "Producing the Superior Self: Strategic Comparison and Symbolic Boundaries among Luxury Hotel Workers." *Ethnography* 6 (2): 131–58.

———. 2007. *Class Acts: Service and Inequality in Luxury Hotels.* Berkeley: University of California Press.

Sheth, Anup. 2010. "Little India, Next Exit: Ethnic Destinations in the City." *Ethnography* 11 (1): 69–88.

Shibutani, Tamotsu. 1955. "Reference Groups as Perspectives." *American Journal of Sociology* 60 (6): 562–69.

Short, Thomas L. 2007. *Peirce's Theory of Signs.* Cambridge, UK: Cambridge University Press.

Simmel, Georg. 1964. *Conflict and the Web of Group Affiliations.* New York: Simon and Schuster.

Small, Mario L. 2004. *Villa Victoria: The Transformation of Social Capital in a Boston Barrio.* Chicago: University of Chicago Press.

———. 2009. *Unanticipated Gains: Origins of Network Inequality in Everyday Life.* New York: Oxford University Press.

Smilde, David. 2007. *Reason to Believe: Cultural Agency in Latin American Evangelicalism.* Berkeley: University of California Press.

Smith, Christian. 1998. *American Evangelicalism: Embattled and Thriving.* Chicago: Chicago University Press.

Snyder, Benjamin. 2012. "Working with Time in Time: A Rhythmic Approach to the Problem of Time Pressure." Paper Presented at the Junior Theorists' Symposium, Denver, August.

Spickard, James V. 1991. "Experiencing Religious Rituals: A Schutzian Analysis of Navajo Ceremonies." *Sociological Analysis* 52 (2): 191–204.

Stack, Carol. 1974. *All Our Kin.* New York: Basic Books.

Star, Susan L., and James R. Griesemer. 1989. "Institutional Ecology, 'Translations' and Boundary Objects: Amateurs and Professionals in Berkeley's Museum of Vertebrate Zoology, 1907–39." *Social Studies of Science* 19 (3): 387–420.

Stark, Rodney, and Roger Finke. 2000. *Acts of Faith: Explaining the Human Side of Religion.* Berkeley: University of California Press.

Stevenson, Charles L. 1944. *Ethics and Language.* New Haven, CT: Yale University Press.

Strauss, Anselm. 1978. "A Social Worlds Perspective." *Studies in Symbolic Interaction* 1: 119–28.

Stryker, Sheldon. 1968. "Identity Salience and Role Performance." *Journal of Marriage and the Family* 4: 558–64.

Stryker, Sheldon, and Peter J. Burke. 2000. "The Past, Present and Future of Identity Theory." *Social Psychology Quarterly* 63: 284–97.

Suttles, Gerald. 1968. *The Social Order of the Slum: Ethnicity and Territory in the Inner City*. Chicago: University of Chicago Press.

Swidler, Ann. 2001. *Talk of Love*. Chicago: University of Chicago Press.

———. 2010. "Remembering Erving Goffman." Available at http://cdclv.unlv.edu//archives/interactionism/goffman/swidler_10.html

Tavory, Iddo. 2010a. "The Hollywood Shtetl: From Ethnic Enclave to Religious Destination." *Ethnography* 11 (1): 89–108.

———. 2010b. "Of Yarmulkes and Categories: Delegating Boundaries and the Phenomenology of Interactional Expectation." *Theory and Society* 39 (1): 49–68.

———. 2011. "The Question of Moral Action: A Formalist Position." *Sociological Theory* 29 (4): 272–93.

———. 2013. "The Private Life of Public Ritual: Interaction, Sociality and Codification in a Jewish Orthodox Congregation." *Qualitative Sociology* 36 (2): 125–39.

———. 2014. "The Situations of Culture: Humor and the Limits of Measurability." *Theory and Society* 43 (3–4): 275–89.

Tavory, Iddo, and Nina Eliasoph. 2013. "Coordinating Futures: Towards a Theory of Anticipation." *American Journal of Sociology* 118 (4): 908–42.

Tavory, Iddo, and Ann Swidler. 2009. "Condom Semiotics: Meaning and Condom Use in Rural Malawi." *American Sociological Review* 74: 171–89.

Tavory, Iddo, and Stefan Timmermans. 2013. "A Pragmatist Approach to Causality in Ethnography." *American Journal of Sociology* 119 (3): 682–714.

———. 2014. *Abductive Analysis: Theorizing Qualitative Research*. Chicago: University of Chicago Press.

Tavory, Iddo, and Daniel Winchester. 2012. "Experiential Careers: The Routinization and De-routinization of Religious Life." *Theory and Society* 41 (4): 351–73.

Timmermans, Stefan, and Mara Buchbinder. 2013. *Saving Babies? The Consequences of Newborn Genetic Screening*. Chicago: University of Chicago Press.

Timmermans, Stefan, and Iddo Tavory. 2012. "Theory Construction in Qualitative Research: From Grounded Theory to Abductive Analysis." *Sociological Theory* 30 (3): 167–86.

Troeltsch, Ernst. 1931. *The Social Teachings of the Christian Churches*. New York: Macmillan.

Tuan, Yi-Fu. 1977. *Space and Place: The Perspective of Experience*. Minneapolis: University of Minnesota Press.

Turner, Victor W. 1974. *Dramas, Fields and Metaphors: Symbolic Action in Human Society*. Ithaca: Cornell University Press.

United Jewish Communities. 2004. *National Jewish Population Survey 2000–01: Strength, Challenge and Diversity in the American Jewish Population*. New York: United Jewish Communities.

Vaisey, Stephen. 2009. "Motivation and Justification: A Dual-Process Model of Culture in Action." *American Journal of Sociology* 114: 1675–1715.

Valins, Oliver. 2000. "Institutional Religion: Sacred Texts and Jewish Spatial Practice." *Geoforum* 31: 575–86.

Venkatesh, Sudhir A. 2006. *Off the Books: The Underground Economy of the Urban Poor.* Cambridge, MA: Harvard University Press.

Vorspan, Max, and Lloyd P. Gartner. 1970. *History of the Jews in Los Angeles.* San Marino, CA: Huntington Library.

Warner, R. Stephen. 1993. "Work in Progress toward a New Paradigm in the Sociological Study of Religion in the United States." *American Journal of Sociology* 98 (5): 1044–93.

Weber, Max. 1978. *Economy and Society: An Outline of Interpretive Sociology.* Berkeley: University of California Press.

White, Harrison C. 1992. *Identity and Control: A Structural Theory of Social Action.* Princeton: Princeton University Press.

White, Hayden. 1987. *The Content of the Form: Narrative Discourse and Historical Representation.* Baltimore, MD: Johns Hopkins University Press.

Whyte, William F. 1943. *Street Corner Society: The Social Structure of an Italian Slum.* Chicago: University of Chicago Press.

Wieder, D. Lawrence. 1974. *Language and Social Reality: The Case of Telling the Convict Code.* The Hague: Mouton.

Wilde, Melissa. 2004. "How Culture Mattered at Vatican II: Collegiality Trumps Authority in the Council's Social Movement Organizations." *American Sociological Review* 69 (3): 576–602.

Wilson, William J. 1987. *The Truly Disadvantaged: The Inner City, the Underclass and Public Policy.* Chicago: University of Chicago Press.

Winchester, Daniel. 2008. "Embodying the Faith: Religious Practice and the Making of a Muslim Moral Habitus." *Social Forces* 86 (4): 1753–80.

Winston, Hella. 2005. *Unchosen: The Hidden Lives of Hasidic Rebels.* Boston: Beacon.

Wirth, Louis. 1928. *The Ghetto.* Chicago: University of Chicago Press.

Wittgenstein, Ludwig. 1953. *Philosophical Investigations.* New York: Macmillan.

Wood, Richard. 2002. *Faith in Action: Religion, Race and Democratic Organizing in America.* Chicago: University of Chicago Press.

Wuthnow, Robert. 1987. *Meaning and Moral Order.* Berkeley: University of California Press.

Yamane, David. 2000. "Narrative and Religious Experience." *Sociology of Religion* 61: 171–89.

Young, Pauline V. 1928. "The Reorganization of Jewish Family Life in America: A Natural History of the Social Forces Governing the Assimilation of the Jewish Immigrant." *Social Forces* 7 (2): 238–44.

Young Israel Community Development Corporation. 1982. *Beverly-Fairfax Neighborhood Revitalization Strategy: Final Report.* Los Angeles, CA: self-publication.

Zerubavel, Eviatar. 2003. *Time Maps: Collective Memory and the Social Shape of the Past.* Chicago: University of Chicago Press.

Index

Page numbers in italics refer to figures.

abductive analysis, 162–66
actor-network theory, 183n2
Adler-Huttler, Miriam, 170–71n4
Althusser, Louis, 6, 167n4
Anderson, Elijah, 125
ANT. *See* actor-network theory
anti-Semitism, 140–43
Apples to Apples (game), 115, 183n21
Aristotle, 186n9, 186n12
Ashkenazi, definition of, 189
Austen, Jane, 155–56

ba'al tshuva (BT), definition of, 189
Bakhtin, Mikhail, 182n10
Becker, Howard, 168n10
Berger, Peter L., 186n18
Beth Medrash Govoha of Lakewood, 34–35, 172–73nn32–35
Beverly–La Brea neighborhood: advertisements in, 124; Ashkenazi Jews predominant in, 180n30; author's residence in, 18–19; author's sources on, 170–71n4; children sent to for Orthodox education, 21, 33, 41; as congenial space, 36; declining synagogue attendance in, 38–39; as dense moral space, 124; density of summoning in, 43, 47, 59, 145; diversity in, 36, 38; as exotic island, 169n1; geography of, 24; guesthouses

in, 18; history of, 13, 32–34; importance of in Orthodoxy, 24; maps of, 25, 125, *126*, 128, 131, 132; navigating profane areas in, 130–34; neighborhood formation narrative and, 169–70n3; non-Orthodox elements of, 3–4, 5–6, 15, 95, 101–2; number of synagogues and Orthodox schools in, 26, 42–43; organizational hooks for yeshivas in, 172–73n34; as organizationally dense Jewish space, 40–41, 42, 173n45; as organizationally greedy neighborhood, 13–14; as Orthodox island, 40–41, 42; as Orthodox-minority neighborhood, 123–24; place entrepreneurship and, 34–35; religious demographics of, 25–26, 171n7; as religious destination, 40, 42, 169n1, 169–70n3; socioeconomic status in, 24, 25–26, 171n5; as strict Orthodox space, 41, 79–80; transcendence of subaffiliations in, 96–97, 175n12; transformation of into Jewish space, 29; two important Orthodox clusters in, 36; viscosity of life in, 59; walkability of, 24, 171n5; walking patterns in, 124–30, 132, 146–47; zoning